A LIFE FOR ANARCHY

A STUART CHRISTIE READER

A LIFE FOR ANARCHY

A STUART CHRISTIE READER

edited by
The Kate Sharpley Library

The Kate Sharpley Library / AK Press

A Life for Anarchy: A Stuart Christie Reader
© 2021 Stuart Christie

This edition 2021 Creative Commons, Kate Sharpley Library
Published in collaboration with AK Press
ISBN: 978-1-939202-37-6
E-ISBN: 978-1-939202-38-3

Kate Sharpley Library
BM Hurricane
London, WC1N 3XX
UK
www.katesharpleylibrary.net
info@katesharpleylibrary.net

AK Press
370 Ryan Ave. #100
Chico, CA 95973
www.akpress.org
akpress@akpress.org

AK Press
33 Tower St.
Edinburgh EH6 7BN
Scotland
www.akuk.com
akuk@akpress.org

Indexing by John Barker
Printed in the USA

If you find mistakes in this publication, please remember that they are there for a purpose. We publish something for everyone, and some people are always looking for mistakes!

FALLS of PEOPLE

CONTENTS

Part 2, Biographical tributes and obituaries by Stuart

Part 3, Tributes to Stuart

Introduction

A life and not a legend

When our friend and comrade Stuart Christie died many people paid tribute to him. They were illuminating in many different ways, and we have included several of them in part three. We hope this book will give you a sense of the richness and complexity of his life. We also hope it will act as a memorial, given that we haven't been able to meet up and celebrate his life. We were slightly troubled by some throw-away comments made after he died about it being a pity he hadn't 'got' Franco. Focussing on the 'legend' like that devalues what he did do. He said himself 'I much preferred to be known as as one of the founders of the Black Cross [...] than one of the many who didn't manage to kill Franco.'[1]

That he didn't kill Franco was inevitably the first fact that people knew about Stuart. He took advantage of that to get publicity, but he did not let it define him. That failed attempt shone a light on the Franco dictatorship, and Stuart came to believe that the 'law of unintended consequences' meant that his arrest was the best possible outcome.[2] He was not one to waste time on repenting something gone in good conscience, nor on repeating the experiment. His life story, if you read his autobiography, is not of a person obsessed with Franco (for all his crimes) but someone returning from the unknown world of Franco's prisons with knowledge – a twentieth century journey to the underworld.

---

1. John Cunningham, 'Anarchist on paper only', *The Guardian*, 5 January 1981.
2. Stuart Christie, *General Franco made me a 'terrorist'* (Hastings: Christie-books, 2003), p. 127.

Stuart's Anarchism

Stuart is a key figure in the history of the anarchist movement from the sixties onwards (a history that is pretty much unwritten). But then, anarchism was also the central impetus of his life. Reading his autobiographies gives us a sense of someone who didn't embrace anarchism as a set of answers, but that it expressed a view of life that was already inside him. His granny really did make him an anarchist! The Carrara conference of 1968 connected him to an international network of anarchist and libertarian revolutionaries committed to freedom and solidarity. Stuart was party to the conflict between 'liberal' and revolutionary anarchists and remained committed to the militant position for all of his life. It would be easy for hindsight to reduce those conflicts to a simple either/or choice (whether your yardstick is 'violence' or 'class') but that would be to simplify Stuart's outlook. Stuart was driven by a strong personal moral choice, and believed in the importance of affinity groups in the wider social struggle. Personally, he was confident, had a sense of humour and without suffering fools gladly was prepared to take people as he found them.

Spain and the sixties

It was his involvement with the Spanish anarchist resistance that put Stuart in the headlines. He saw the continuing existence of Francoism as 'unfinished business'[3]: to him anti-fascism was a moral imperative in the shadow of the Second World War. He called the Spanish Civil War 'the most important moral reference point in the whole of the 20th century.'[4] But the execution of Delgado and Granado in 1963 was the immediate impetus for his

---

3. Andrew Stevens, 'Looking back at anger' interview with Stuart Christie, 2004, http://www.3ammagazine.com/politica/2004/apr/interview_stuart _christie.html.
4. 'On anarchist resistance', unnumbered page before introduction of *General Franco made me a 'terrorist'*.

involvement with the plot against Franco.[5] He found once imprisoned, that the attitudes he had formed in Scotland connected him perfectly with anarchists old and young in Spain – and worldwide.

The 1960s and 1970s were a time both of conflict and optimism across the world. Britain (and other countries) saw high working-class self-confidence. It was much easier to walk out of one job and into another. You could live on unemployment benefit. Strikes meant higher wages. For many people, breaking with capitalism was not just necessary but possible. The anarchist movement grew. New ideas were arising and being tested, leading to new conflicts. For 'liberal' anarchists both revolution and class were outdated ideas. The explorations of intellectuals would guarantee that society gradually but inexorably became more and more reasonable. For other anarchists revolution was not just desirable, but near. There was an opportunity to get rid of the state and capitalism and to start building a free society. Stuart identified with this revolutionary tendency and in 1974 said he expected to see Anarchy in his lifetime.[6] Upholding the anarchist tradition of revolt, they wanted more than to repeat the slogans of the past. For them, people were to be judged far more on what they did than what they said. This led them into conflict with some veterans of the movement: the revolutionaries were dissatisfied with grand but empty phrases uttered by unaccountable 'notables'. This conflict played out at the Carrara conference, but its roots lay in part in the organisational trauma of the exiled Spanish anarchists.

The Spanish anarcho-syndicalist union, the CNT, had suffered defeats and repression before but remained a union and a revolutionary organisation. After 1939, and after the chaos of the Second World War, what was the aim of the CNT, and what

---

5. Two Spanish anarchists executed for a crime they did not commit. See the note on 'Delgado and Granado' in glossary.

6. See the introduction to *MAN!* on page 62.

tactics should it follow? Would the allied powers follow up their anti-fascist slogans by getting rid of Franco? Divisions over tactics were exacerbated by the control of the CNT by figures like Federica Montseny and Germinal Esgleas. Their sabotage of the resistance to Franco would lead to revolutionary anarchists increasingly operating outside the official structures of the CNT and give rise to the First of May Group.

Publications and networks

His skill as a social networker (as well as the breadth of his interests) showed in his and his life partner Brenda's publishing efforts, in particular with Cienfuegos Press. It was the death of his close comrade Albert Meltzer in 1996 which started him on a new phase of publishing activity, taking advantage of new technologies, just as he had in the 1960s and 1970s. Under the imprint of the Meltzer Press he published his study of the Federación Anarquista Ibérica *We, the anarchists*.[7] The moral and social foundations to his anarchism remained the same, but the desire to commemorate his comrades and lost generations of anarchists grew stronger. Tony Blair's ascendency and in particular the 2003 invasion of Iraq provoked a look at his own personal history, and his three volumes of autobiography, *My granny made me an anarchist, General Franco made me a 'terrorist'* and *Edward Heath made me angry*.

We encourage you to go and read some of Stuart's books. We haven't gone through them for extracts for this reader, but we hope it will complement them. There is one book of Stuart's that we do want to talk about, since you're unlikely to find it on the shelves of your local library.

In 1983 Stuart wrote *The investigative researcher's handbook*. Produced before word processing, let alone the internet, it contains social network analysis done by hand: proof that as well

---

7. We have reprinted Stuart's introduction on page 110.

as being intelligent, Stuart was not afraid of hard work! He also advises the researcher to 'include in your friendship network key people who know everything and everybody – "sociometric stars". You'll often be surprised at just who some of your friends and acquaintances do know.'[8] Stuart himself came into that category!

The *Handbook* also contains this warning to the researcher:

> In a vendetta investigation all you waste is your time and money, but a conspiracy investigation can seriously damage your mental health. This has nothing to do with whether or not conspiracies exist or don't exist. Conspiracies occur all the time, but they are rarely, if ever, as ubiquitous, all powerful and pervasive as the obsessives who believe in them make out. [...]
>
> The maze-like trap of all conspiracy investigations (and trials) is that one lead takes you to another and so on interminably until everyone you come across – or wish to involve – is inextricably linked with the conspiracy. It can be a nightmare world for the investigator – and the investigated, – so unless you have a healthy, sceptical and open mind try to avoid getting sucked into conspiracy theories if you want to keep your sanity.[9]

That's obviously a nod to Stuart's experience in the 'Stoke Newington Eight' trial. Presented by the police as mastermind of the Angry Brigade, he was acquitted of charges of conspiracy to cause explosions and possession of 'explosive substances' after sixteen months of imprisonment on remand. That acquittal gave him the opportunity (and maybe a self-imposed obligation) to try and explain the Angry Brigade in the context of its times.

---

8. Stuart Christie, *The investigative researcher's handbook* (London: Refract, 1983), p. 16.
9. *The investigative researcher's handbook*, p. 12.

What if?

It has been hard, when putting this collection together, to have so many things we would like to and cannot ask him about. We know that Stuart was a fine comrade and friend, loyal and supportive as well as tenacious and sometimes maddening. Beyond those human qualities we would like to try and show his contribution to anarchism. It's a hard thing to measure what one person brings to a social movement. We're glad he wasn't executed by the Franco regime. But what if he had 'retired' from the anarchist movement in 1967 after his imprisonment in Spain? Thinking about that gives a sense of what a difference he made.

Would *Black Flag*, 'excitingly irregular' at times but funny and committed, have appeared or been what it was without Stuart? Without Cienfuegos Press (1974–1982) and Stuart's other publishing efforts we would know much less of anarchism. Who would have given voice to half of those lives and ideas?

What would Albert Meltzer's autobiography *I couldn't paint golden angels* look like? The more we look, the more Stuart becomes a key figure in Albert's life. Mark Hendy said 'Albert before 1967 was Albert without Stuart. From late 1967 onwards he was Albert with Stuart – two very different beasts!'[10] Though the temptation is to see them as 'indelibly joined as Marx and Engels, or perhaps more appropriately Laurel and Hardy,'[11] their great partnership does not mean they saw things the same way at all times. Stuart was enjoying Charles Radcliffe's revolutionary/ countercultural *Heatwave* in prison, while Albert was fuming at him as one of the 'lunatic middle-class "militants"' disrupting anarchist meetings at the Lamb and Flag pub in London.[12]

Without Stuart's character and contacts, would the Anarchist

---

10. Email of 28 December 2018.
11. Albert Meltzer, *I couldn't paint golden angels* (London: Kate Sharpley Library and AK Press, 1996), p. 269.
12. '"Lamb & Flag" meetings' *Freedom* 12 November 1966.

Black Cross have been relaunched? Miguel Garcia, the resistance veteran who became International Secretary of the ABC, said of Stuart that he was 'rancho aparte' (meaning that he 'goes his own way') which is undoubtedly true, and worth remembering alongside his charm and friendliness. Had Stuart 'retired', would Miguel Garcia have come to London and written *Franco's prisoner* with Albert Meltzer? And if Miguel Garcia is 'in some ways, perhaps every way, the reason why the Kate Sharpley Library exists',[13] then were would we be?

Aims and process

This is a selection of Stuart's writings and there are several interesting articles we didn't have room for. We wish that Stuart had written more, even if only introductions to some of the books he published. But obviously, to publish, to 'get it out there' was often enough, without Stuart needing to add his own commentary. Once he had access to a website, Facebook, short-run printing and ebooks it's hard to keep track of everything he did publish. If you look at Christiebooks or his Facebook page, Stuart was as happy to share the words of a comrade or friend as to write his own.

The first part of the reader contains a selection of Stuart's short political writings. They hopefully reflect some of the optimism, as well as some of the conflicts, of when they were written. We have given each of these a brief introduction to set out their context. They are in chronological order, but this is not a comprehensive selection, since he never stopped writing political articles.

The second part contains some of Stuart's biographical tributes to his friends, mentors and comrades, beginning with that of his good comrade Albert Meltzer. These are in chronological

---

13. 'Dar la vida, por la vida (Give a life for life): Miguel Garcia Garcia (1908–1981)', introduction to *Looking back after twenty years of jail: questions and answers on the Spanish anarchist resistance* (London: Kate Sharpley Library, 2002).

order, except that the two pieces about Flavio Costantini have been put next to one another. We have also put his tribute to Brenda at the end of that section. In some ways, it's the most important piece there.

These biographies contain the warmth of comradeship and hint at Stuart's importance in connecting an older generation of anarchists to a new one, not to mention creating international links, reflecting Stuart's own internationalism. They also record the world-view of an anarchist tendency which continued the tradition of revolt in new circumstances. We have tried to provide a balance in both parts between British and European pieces and hope they act as building blocks for an otherwise unknown anarchist history.

Stuart in the Cienfuegos Press Office on Sanday, Orkney, 1979.
Photo from the Stuart Christie Memorial Archive.

The third part contains a selection of tributes to Stuart, in a loosely thematic order. It starts with two tributes from the Kate Sharpley Library. Ones from his Spanish comrades are followed by those of historians. Tributes from other British comrades come next. We have kept together the eulogies read at the funeral. The section ends with details of the Stuart Christie Memorial Archive. We give the last word in the book to Stuart, with his 1983 article 'A time for anarchy' which we think gives a concise view of his political viewpoint and of his life.

We have, to the best of our abilities, corrected errors silently and put footnotes in to explain the context of the pieces (and sources of quotations). We have also attempted to keep the notes under control. Many of the people mentioned need a book of their own but we have tried to give a sense of who they are and where they came from. We have given nationalities to show where people started out. Their lives will be richer than we can tell in a few words. We hope that the glossary of people and groups that regularly reappear helps you to find your way around. We would like to borrow one last quote from Stuart's writings. 'If you find mistakes in this publication, please remember that they are there for a purpose. We publish something for everyone, and some people are always looking for mistakes!'[14]

We know that this is not the final word on Stuart's life. Seeing the materials that people are sharing with us and the Stuart Christie Memorial Archive, we feel as though we are constantly learning more. We hope this reader gives you a sense of the breadth of his experiences, and celebrates his humanity, his morality and his intuitive grasp of anarchism.

Kate Sharpley Library collective

1 May 2021

---

14.   *The investigative researcher's handbook*, p. ii.

Acknowledgments

Firstly, to Stuart's daughter, Branwen: thank you for your enthusiastic agreement to the idea of a memorial volume. We hope you get some pleasure and comfort from it.

We would like to thank all of the writers whose work appears in part three for allowing us to reprint it here.

Thanks also go to our friends and comrades who have shared material, looked for articles, provided copies and answered questions. Thanks also to the librarian and archivist colleagues and comrades whose resources we have used. Christiebooks.co.uk is full of treasures, but we have also used these (and have probably forgotten some):

Anarchy Archives (dwardmac.pitzer.edu), Archive.org, www.archivesautonomies.org, Centre de Recherche pour l'Alternative Sociale (CRAS, www.cras31.info), Center for the Study of Political Graphics (www.politicalgraphics.org), Centre international de recherches sur l'anarchisme (CIRA, www.cira.ch), Dictionnaire international des militants anarchistes (militants-anarchistes.info), Fédération internationale des centres d'études et de documentation libertaires (FICEDL, ficedl.info), *Fifth Estate* (www.fifthestate.org), Freedom Press (freedomnews.org.uk), *The Guardian* (www.theguardian.com), Kate Sharpley Library (www.katesharpleylibrary.net), Libcom.org, Library of Congress (www.loc.gov), Los de la Sierra (losdelasierra.info), Modern Records Centre (warwick.ac.uk/services/library/mrc), *Sicilia Libertaria* (www.sicilialibertaria.it), The Sparrows' Nest (www.thesparrowsnest.org.uk), Spirit of Revolt (spiritofrevolt.info), Splits and Fusions (splitsandfusions.wordpress.com), Union of Egoists (www.unionofegoists.com), Wordcat.org.

'Review of *Anarchism* by George Woodcock' is reprinted from *Time Out* No.273, 612 June 1975.

Stuart's tribute to Flavio Costantini was originally published in *Illustrators 50* (1976), published by the Association of Illustrators https://theaoi.com.

'Freedom is a fiction: Stuart Christie looks at how radical publishers are surviving the recession' was originally printed in *The Times Higher Education Supplement* 16 October 1981, and issued as a leaflet by the Friends of Cienfuegos Press for the Socialist Book Fair 1981.

'A time for anarchy...' is reprinted from *City Limits*, 22–28 April 1983.

We have tried to accurately credit authorship and publication information. Please contact us with corrections and additions.

Bibliography

A short bibliography of books and periodicals written, translated or edited by Stuart Christie

1969–1982 *Bulletin of the Anarchist Black Cross*, later *Black Flag* (editor).

1970 *The floodgates of anarchy* (with Albert Meltzer) published by Kahn & Averill. New editions Sphere Books, 1972; Kahn & Averill, 1979 and 1984; PM Press, 2010. Spanish-language editions Editorial Proyección, 1971; Centro Iberico, 1976; Descontrol, 2015.

1974 *Sabaté: guerrilla extraordinary* by Antonio Téllez (translator) published by Davis Poynter Ltd., with a paperback by Cienfuegos Press. Later English-language editions Elephant Editions, 1985; Elephant Editions and AK Press, 1998.

1976–1982 *The Cienfuegos Press Anarchist Review* (editor).

1979–1981 *The Free-Winged Eagle* (editor).

1980 *The Christie file* published by Partisan Press and Cienfuegos Press.

1983 *The investigative researcher's handbook* published by Refract.

1984 *Stefano delle Chiaie: portrait of a 'black' terrorist*[1] published by Anarchy Magazine and Refract.

1986 *The anarchist encyclopedia* (editor).

1996 *We, the anarchists: a study of the Iberian Anarchist Federation (FAI), 1927–1937* published by the Meltzer Press. Later editions The Meltzer Press and Jura Media, 2000; AK Press, 2008. Spanish edition Universitat de València, 2010.

2002 *My granny made me an anarchist: the Christie file, part 1, 1946–1964. 'the cultural and political formation of a west of Scotland "baby-boomer"'* published by Christiebooks.

---

1. In this context 'black' is a reference to fascism (as in Mussolini's blackshirts).

2003 *General Franco made me a 'terrorist': the Christie File, part 2, 1964–1967. 'The interesting years abroad of a west of Scotland "baby-boomer"'* published by Christiebooks. Spanish-language edition Temas de hoy, 2005.

2003 *The Angry Brigade: the cause and the case* by Gordon Carr (editor of the expanded second edition) published by Christiebooks. Later edition, PM Press, 2010.

2004 *Edward Heath made me angry: the Christie file, part 3, 1967–1975. 'The later memoirs of a west of Scotland "baby-boomer"'* published by Christiebooks.

2004 *Granny made me an anarchist: General Franco, the Angry Brigade and me* published by Scribner. Later editions, Scribner, 2005; AK Press, 2007. German-language edition, Nautilus, 2014.

2005–06 *The Hastings Trawler* (editor, under the pseudonym Francisco Ferrer i Guardia).

2009–12 *Arena* (editor). Three issues: 1, 'On anarchist cinema', guest edited by Richard Porton; 2, 'Anarchists in fiction' (Ebook published PM Press, 2011 as 'Noir fiction'); 3, 'Anarchism in Music', guest edited by Daniel O'Guérin.

2009 *¡Pistoleros! 1: 1918* (The chronicles of Farquhar McHarg) published by Christiebooks. Later edition, PM Press, 2011.

2010 *¡Pistoleros! 2: 1919* (The chronicles of Farquhar McHarg) published by Christiebooks.

2012 *¡Pistoleros! 3: 1920–1924* (The chronicles of Farquhar McHarg) published by Christiebooks.

Glossary

Glossary of recurring groups, people and terms

ABC Anarchist Black Cross: Anarchist affinity group and then network dedicated to revolutionary solidarity and prisoner support, initially drawing on Stuart's contacts in Spain. Named after an earlier group with the same aims, which had originally been called the Anarchist Red Cross.

Alberola, Octavio: Spanish anarchist, coordinator of Defensa Interior, member of the First of May Group and writer. See his tribute on page 221. A biography by Agustín Comotto *El peso de las estrellas: vida del anarquista Octavio Alberola* was published by Rayo Verde, 2019 (translation forthcoming as a joint KSL/AK publication).

Angry Brigade: British group (1970–1972) which applied the armed protest tactics of the First of May Group to international solidarity and opposition to the Conservative government of Edward Heath. Best known for the long and confrontational trial of the 'Stoke Newington Eight' (1972).

'Apaches'/ the Apache sector: The parts of the Spanish anarchist movement involved in the resistance, as opposed to the official leadership. 'Apache' was early twentieth century slang for a member of the Parisian underworld: Albert Meltzer in 1968 called the 'Bonnot Gang' (anarchist expropriators, 1911–12) 'the last of the Apaches'.

Busquets Vergés, Joan (Juan): Spanish anarchist and guerrilla, arrested in 1949. Stuart and Busquets met in prison in Spain. See Stuart's tribute on page 166, and the tribute by Busquets on page 219.

Centro Ibérico/ the International Libertarian Centre: From 1971 Miguel Garcia and other anarchists got involved in the Centro Ibérico which met in a parish hall in North London. From December 1973 to September 1976 the Centro was run as an anarchist club at 83a Haverstock Hill. Books, pamphlets and periodicals (including *Black Flag* and *Colectivo anarquista*) were printed and published there.

Christie, Brenda: (Brenda Earl, 1949–2019) British anarchist, publisher and member of the First of May Group. Stuart's partner from 1968. See his tribute on page 196.

CNT Confederación Nacional del Trabajo: (National Confederation of Labour) Spanish anarcho-syndicalist union, founded 1910.

Delgado and Granado: Joaquin Delgado Martínez (1934–1963) and Francisco Granado Gata (1935–1963) were two Spanish anarchist members of Defensa Interior. They were executed for a bombing that the police knew they had not carried out. See the tribute to Antonio Martín Bellido on page 182.

DI Defensa Interior: (Interior Defence) Secret branch of the CNT in exile tasked with assassinating Franco and using armed protest actions to maintain international pressure on the Franco regime. Established in 1961 but choked of funding and resources and wound up in 1963. The First of May Group continued its armed protest actions.

Edo, Luis Andrés: (1925–2009) Spanish anarchist and writer, member of the First of May Group (and cellmate of Stuart's). See Stuart's tribute on page 148.

ETA Euskadi Ta Askatasuna: (Basque Fatherland and Liberty), Basque nationalist armed group founded in 1959.

Facerias, José Lluis: ('Face', 1920–1957) Spanish anarchist and guerrilla, killed in a police ambush in Barcelona.

FIJL Federación Ibérica de Juventudes Libertarias: (Iberian Federation of Libertarian Youth) also known as Juventudes

Libertarias (JJLL, Libertarian Youth), founded in 1932. FIJL members were central to the various phases of the anarchist resistance to Francoism.

First of May Group: (Grupo Primero de Mayo) Anarchist group, successor to Defensa Interior, carrying out armed protest actions against Francoism and other regimes from 1966 onwards. See *The International Revolutionary Solidarity Movement: First of May Group*, edited by Albert Meltzer (Cienfuegos Press, 1976).

Franco, Francisco: (1892–1975) Spanish general who became dictator after victory in the Spanish Civil War. Franco was the lynchpin of an authoritarian coalition comprising the army, fascists, nationalists, capitalists and the Catholic Church.

GARI Grupos de Acción Revolucionaria Internacionalista: (Internationalist Revolutionary Action Groups) a collective of groups, following the armed protest tactics of the First of May Group. Responsible for the Suárez kidnapping. The French examining magistrate on that case (Pinsseau) defined GARI as 'an international structured coming-together of various anarchist grouplets coordinating their activities with a view to mounting of a series of spectacular attacks designed to support the struggle under way against the Francoist regime and on behalf of Spanish political prisoners.' [from *Lucio l'irréductible* (Flammarion, 2000) by Bernard Thomas; Translated as *Lucio Urtubia: the indomitable anarchist*, available as an ebook from Christiebooks.]

Garcia, Miguel: (1908–1981) Spanish anarchist, forger and guerrilla. Arrested in 1949, he served twenty years, and met Stuart in Carabanchel Prison (Madrid). On release in 1969 he moved to London and became the International Secretary of the Anarchist Black Cross. He was the mainstay of Centro Ibérico. See *Franco's prisoner* (Rupert Hart-Davis, 1972) and *Miguel Garcia's story* (Miguel Garcia Memorial Committee and Cienfuegos Press, 1982). See Stuart's tribute on page 157 and the extract from *Franco's prisoner* on page 206.

Libertarian: Used as synonym for anarchist, also used more broadly to cover anarchists and libertarian socialist, non-Leninist 'neighbours', like libertarian communists, etc.

Massana Bancells, Marcelino: ('Pancho', 1918–1981) Spanish anarchist and guerrilla. He survived because he 'retired' from the guerrilla struggle. Having disarmed some French border guards (in 1950), a French court banished him from the border region.

Meltzer, Albert: (1920–1996) British anarchist, writer and publisher. Worked closely with Stuart on the Anarchist Black Cross, *Black Flag* and Cienfuegos Press. See Stuart's tribute on page 118 and Albert's review of *The Christie file* on page 209.

MIL Movimiento Ibérico de Liberación: (Iberian Liberation Movement) Anarchist and libertarian communist action group. Dissolved in 1973. A pamphlet on *Salvador Puig Antich and the MIL* was published by the Kate Sharpley Library in 2008. AK Press published *Salvador Puig Antich: collected writings on repression and resistance in Franco's Spain*, edited by Ricard de Vargas Golarons, translated and introduced by Peter Gelderloos in 2021.

Pinelli, Giuseppe: (1928–1969) Italian anarchist and secretary of the Milanese Anarchist Black Cross, the Croce Nera Anarchica. He was murdered by the police following the Piazza Fontana bombing (12 December 1969), carried out by fascists in conjunction with parts of the Italian security services as part of the 'Strategy of Tension'. A short biography by Paolo Finzi is on the Kate Sharpley Library website (www.katesharpleylibrary.net/f7m14m).

Puig Antich, Salvador: (1948–1974) Spanish anarchist and member of the MIL, executed by the Francoist regime. See also MIL Movimiento Ibérico de Liberación.

Suárez, Ángel Baltasar: manager of the Paris branch of the Banco de Bilbao, who was kidnapped on 3 May 1974 by GARI. Their demands, given in a statement of 8 May 1974, were that the Franco regime release five MIL members (Oriol Solé Sugranyes

[1948–1976, shot dead after a mass prison breakout], José Luis Pons Llobet [part of the same breakout, recaptured but amnestied in 1977], Santiago Soler Amigó [1943–1999, journalist and member of anti-authoritarian and libertarian documentation centre CEDALL], Francisco Javier Garriga Paituvi and Maria Angustias Mateos Fernandez) and that the law of conditional liberty be applied to political prisoners. Suárez was released unharmed.

Téllez, Antonio: (1921–2005) Spanish anarchist, guerrilla and writer. The central figure in recording the history of the anarchist guerrilla resistance to Francoism after the Spanish Civil War. See Stuart's tribute on page 134.

UGT Unión General de Trabajadores: (General Workers' Union), Spanish Socialist union federation.

Part 1

Articles by Stuart

The Factory for Peace

The 'Factory for Peace' (also known as the Rowen Engineering Company) was established by Tom McAlpine (1929–2006) in 1963. McAlpine was closely involved in the campaign against nuclear weapons (he left the Labour Party over the issue in 1967, joining the Scottish National Party). Announcing the 'Factory for Peace' project in *Anarchy* 26 (April 1963) he said 'we intend to try new industrial experiments in co-operative ownership where all workers will have equal say in decisions affecting wages, new products, profits and other policy matters. This presents problems but we are convinced that workers' participation is vital.' Here Stuart, highlighting the top-down control of the project by McAlpine, criticises the distance between the aims and reality of the project.

Tom McAlpine, visionary – or waster? This has been a topic of conversation in libertarian circles. He has been lauded by the Christians, Social Democrats and pacifists; but this is only to be expected, as it seems to them that if the Factory for Peace succeeds (as it will not) there will be no need for the revolution which they all fear. The left wing press have dedicated whole pages to this subject and there have been TV films made about this experiment below the co-operative sausage factory off Scotland Street, Glasgow.

I worked in the Factory for a month – enough for me to get an insight on its nature. I was paid £2 10s. for three days' work, the idea being that on alternate days we would sign on at the labour exchange, thus giving us added income.

The manager, according, to the constitution of the factory, was supposed to be elected by a meeting of the workers, and so Tom became manager. A mystery exists here – who elected Tom McAlpine? This question is comparable only to that of the *Marie Celeste*.

A foreman was elected (by Tom) and then part-time labour was introduced in order to begin production. This system of part-time labour worked well for a week, and then, when production had to be stepped up, the manager asked the other boy who was working part-time to come into his office. When he came out I was called in and asked whether I would be willing to work full time for a wage to be decided.

I had not been informed what the other boy had been offered and, as I had no knowledge of engineering, felt £7 would be enough. Later, when I talked to this other boy, I discovered McAlpine had offered him £10, but when McAlpine discovered I would work for far less, he reduced it to £8. This boy told the manager he was quite happy with the present state of affairs and would not work for less than £10 a week, as he was a fifth-year engineering apprentice and entitled to more.

Stuart (in white mac) and other Glasgow anarchists heckle Labour Party leader Hugh Gaitskell, over nuclear weapons at the May Day Rally, Queen's Park, Glasgow, 6 May 1962. From the Stuart Christie photo album on the Kate Sharpley Library website.

This obviously annoyed McAlpine and at the Council Meeting the following Friday he proposed that the boy should be given a week's notice. As two other young lads had started work that week, they voted with us and McAlpine's proposal was flung out of the window. He told the meeting he would bring this up the following week and, if it was rejected again, would take it to a higher authority. This higher authority is a Council which has nothing to do with the shop floor, but to make sure we don't make any H bombs, and who also decide the wages of the personnel.

The following week, just as we were going into the meeting, I was told by McAlpine that he was sorry, but he had forgotten to tell me that my friend and I were not allowed to vote. Seemingly it is in the constitution that only those who had worked for three months were allowed to vote. If that were the case no one would be allowed to vote *as the factory had only been opened a fortnight previously*. This friend of mine resigned after that; can you blame him?

Another boy whose work was exactly the same as mine was being paid a pound more, because he was 21 and I was not. I brought this up at a meeting and McAlpine said he was not willing to raise my wages, but would rather lower the other boy's. A shocked silence followed. A so-called socialist lowering wages already below subsistence level! I pointed out that I did not wish this boy's wages to lowered, as I had already guessed that this would have been the answer, but the reason why I brought this up was because I wished to show the bourgeois elitist nature of the Factory for Peace.

A young socialist who worshipped McAlpine with naive sincerity had been working in the factory since its opening. This young socialist had no previous experience in sheet metal work, but because he paid homage to the Court of McAlpine he was paid according to needs. While fully-apprenticed tradesmen were getting less than £12, he was paid a salary of £56 per month. This caused quite a stir among the rank and file.

He defended his position by saying he had a family to support – a mother and dog, and his mother had a private income! Only two people were paid according to needs – McAlpine, £19 per week, and this young socialist. Needless to say they were the highest-paid members of the factory. As I lived more than 14 miles away, almost beside Tom McAlpine, I arrived every morning at nine o'clock precisely. He kept nagging at me about my late coming and eventually brought it up at a council meeting. When he had finished his diatribe I asked at what time he arrived in the morning. There was a hushed silence when he answered between 10.30 and 11 a.m. I just left it at that.

These points show only too clearly the fallacy in the idea of *giving* the workers control.

The workers had no impetus, they did not look upon the machines as theirs. One boy took a morning off the first week he was there to go and look for another job, which shows how effective is McAlpine's brand of industrial democracy.

Last of all, McAlpine himself told me that the factory was not under workers' control and never would be, unless the workers took it over themselves and, as far as he was concerned, it was just an industrial experiment.

'Peter Piatkov'[1]

From *Direct Action* July 1964 vol.5, no. 7 (whole number 37)

---

[1].   Pseudonym of Jānis Žāklis (1883–?) Latvian (ex-Social Democrat) anarchist. Subject of Philip Ruff's *A towering flame: The life & times of 'Peter the Painter'* (London: Breviary Stuff Publications, 2019).

Speech at Carrara Congress, 1968, as delegate of the Anarchist Federation of Britain

After his return from imprisonment in Spain, Stuart became much more closely involved with the international anarchist movement. He was chosen as delegate of the Anarchist Federation of Britain to the Anarchist congress held in Carrara from 31 August to 3 September 1968. The prospect of a conference in Carrara had been raised as far back as October 1965 by the exterior delegation of the Iberian Federation of Libertarian Youth (FIJL) to coordinate the work of active militants. Eventually it was to happen in the wake of the revolutionary situation in Paris in May 1968.

This piece reflects the tension at the congress between a formal tendency of organisation-building and one much more focussed on action. More than a divide between generations, the conflict came from disagreements about what anarchists should do (and who they should work with). On one hand, the congress resulted in the founding of the International of Anarchist Federations (IFA). On the other, for those who withdrew from the official congress, it cemented lasting connections between anarchist militants. Stuart returned from Carrara with a network of like-minded comrades who he could work with. This network was key to the achievements of the Anarchist Black Cross and of Cienfuegos Press. It's worth noticing that, looking back, Federica Montseny[1] of the CNT remained a target of Stuart's ire.

The Anarchist Federation of Britain sends Congress fraternal

---

1. Federica Montseny (1905–1994) was one of the CNT 'notables' who took government posts during the Spanish Civil War. After the Second World War she was part of the leadership of, and lived off paid organizational positions in, the CNT in exile. A divisive figure, whose opponents saw her anarchist 'purism' contradicted by her actions.

greetings both to those comrades who were invited to attend and to those who were excluded.

As anarchists, we have no sympathy for rote speeches and parliamentary procedures. More important to us is the exchange of experiences, views and ideas, with a view to creating a truly effective international anarchist organisation. We do not believe that the spirit in which this Congress was convened reflects the true ethos of anarchism. We note, sadly, that a number of the most active anarchist groups and organisations, such as the Iberian Federation of Libertarian Youth (FIJL), Noir et Rouge,[2] the 22 March group,[3] and the Paris Local Federation,[4] are not represented here. We propose, therefore, that this Congress be declared open to all observers from all anarchist groups and organisations, be they affiliated or not to 'national federations'.

Our movement should not be divided along nationalist or racist lines. For ourselves, we roundly refuse to embrace such bourgeois notions that undermine the very roots of international revolutionary solidarity.

We will have no truck with an international secretariat that liaises with the range of international bodies such as we have seen in the proceedings and convening of this Congress. We support, enthusiastically, the example of the Parisian workers and students and are actively encouraging similar stances in Britain. We must, however, scrutinise, dispassionately, the successes and the shortcomings of our French comrades if we hope to succeed in any attempted international social revolution. The British movement considers it

---

2. *Noir et Rouge* (1956–1970) anarchist periodical. Subtitle 'cahiers d'études édités par les Groupes anarchistes d'action révolutionnaire', later 'cahiers d'études anarchistes communistes' and 'cahiers d'études anarchistes'. Online at https://archivesautonomies.org/spip.php?article188.

3. Mouvement du 22 Mars, Nanterre libertarian/anarchist group (Daniel Cohn-Bendit and Jean-Pierre Duteuil were members).

4. The Paris Local Federation of the CNT of Spain in Exile.

essential that the international movement builds upon sound foundations, and so the first task facing each organisation and group is to consolidate and grow naturally. It is our firm belief that fictitious organisations, such as some of those represented here today, conjured up simply to raise the media profile of the Congress, are utterly pointless, and indeed harmful in the extreme. One example is that of the Iberian Anarchist Federation (FAI), represented here today by former government minister Federica Montseny; another is the imaginary Bulgarian Federation, represented by Balkanski.[5]

The speech was published in *Esfuerzo*, the Internal Bulletin of the Paris Liaison Commission: Year 4, No 11, December 1968, p. 24 (Translated by Paul Sharkey).

The Congress continues
As reported in *Freedom* (21 September 1968)

After his speech, Failla[6] (Italy) asked that a vote be taken by the conference.

He was answered by another delegate from the Italian Federation, saying he was against a vote being taken, as the constitution of the Congress had been decided on beforehand by the Preparatory Commission. Marzocchi[7] then went on to propose a motion condemning aggression in Czechoslovakia and Vietnam: Christie got up again and demanded the dais, saying we were opposed

---

5. Georges Balkanski was the pseudonym of the Bulgarian anarchist Georgi Grigoriev (1906–1996). In exile he was active in the Bulgarian Anarchist Union.
6. Alfonso Failla (1906–1986) Italian anarchist and writer, member of the Federazione Anarchica Italiana (FAI: Italian Anarchist Federation).
7. Umberto Marzocchi (1900–1986) Italian anarchist and writer, member of the Federazione Anarchica Italiana (FAI: Italian Anarchist Federation).

to any motion of this nature as we were completely powerless to enforce it. By stooping to such methods we merely imitated the procedure of Harold Wilson and similar politicians. It was up to anarchists, surely, to show their disgust and contempt for military aggression by revolutionary direct action.

Stuart looks back at the Carrara Conference

The following notes come from an email of Stuart's to an Italian comrade (November 2011). The Anarchist Federation of Britain conference in October 1967 certainly discussed the Carrara conference: 'Carrara was discussed, and its authoritarian organisation criticised. Consensus was in favour of such a conference, but against the present method of organisation.' 'It was also agreed that the AFB Conference next year should be held prior to Carrara in order to "brief" any comrades attending.'[8] There may also have been an informal AFB meeting in the summer of 1968. The 1968 AFB conference took place in Liverpool in September.

With regard to your questions on Carrara, I should reiterate that the Anarchist Federation of Britain did exist (albeit very loosely) and that in the early summer of 1968 I was mandated to attend the Carrara Congress as the (only) official British delegate with full power to endorse members of both the FIJL (Juventudes Libertarias) and the March 22 Group as AFB delegates (they had been refused recognition as delegates by the Congress organisers because – although activists and constituting the most dynamic elements of the anarchist/libertarian movement of the time – they did not belong to or were answerable to any of the moribund 'national federations' such as the MLE[9] (FAI-

---

8. *Freedom* 14 October 1967.
9. Movimiento Libertario Español / Mouvement Libertaire Espagnol, umbrella organisation of the exiled CNT-FAI (Confederación Nacional del Trabajo and Federación Anarquista Ibérica). The FIJL distanced itself from the MLE from 1965 onward.

CNT), the FAF,[10] the Bulgarian Federation, or the other 'phantom' sclerotic bureaucratic institutions of the time, including Giovanni Baldelli's[11] British 'secretariat'). The reason was, as you point out, because the representatives of the various disparate groups that constituted the British movement at the time came together at a packed AFB meeting that summer (of 1968) in the offices of the ACTT union (The Association of Cinematograph, Television and Allied Technicians) in Soho Square and agreed, unanimously, to reject the principle of national federations (most of whom had no organisational base and were answerable to nobody). Hence the decision to allow me to grant 'British nationality' to representatives of the excluded activist groups. [...]

There certainly was no intention on our part to split the congress, but it was clear to us very early on – as a result of the blatant hypocrisy and the behind-the-scenes political machinations of Montseny and company – that it was pointless to engage further with them – hence our decision to continue our own Congress of activists at Marina di Carrara. In fact it was there that we extended the foundations of the international revolutionary solidarity movement/network that became the International Anarchist Black Cross (we had formally re-launched the Anarchist Black Cross in London the previous autumn [1967] at a meeting of the Anarchist Federation of Britain).

---

10. The Fédération Anarchiste, the French Anarchist Federation.
11. Giovanni Baldelli, aka 'John Gill', (1914–1986), London-based Italian anarchist and writer, ran the Secretariat of the International Anarchist Commission (Commission Internationale Anarchiste: CIA), established at the International Anarchist Congress, London, July 1958. The Commission published a bulletin from 1959–1961. After that, it was inactive until Baldelli helped to organise the Carrara conference, ensuring it was limited to national federations only.

Statement by the Black Flag Group to the Liverpool Conference of the Anarchist Federation of Britain, Sept., 1968

Working in London with Albert Meltzer, Stuart was a key figure in the creation and development of the Anarchist Black Cross and *Black Flag*. This 1968 statement lays out some of the conflicts and criticisms between what they saw as revolutionary and 'liberal' anarchists. It arises from various polemics in the anarchist press, especially *Freedom* and *Anarchy*. Efforts by the 'liberal' anarchists to make anarchism 'relevant' to modern society were seen as acquiescing to it. *Black Flag* gave voice to the revolutionary tendency.

Anarchism is a revolutionary method of achieving a free non-violent society, without class divisions or imposed authority. Whether this is a 'utopian' achievement or not is irrelevant; the Anarchist, on any normal definition, is a person who, having this aim in mind, proceeds to get rid of authoritarian structures, and advances towards such a society by making people independent of the State and by intensifying the class struggle so that the means of economic exploitation will be weakened and destroyed.

Confusion

There should be no confusion between anarchism and liberalism however militant the latter might be (e.g. movements towards national liberation). The liberal seeks greater freedom within the structure of society that he finds himself; he rejects the methods of class struggle which relate to the economic divisions of society. Since there is such a confusion, however, we find that there are now TWO contrary conceptions of anarchism.

There are not 'as many conceptions as there are anarchists' nor 'a thousand fragments' but there are TWO, both of which are probably represented at this Conference. One, which we support and intend to give coherence to as an organisation, is what we are obliged to call Revolutionary Anarchism (though anarchism should not need such a qualification) which says that there can be no compromise with the State; that there is a class struggle, and that there is nothing to be gained [by] adapting to class society. There can only be a revolution, in the streets and in the factories. The other conception we call Liberal Anarchism (though it may regard itself as revolutionary, while more usually deriding the word) which seeks to adjust to present day society, without the need for overthrowing the State (regarded as an unlikely contingency). Such adjustment could, of course, be to Capitalism or even in some circumstances to State Communism; and there are many different ways in which it could be made.

Peace Movement

In the main, so far as this country is concerned, such social-liberal ideas have come into the Anarchist Movement by way of the Peace Movement which has questioned, or perhaps never understood, certain basic anarchistic conceptions. In saying this, we are not denying that pacifists can be anarchists (though for the sake of coherent action we would exclude them from our own group). So long as their viewpoint does not become a mainstream tendency we can no doubt work with them within the AFB.

We regard the principle of pacifism as irrelevant and on the whole unanarchistic (as would be making a cult of temperance or vegetarianism or taking pot or 'dropping out' – these are all matters for personal decisions, and while often escapes from the main social issues, only become absurd when made into a cult that all are exhorted to follow, and elevated to becoming the main social issue among ourselves and within society as a whole, with matters such as the class struggle relegated or ignored.) Even so, the issue we face in this conference is NOT pacifism as such but the fact that it has opened the door for so many liberal assumptions. For instance, that prisons can be reformed and are incapable of abolition (Vine[1]; Willis); that we should go to the extent of collecting money for policemen injured on demonstrations (Featherstone)[2]; that the police are a necessary crutch to society (Rooum)[3]; that criminals are the only free people but that we should call on the services of the police if necessary (Schweitzer-Mariconi)[4].

Liberalism

Once one accepts that 'anarchism must be related to contemporary society', capitalism (Ward)[5] one may accept participation in management (Topham through to Ostergaard)[6]; or the neces-

---

1. Ian Vine wrote on on crime and the law in *Anarchy* 59 and 'Anarchism as a realist alternative' *Anarchy* 74.

2. See Godfrey Featherstone's letter in *Freedom*, 20 April 1968 and the response in the following issue from Stuart Christie, Adrian Derbyshire, James Duke, Ross Flett, Albert Meltzer and Martin Page.

3. Donald Rooum (1928–2019) British anarchist and writer. 'A police force is something like a pair of crutches. If everyone would stand on his own feet they wouldn't exist. We anarchists are striving towards a situation where everyone can stand on his own feet; but at this present moment, supposing it were possible to kick the police force from under the people, it would do more harm than good.' From his account of being framed by the police (the Challenor case) 'I've dislodged a bit of brick' in *Anarchy* 36.

4. Jean-Pierre Schweitzer's 'Prolegomena to an Anarchist Philosophy: 3 – Politics', *Minus One* no. 13 talks about 'the criminal is the (an)archist "par excellence"'.

5. Colin Ward (1924–2010), British anarchist, writer, architect and editor of *Anarchy*. His preface to *Anarchy in action* (1973) says that his interpretation of anarchism 'is a description of a mode of human organization, rooted in the experience of everyday life, which operates side by side with, and in spite of, the dominant authoritarian trends of our society.'

6. Tony Topham (Institute for Workers Control) was not an anarchist; Geoffey Ostergaard (1926–1990) wrote about Workers' Control in

sity for psychological and sociological adjustments to living in the rat race (various, *Anarchy*); or that taxation is necessary to help the poorer classes (Richards);[7] or that we need merely be in a condition of permanent protest against abuses within society (Sydney Libertarians); adjusted to non-violent methods (*Peace News*) or to such authoritarian bodies as the Catholic Church (Hennacy)[8] or even make our peace within the Communist State (Jeff Robinson)[9].

Anarchism so diluted may be recognised by the monarchy (Read)[10] or be compatible with voting Labour (Melly);[11] or it can be reduced to a mere imaginary mind process leading to intellectual salvation (various, *Minus One*)[12]. Those who reject the revolutionary concept may have various views, ranging from a rejection of contemporary values and a mere ignoring of the State hoping it will go away (hippies, diggers) to deliberate provocation of it to use its full repressive powers without, however, preparing for any effective resistance (some at least of the Provo-Situationists).[13]

Anarchy nos. 2 and 80.

7. Vernon Richards (1915–2001), British anarchist, writer and publisher. Self-effacing but controlling, he had little sympathy for the new generation of militant anarchists of the 1960s. As owner of Freedom Press he was blamed for the 'liberalism' of *Freedom*.

8. Ammon Hennacy (1893–1970), American anarchist and Catholic.

9. Jeff Robinson wrote 'Inner freedom is possible in the modern world even in a prison cell' ('A statement', *Freedom* 29 July 1967) but we have not seen him suggesting we 'make our peace with the Communist State'.

10. Herbert Read (1893–1968), British anarchist and writer, accepted a Knighthood in 1953.

11. George Melly (1926–2007), British anarchist, jazz singer and writer.

12. *Minus One* ('Individualist Anarchist Review') see https://www.union-ofegoists.com/journals/minus-one-1963.

13. Provo was a Dutch counter-cultural movement (based on playful provocation) which inspired groups elsewhere. Situationism was a critique of the world where capitalism was so successful even the idea of revolt could be turned into a commodity (the Situationist International criticised

We do not recognise what we call Liberal Anarchism to be genuine Anarchism, but since it exists, we are obliged to describe ourselves as Revolutionary Anarchists. We do not know to what extent there is general agreement with us in the AFB. Our present intention is to be a membership organisation, within the AFB and local groups. If on the other hand we represent the bulk of the membership of the AFB there is no reason why the organisation cannot take over our programme. Those who have followed controversies in the Libertarian Press, at least, will know what this leaflet is about. Those who have, by reason of their contemporary experience, rejected the name anarchist, thinking they would identify themselves with what we here call Liberal Anarchist, are invited to re-think their position

International

The situation internationally, has similarities with Britain except that there the tendency to fit into the framework of society comes from an institutionalised syndicalism, or where exile movements have become bureaucratised. This is what the clash at Carrara[14] was about. But it was also a clash between a revolutionary policy and one of 'fitting in'. We aim to work out a revolutionary programme, as a group having no preconceived programme of working-class organisation but accepting the principle of direct action and working with people on the basis of their beliefs and actions rather than on the mere labels they give themselves, although retaining our own identity.

(Original signatories) A. Meltzer, Ross Flett, Adrian Derby-

Provo). It was discussed by writers such as Guy Debord (1931–1994) and Raoul Vaneigem of the Situationist International. The target here is not so much Provo or the Situationists but people (in Britain and elsewhere) inspired by both.

14. Carrara International Anarchist Congress, 31 August to 3 September 1968 (see previous article).

shire, Stuart Christie, Roger Sandell, Mike Walsh,[15] Jim Duke,[16] Ted Kavanagh.[17]

Comments are invited upon the draft "Aims & Principles of Anarchism".

Issued by the BLACK FLAG GROUP, 735 Fulham Road, London, S.W.6.

The first conference of the "Black Flag" group will be held in Brighton in the autumn. Discussion on the formation of another anarchist newspaper

---

15. Mike 'Digger' Walsh. British Anarchist involved with the strike paper *Ludd* in 1966.
16. James Herriott Duke, (1939–1992). Australian anarchist and poet, involved in *Cuddon's Cosmpolitan Review* and the Wooden Shoe anarchist bookshop (1966–1967). There is a biography of him by Nick Heath at http://libcom.org/history/duke-james-herriott-1939-1992.
17. Australian anarchist involved in Coptic Press, *Cuddon's Cosmpolitan Review* and the Wooden Shoe bookshop.

A Special appeal to all who consider themselves to be revolutionaries

When Stuart Christie and Albert Meltzer revived the Anarchist Black Cross their aim was to encourage solidarity with prisoners of the Franco regime, but also revolutionary action. The ABC encouraged direct connections of solidarity (rather than collecting and forwarding donations themselves) to avoid creating a charity or a bureaucratic organisation. While they could publish the names and addresses of prisoners, this would not work for the resistance. This article asks revolutionaries for concrete solidarity in the form of financial support for the resistance in Spain.

We were conscious that when we began the work of the ANAR-CHIST BLACK CROSS once more that we were tackling an immense task: we have to face innumerable problems all over the world and are obliged to try and specialise on particular issues. 'Amnesty' already exists to help those imprisoned for conscience's sake or unjustly detained for their opinions. (Though we ask supporters of Amnesty and the NCCL[1] to look into the case of Alan Barlow now in prison and refused bail solely because a police officer disliked his expressed opinions).[2]

Our aim has been twofold: to help political prisoners, especially in Franco's Spain, who had fought to resist the Franco dictatorship; and to help the work of the Resistance Movement in

---

1. National Council for Civil Liberties, formed in 1934.
2. Alan Barlow and Phil Carver were arrested on the 15 March 1969 for carrying out a First of May Group attack on the Banco de Bilbao in Covent Garden. See also 'Letter to the Home Secretary' in *Black Flag*, vol. 1, no. 4 April 1969, by Albert Meltzer on behalf of the Anarchist Black Cross.

Spain. We now realise that many, especially pacifists and humanitarians, who would have supported the former aim, have been reluctant to assist us because of the fear that funds would be used to assist the 'violent' Resistance. For this reason we are dividing our work, and this decentralisation will help us to cut out overhead costs of postage etc, which becoming crippling; it will also show wider solidarity and enable parcels to get through.

In future we ask all sympathisers with those suffering in Spanish prisons to send parcels direct to Spain. (Elsewhere in this issue we give details of how to do so; current addresses may be had from us). We want to avoid becoming a 'charity'; everybody knows charities are rackets, anyway. Send parcels direct, from individuals and groups, and let the prisoners know that they are not forgotten. Even our Quaker friends will admit that those suffering ten or twenty years in Spanish prisons for their resistance to Franco are not less worthy of support than those in prison merely by accident, who happen to have offended the dictatorship without doing anything about it, or those convicted of criminal offences, who were in it for the cash. I myself was very grateful for a stream of parcels which came to me during three years in a Spanish jail, as a result of wide publicity which has not been given to many Resistance fighters, outside Spain, solely because they were Spaniards. Anarchists, socialists, Peking-line communists, and Basques, share their food and medical parcels from outside, in a prisoners' commune. There needs be no sectarianism in sending aid and succour to the victims of Franco's penal laws, running the gamut from left catholic to anarcho-syndicalist (but excluding Christian Democrats, Moscow-liners and dissident Falangists,[3] who are not in the commune).

So far as the work of resistance to Franco is concerned, we are

---

3. Members of the ruling party, the Falange Española Tradicionalista who had fallen out with Franco.

asking friends and sympathisers to help us send material aid to the activist groups. With this issue we are launching a special fund to enable us to finance directly the task of resistance against Franco. We have received many requests from militant groups, which we have been unable to do anything about, since up to now our funds have been low and earmarked for a special purpose. From now on, we ask our readers to take over the job of sending aid to prisoners; and such aid, coming locally, is more likely to get through and shows wider solidarity. The funds that we receive will go directly to actively supporting the groups that inside Spain and scattered elsewhere are about to make the breakthrough in the overthrow of the regime. The coming months are critical. Every open act of militant defiance now is a crack in the regime of the ageing dictator. The issue now is no longer whether Franco CAN be overthrown, for what keeps him in power is solely the divided opinions as to what will happen next. The issue is: WHAT WILL FOLLOW? Will it be a continuation of the dictatorship, perhaps in a worse form, perhaps under another party? Or will there be a breakthrough of the revolutionary forces? Every blow that is struck now against the Franco regime is a nail in its coffin, and *also a warning to the next aspirant for power.*

Stuart Christie, Fairfield Gardens, London, 1968. From the Stuart Christie photo album on the Kate Sharpley Library website.

The Resistance Movement lacks everything. It has no means of collecting subscriptions; it cannot pass round the hat. It has for long been dependent on emigré groups, support which it has sometimes received and sometimes not. It needs duplicators and typewriters no less than it needs incendiaries and guns. Far be it from us to break the law by suggesting that funds should be collected in this country to buy explosives; but the best way to get these into Spain is not by hitch-hiking, and we would not like to see French Railways being tricked of their just due in rail tickets.

May I make a special appeal to the not inconsiderable number of people who consider themselves libertarians at little cost to themselves. Usually the same people fork up money they cannot really afford; as attend demonstrations and carry on militant work and devote their time to revolutionary activity. Meanwhile there are many who can easily afford to give large sums – who give such sums to phoney charities and liberal causes and devote none of their time to revolutionary activity – who like to think of themselves as libertarians because it eases their consciences. It may even help their careers as they casually drop the correct phrases into broadcast talks or newspaper articles or around the pop world or write the occasional learned, impartial comment on someone who spent their whole life in militant struggle. There is often little such people can do. But the struggle in Spain about to break out as fiercely as ever is your touchstone. If you fail now, at least have the grace to be silent henceforth.

What Spain needs today is AUDACITY, the audacity by which a conquered people gets up and strikes the ruling class such a blow that it will never again repeat the atrocity of Police State Rule. It does not lack the people prepared to take the initiative, at home and abroad; they are circumscribed by sheer lack of any funds not safely tucked away by bureaucrats, properly audited and never available. What the sympathisers with Spain lack is A CONCRETE PLAN OF ACTION. *In the events that will take place in Spain within the next year, the possibility for action is there.* Let us provide the sinews of battle.

From *Bulletin of the Anarchist Black Cross*, Vol. 1. No. 5, June 1969.

Reprinted in *Attentat* No.2 (Chicago, Solidarity Bookshop). 'Both the Special Appeal and the aid to Spanish prisoners are reprinted from the ANARCHIST BLACK CROSS BULLETIN. Write to the Anarchist Black Cross, 735 Fulham Road, London S.W.6, England for further information.'

The Carr Bombings:
Angry Young Scots?

The 12 January 1971 saw large demonstrations against the Conservative government's Industrial Relations Bill, designed to reduce
the number of strikes. That evening, there were two explosions at
the home of Home Secretary Robert Carr. They were claimed by
the Angry Brigade's communiqué 4. This led to much press comment, much of which was uncritical repetition of police theories
about who was to blame. This 'Christie-watching industry' would
lead to Stuart standing trial at the Old Bailey.

Dominating the news has been the spate of bombings, arson and
personal attacks upon Ministers, Ministries, police and senior
civil servants. The motif has obviously been political and is connected with the Industrial Disputes Bill but also, it seems, the
whole of Government policy including criticisms of the Spanish
fascist regime made by way of force. We may dismiss as fanciful
the Machiavellian comfort of the Left ('it's probably the National
Front trying to stir it up and make out how wicked we are'). The
whole matter seems too widespread for that. The National Front is
only a front for the right wing Tories and they do not (like Charles
Lamb's Chinaman)[1] burn down their houses to roast pigs to get
roast pork. There are simpler ways than that. And how important
is the 'Angry Brigade' (if it exists)?

Let us take the valuation current in everyday society – hard
cash and effort. Many Jewish people feel strongly that the mass

---

1.   A reference to the humorous essay 'A dissertation upon roast pig' in *Essays
      of Elia* by Charles Lamb (1775–1834).

murderer Dr Josef Mengele is still alive and well.[2] The Israelis would like to get him as they got Eichmann.[3] A reward is offered of £20,000. To capture this multi-thousand murderer, you must proceed at risk of life, health and liberty over swamp and forest and then try to kidnap him in the teeth of the Paraguayan police.

Half the price as is offered for this unspeakable monster is offered by the *Daily Mirror*, and few risks are involved. All you have to do is to say that on such-and-such a night you saw Mr. X. put a bomb in Mr. Carr's house at Barnet, and provided your victim fits neatly into New Scotland Yard's category of Dangerous Thoughts Extremist, you can sit back comfortably the rest of your life. Let us hope you do not select from 'clues' obligingly planted by criminal reporter John Stevens of the *Evening Standard*!

Comparisons of value

Perhaps it sticks in the gullet to commit perjury? Well, for £5,000 you need do no more than perform your common law obligations. This sum will be made by the *People* to anyone passing on a clue leading to the conviction of any one of half-a-dozen particularly vicious sex crimes probably committed, as is usual in these cases, by supporters of the Tory Party. (In the event of conviction, political affiliation will be concealed. It might prejudice the jury to know the accused were self-confessed Conservatives).

The Angry Brigade

This tells us that the outrages of the 'Angry Brigade' are regarded seriously, and members of parliament are getting worried. The press does not ask the real issue: how is it that people can feel so strongly about issues that affect them, [like] the Industrial Relations Bill,

---

2. Josef Mengele (1911–1979), the 'Angel of Death' of Auschwitz died in hiding in Brazil.

3. Adolf Eichmann (1906–1962), one of the major organisers of the Holocaust, was abducted from Argentina, tried in Jerusalem and executed.

that they can risk life and liberty? But the M.P.s ask each other anxiously – if they can do *that* over the Industrial Relations Bill, what would 'they' do over a plan to send them to concentration camps? They shout confidently about the possibility of a Right Wing backlash. But privately they are terrified little men. Sir Peter Rawlinson, for instance, the Attorney General, made the press conceal the attack on his home. Had the perpetrator been found before the 'Angries' revealed the fact themselves, would he have prosecuted not declaring his interest in the case? This is what Heath's boys are reduced to. ('Sorry, I didn't want to frighten my children.')

The government announced it was going to take a tough line. It would have 'no nonsense'. It was going to tackle unofficial strikers. The Yachtsman[4] spoke glibly of Civil War. Like public school bullies, they come back crying at the first bloody nose... 'Tisn't fair! We're prefects!' The minister for employment made a great thing of attacks on power workers during their strike. Some were beaten up or their car tyres or house windows were slashed; their wives were refused service in shops (some shopkeepers have since seen a great light, following a boycott) or their children sent home crying from school.... Serves them right, suggested the Minister. Now they know where public opinion lies. So do you now, said someone anonymous.

The Eunuch[5] cries for Rivers of Blood. Pakistani homes are blown up in London. The Right Wing makes it clear how *they* intend to divide the workers, to prepare for civil war, by racial conflict. Is it so very surprising someone has 'introduced violence into British politics', as the Tory M.P.s say – for as it never affected them before, they do not know it existed before. Did they ever have to get the kids to bed while Mosley[6] was holding a

4.   The Conservative Prime Minister, Edward Heath (1916–2005).
5.   Enoch Powell (1912–1998), racist Conservative MP. His 'Rivers of blood' speech was given in Birmingham on 20 April 1968.
6.   Oswald Mosley (1896–1980), leader of the British Union of Fascists.

demo outside the East End tenement windows? As nobody ever marched to Mosley's country home, they assume that violence never existed – well, of course, not so far as 'WE' are concerned....

Does the 'Angry Brigade' exist?

And yet for all this I am sceptical as to whether the Angry Brigade, so-called, exists. The police have told so many lies and made so many evasions it is impossible in this case to rely on any single piece of evidence.

The Establishment can tolerate an Underground that is as devious as the Bakerloo Line. What it dreads is that working-class youth with concern about industrial relations, international affairs, working class solidarity and so on, should adopt the type of urban guerrilla tactics seen in this sort of thing. It can face the duchess's daughter taking up with the hippies and going off to Katmandhu chanting Non Violent Revolution – or even violent if it comes to that – it looks with dismay at the casting off of bourgeois values by those who can stand up and fight for their interests one minute and go back to delivering (or not delivering) the post the next.

They can bear to think of strikes, especially when it happens to hit a competitor. The ruling class can even bear to think of the police battling with demonstrators. As a famous Tory Duke once told his tenants in far-off Ireland: 'You little think to know my temper if you think I will mitigate my just demands in rent by your shooting my bailiff'.[7] But the 'Angry Brigade' have made it all just a little more personal.

Yet, I repeat, IS there such a thing? Or are we really facing a new trend, a development of young working class thought? The police of the day confronted with the Luddites,[8] thought it

7. Rufus Edmonds Shapley included a similar anecdote in his *Library of wit and humor, prose and poetry; selected from the literature of all times and nations* (1884), saying 'I believe the story is an old one'.

8. Artisan textile workers revolting against deskilling and pauperisation.

was necessary to find a 'leader' and they sought for Capt. Ludd. Once again, reports suggest they seek a 'leader'.... and (as someone is said to have found a farm labourer called Ned Ludd, who got the blame for the Luddites) one crooked journalist 'discovered' a certain angry young Scot... but perhaps *we are all angry young Scots....?* Those who worked out neatly that if a certain young Scot did so-and-so, and this is in line with that, then all we have to do is offer a reward for proving it, have slipped up. The fact is that he was not a leader but he might have been a prototype? What was unheard of in 1964 may be very much the fashion in 1972 if we move remorselessly forward to '1984'.

Anyone in public life can make the news which otherwise they might lack by phoning the police and saying they received a kidnap threat by post. Even the clown Nabarro[9] claimed someone wanted to kidnap his daughter (reaction of police was said to be 'What for?'). We can hardly judge the motives and actions of the present direct actionists by what anyone can write or phone on their behalf. It is only reasonable to judge on what is apparently happening. The Establishment seems prepared to be tough, and at the same time it is shitting itself. If this is what is happening as a result of the 'aggro' going in the right direction for a change, we will not be so hypocritical as to condemn it. We should not make the mistake of emulating the violence of the 'Angry Brigade', if such a thing exists, or the many intelligent young people impelled into action. But one must respect their integrity. They are translating our 'fantasies' into reality.

From *Black Flag*, vol.2, no. 2 February 1971

---

9. Sir Gerald Nabarro (1913–1973), Conservative MP. The 'threat' was reported in April 1970.

Violence is not the yardstick ...

The actions of the Angry Brigade led to much discussion in the radical press about the definition of 'violence' and the wisdom or otherwise of violent tactics.

Bismarck was said to be worried when he heard that the Socialist Party had been treated to a long diatribe against violence. Did it mean they would no longer acquiesce in plans for conscription, military aggression, a stricter police force? He was assured they had no such thing in mind. It was what later became a ritual of German Socialism: a denunciation of *anarchist* violence, which consisted then of attacks on military and police establishments and which they felt in their pedantic way was trying to destroy the State building by building.... Naturally, they accepted *State* violence.

Nationalist violence is State violence without State power. Fascist violence is singling out one minority so as to terrorise another, and gaining power by leapfrog. Anarchist violence is the destruction of authority: since it sometimes holds the individual responsible for his actions it has the worst press, since the bourgeoisie can calmly look on the death of millions but the idea of holding someone in authority responsible causes them the utmost horror. They take his views at face value.

Given sufficient mental conditioning one can have authoritarianism without violence (Gandhi, for instance). Normally, authority requires force of some kind, usually violent but it prefers hypnotism and persuasion when these are possible (though even so they do not preclude violence: note the Indian Army reconstructed in Gandhi's new order).

When the intelligent middle class takes a long hard look at current society, it realises that capitalism and the State have landed us in such a position that to support them means support-ing death. But after their long hard look at revolution, they find it is too hard and too long and it cannot be visited over the week-end and get back in time for the office on Monday. That is why radicalism is trendy and that is why the trendiness stops short of action. This applies quite as much to those who apply the yard-stick of 'violence' as those who apply that of 'non-violence', for the real yardstick is freedom and class struggle and how these can be advanced.

Once you get a negative yardstick, you get the romantic apos-tles of revolution as well as those of pacifism but to keep it roman-tic you have to keep it out of your own backyard. That is why so many rave about nationalism – someone else's.

National liberation is a great thing providing it is at least di-vided from us by a stretch of water (though Ireland is a bit uncom-fortably near).... Venezuela is an ideal place, now. Or guerrillas in Czechoslovakia! That would be something! We could all claim them for our own without any fear of anyone calling our bluff! But let spontaneous action happen here and it calls everyone's bluff. They cannot say they are the leaders for then they would face trial. They could at least admit the courage of the many, growing, and obviously numerous unknown people who feel so strongly about some things that they will revolt here and now, without space or time to justify them. But they do not do so for fear the police need further fall guys. Hence the pseudo left attacks on the Angry Bri-gade and its imitators.

ONCE AGAIN the old despicable excuse. The Van der Lubbe[1] excuse.

One month the Red Front marches, fists clenched, through

---

1. Marinus van der Lubbe (1909–1934) was a Dutch council-communist who burnt the Reichstag on 27 February 1933 in an attempt to incite an anti-Nazi revolt. The Communist Party falsely accused him of being in the pay of the Nazis.

Berlin, shouting slogans... next month the Nazis take over and no one breaks so much as a window, but one man, Van der Lubbe burns the Reichstag, and the Left screams 'Police spy!' an echo that is with us to this day.

The imagination that sees police spies everywhere is the reverse of the coin from that which sees us offering flowers to the State as it withers away... The yardstick that counts is not the preconceived, authoritarian idea of how much one conforms to an idealised theory. It is whether or not one is learning to be free. The State has bred enough conformists for authority is based upon the obedient and the meek. If people will say TO HELL WITH THE STATE then at least wish them well.

From *Black Flag*, vol. 2, no. 5 May 1971

Reflections on Commando Raids

The Second World War cast a long shadow over the end of the twentieth century, for radicals as much as anyone else. Commando raids and the attack on Dieppe (1942), which preceded D-Day (1944) are here used as a comparison to point out what the Angry Brigade's attacks could and could not achieve. The article also points out the limited value of criticism of methods from people with completely different aims to those carrying out the attacks.

Are individual attacks on capitalism right or wrong? It is impossible to discuss the question except in context of the class struggle.

Were the individual raids on German-hold territory during the war right or wrong? Was it correct or incorrect military strategy to raid French coastal towns? This was doubtless raised and discussed at the time. But such discussions must have supposed that those participating had the same views.

What value had the opinions of the German High Command? Well, a certain value. Obviously they did not want action that would lead to success. As for those who opposed the war anyway, the whole matter was crazy, fanatical and a mere exercise in suicide. Those who supported Russia above all had a vested interest in escalation which was not necessarily that of the raiders – and to them it was a mere evasion of 'D Day'.

Why raid friendly towns at all? Why not just go over as we do today, and have a nice day out? Why be 'fanatics' and 'lunatics' about it? All this is naive in the light of those who planned Allied strategy. But those who discuss and presume to condemn the 'Angries' of today have just the same naiveté. They think the class war does not exist. So any 'commando' action is lunatic or criminal, just as raids on Cherbourg or Dieppe would be... today! Persons not supporting their aims and pretending no conflict exists, talk as if some imagined that by individual raids they could change ministerial policies or even overthrow governments.

No, they are not quite so simple. Fanatics, maybe; idiots, no. Neither did the British General Staff imagine that by a Marine raid on a coastal town they would get Hitler to resign or sign a non-aggression pact. Each time they retreated the German Press hailed it with glee as a defeat, as if they had planned D Day that week-end. Neither has the 'Angry Brigade' planned D Day for next week-end, nor does it suppose that its commando actions will do more than bring about the climate in which the D Day of the class war will exist.

In terms of the class war, they are no more nor less eccentric or fanatical than any of the outfits that abounded in the militarist war, such as 'Popski's Private Army'[1] or Wingate's.[2] As they are against the State, however, they are denounced by those who would laud them if they did the same deeds but in terms of State acceptance (on patriotic or nationalist grounds).

The between-wars generations were forced on to the defensive. They dared not provoke further capitalist aggression, for the Communist Party had weakened the front of working-class aggression by itself becoming a major Imperialist power. They were obsessed by the real fear of fascism. The fear of a right wing backlash was still over the heads of the post-war generation, and is still vainly threatened by the Right Wing. The CND movement was then touting the myth of a non-violent revolution in which the governments of the world would give up not only the H Bomb but anything else that gave them power. Today we have come back to reality, and we have also the confidence – born out of the

---

1.   British special forces group, active in North Africa and Italy.
2.   The Chindits, commanded by Orde Wingate (1903–1944) carried out jungle warfare against Japanese forces in Burma.

realisation of what causes fascism, war and unemployment and that is our weakness – to know that our generation can once again take the offensive.

As working-class offensive arises, so we will find ourselves in guerrilla warfare, in industrialised countries no less than in peasant wars. It is an open struggle that has not yet really begun, so far as 'D Day' is concerned, but clearly recognised. As Mr. Heath said at UNO, it is a struggle between the governments of the world, whatever their political credo, and those who do not believe government – indeed, of all those whom the former oppress.

Some cannot wait for the balloon to go up. Like John Brown at Harper's Ferry – whose individual actions and whose Angry Brigade sparked off the Civil War in the States, or at least determined that slavery would be one of its issues – they are jumping the gun ... literally. Like the Commando raids, they are preparing the way. It may be, strategically, that they are wrong. That is worth discussion. It must be a discussion, however, that treats the views of the enemy for what they are worth.

From *Black Flag*, vol.2, no. 7 (July/August 1971), p. 5–6.

The Black Cross:
persecuted by Special Branch

Stuart Christie was arrested on 21 August 1971. This article, covering the origins, activities and harassment of the Anarchist Black Cross appeared when Stuart was on trial as one of the 'Stoke Newington Eight'. He, like all the defendants, was charged with conspiracy to cause explosions, and also with possession of explosives (the detonators that he successfully argued were planted by the police). Presumably written after his arrest, it obliquely suggests that his arrest was a result of complaints by the Spanish political police to their British brethren. In *Edward Heath made me angry*, Stuart recognised that Special Branch had their own reasons for attacking him.

During my 3½ years imprisonment in Carabanchel and Alcala I was shocked to discover that the only political prisoners who received any support either moral or financial were the members of the Spanish Communist Party and the Jehovah's Witnesses. Amnesty International would not concern itself with men who had taken a positive position against fascism such as the FIJL, ETA, the MLCP of Spain (and some trot groups), and the CNT.[1]

To live in prison we had to depend on our own friends and solidarity from our own groups both in the interior and in exile, such as the committee pro-presos in Toulouse.[2] The knowledge of the existence of such aid groups was more or less confined to the Spanish groups in exile, and our attitude was that we had to broaden the spectrum of support for political prisoners (as

1. FIJL – Spanish Libertarian Youth; CNT – National Confederation of Labour (Anarcho-Syndicalist Union); MLCP – Maoists; ETA – Basque Nationalists [Original note by *Black & Red Outlook*].
2. Comite pro-presos, prisoner support committee.

opposed to liberals) which as far as we could see was confined to Spaniards in exile and in the interior, to include libertarians from all over the world. It was not solely to be confined to the Spanish victims of the class struggle, but at that point in time, 1967, the repression that was quickly to spread throughout Western Europe was still the monopoly of the Franco regime.

On my return to London I had long discussions with comrades about the idea – especially Albert Meltzer who had been one of the militants who had remained in the forefront of activity since 1935. Albert had been involved in liaison with comrades for some time – especially with comrades on the Chinese mainland – and as a result of discussions we decided to form an organisation which could act as a clearing house for information and counter-information on the number, condition and whereabouts of political prisoners also the nature and details so far as we were able, of the people and agencies responsible for the repression throughout the world. The International Anarchist Black Cross was formed in late '67. Firstly, we put out an appeal for funds to which people responded very well but after a number of food parcels were returned by the Spanish Prison authorities, it was decided that the answer was to print the names of prisoners and their location in the Black Cross bulletins and have people contact prisoners on a more personal level. On a different level we used information and letters smuggled out of prison to maintain pressure, through the national press, on the Spanish authorities who were, and still are, particularly sensitive to any reference in the foreign press to their political prisoners and the brutality of the Spanish Special Branch. This aspect was particularly successful, not so much in the coverage such stories got in the British and international press but in the reaction of the Prison authorities to these stories, and consequently in the rise in morale of the prisoners who discovered the existence of these stories after being interrogated by Franco's officials as to how the letters were being smuggled out of the prisons. On a number of occasions articles were found inside the prisons which related to escape attempts and the Black Cross became more of a bugbear to the Prison authorities as the existence of them, when found, was blamed on us. Not that this worried us – anything to be of service – but the effect that this had on us was direct and hard. For a number of years the Spanish Secret Police had been working in close contact not only with the French Police but also, as I discovered, with the British Secret Police, the Special Branch!

This photo was taken during a visit with Stuart when he was on remand in Brixton prison. From *Inside Story* no. 7 (January–February 1973). Digitised by The Sparrows' Nest.

Shortly after my arrest while I was being held in the Dirección General de Seguridad by the Brigada Politio-Social, I was shown a number of photographs of young militants in exile (none of whom I recognised, obviously) – then two days after my arrest a new interrogator was brought in. This policeman spoke perfect

English without any trace of an accent whatsoever. He was extremely polite and introduced himself (the name slipped my mind almost immediately afterwards). He then went on to say that he had been flown over from London especially to conduct the interrogation and had been based in London for the previous 12 years. He spoke for some time on the usual 'barrier breaking' chat on the English way of life and, as a passing comment on the qualities of the English Police with whom he collaborated closely! Shortly after he produced a photograph of myself [at] Hyde Park (Speakers' Corner) with two young Spanish comrades. I was asked if these were the men who had put me 'up' to the job of bringing explosives which I denied. He then went on to say that these two men (and myself) were well known to Scotland Yard as 'troublemakers'. Obviously the relationship between the Home Office and the Spanish Embassy is not confined to the cocktail circuit.

The first direct evidence of a close collaboration with the Spanish Police came when the Special Branch raided my home in London with an explosives warrant.[3] This was before any explosions had taken place! No explosives were found but a watch was kept on my house for the next few days. The following Saturday night two explosions took place, one at the Spanish Embassy and the other at the American Officers Club.[4] This was claimed by the Revolutionary Solidarity Movement-1st May [Group]. The Spanish police had received information that attacks would be made on their Embassies shortly in European Capitals and had passed the information on to the Scotland Yard to do the dirty work for them. From that date onwards it became apparent that the British Political Police would, when the first opportunity presented itself, attempt to frame me. I came to the decision that I could not become actively involved in domestic political activity apart from, of

---

3. 27 February 1968.
4. 3 March 1968.

course, general propaganda work. They were itching to get their hands on me and made it only too obvious. The facade of a disinterested British Police was cracking.

I later discovered a possible reason for the growing interest in Albert and myself when comrade Miguel Garcia was released after spending 20 years in Spanish prisons. Miguel informed me of the aforementioned interviews with prison authorities over escape attempts and smuggled letters of complaint appearing in the international press – which were conveniently blamed on the A.B.C. From what I can gather from journalists and other sources the Spanish Government made strong complaints about the activity of the A.B.C. – certainly through the Police Force (Interpol). The result of these complaints may be guessed.

ANARCHIST BLACK FLAG Organ of Revolutionary Anarchism: Subscription for 12 issues 75p. 10, Gilbert Place, London W.C.1

From *Black & Red Outlook* (published by the Anarchist Syndicalist Alliance) no. 7. undated but advertised in *Freedom* from 23 September 1972 on. *Black Flag* v. 2, no. 14 (October 1972) reported police harassment of ASA members possessing this issue.

Translator's Introduction to
Sabaté: guerrilla extraordinary

During the 'Stoke Newington Eight' trial, while on remand in Brixton prison, Stuart translated Antonio Téllez's groundbreaking biography of Francisco Sabaté (1915-1960), whose death in action marked the end of one phase of the anarchist resistance to Franco. Sabaté was not the last guerrilla – Ramón Vila Capdevila, known as 'burnt face' or 'long strides' was killed in action in 1963 – but, as Stuart shows, the next phase would not be limited to the territory of the Spanish state. Stuart recognises the limited, defensive role that the guerrilla can play; without forgiving those radicals who called the Angry Brigade 'elitists'. *Sabaté: guerrilla extraordinary* would be the first publication of Cienfuegos Press. This article reflects some of the connections that made Cienfuegos possible.

It was in Madrid's Carabanchel Prison that I first came into contact with men who had been active in the Spanish Resistance during the period covered in this book. One name was constantly brought up – that of Sabaté. His name is almost unknown beyond the Pyrenees.

There is a chapter in Professor Hobsbawm's book on *Bandits* (Weidenfeld and Nicolson 1969) where he relies on facts gleaned from the author of this book to illustrate his own thesis. There is a Hollywood film very loosely based on the life of Sabaté, but which portrays the protagonist as a smuggler – *Behold a pale horse*,[1] starring Gregory Peck and Anthony Quinn. A better introduction

---

1. *Behold a pale horse*, directed by Fred Zinnemann (1907–1997), released in 1964. It was based on the 1961 novel *Killing a mouse on Sunday* by Emeric Pressburger (1902–1988).

to the struggles of the Sabaté brothers is given in Miguel Garcia's book *Franco's prisoner* (Rupert Hart-Davis 1972).

Antonio Téllez's life of Sabaté gives some insight into the motivation behind urban guerrilla action and, most important of all, shows us how everyone – no matter how difficult his or her position may be or how despotic the regime – can fight for justice and liberty, if they so choose.

The story does not end in San Celoni with the death of Sabaté. Almost the same day he was gunned down by the Militia and the Guardia Civil, his struggle – that of free men against tyrants – was taken up by other men and women who must remain anonymous. They profited by both his experience and his mistakes, not only in Spain but throughout the world, under the banners of the First of May – a day of international working-class solidarity.

Within one month of Sabaté's death the DRIL (the Revolutionary Directorate of Iberian Liberation) was formed, later to develop into the Iberian Liberation Council (CIL). This Organization was responsible for, among other things, the first political hi-jacking and kidnappings in recent history. One example was the arrest of the Portuguese liner *Santa Maria* on the high seas in 1961. In Milan, Italy, libertarian activists staged the first in a wave of successful abductions with the kidnapping of the Spanish Vice-Consul in that city, Sr Elias, in 1962 – to prevent the execution of Jorge Cunill Vals, of the Iberian Federation of Libertarian Youth (FIJL).

A number of foreign political prisoners being held on sentences ranging from twenty to thirty years were released following the kidnapping of the Ecclesiastical Adviser to the Spanish Embassy in the Vatican City, Mgr Marcos Ussia, in 1966.[2]

---

2. His kidnapping was the first action of the First of May Group. He was held from the 29th of April to the 11th of May, 1966 and released unharmed.

Kidnapping and the holding of hostages is repugnant to Anarchists. It savours of the prison system we want to abolish – our aim is to smash the power of the ruling class, not to imprison them. On the other hand, however, how does one prevent comrades from rotting in prison? In future, the State that takes political hostages must expect political hostages to be taken in return – no longer is the game being played according to the rules which *they* laid down to make it easier for *them* to keep the upper hand.

The question often posed – how does one abolish political violence? – is an easy one to answer. Abolish political tyranny and it will be gone with the wind. There is a climate of opinion, especially among my generation, which questions the rules, sanctified by time, according to which all the games have been played. For this reason, they are willing to listen to such divergent ideas as anarchism, the New Left and even mysticism.

In the thirties and forties the essential political struggle appeared to be between two poles of dictatorship – State Communism and Fascism – which made decentralism seem irrelevant. Then, until the late fifties, the struggle appeared to be between one power bloc and another – making the idea of free communities appear irrelevant. Now it is evident, even to the politically illiterate journalist who confuses the climate of opinion with anarchism itself, that the issue of our times is between the State – call it 'law and order' or 'mass genocide organization' as you like – and anarchism.

It is the recognition of this that leads to collaboration and conspiracy between the international police forces – and how this affected Sabaté is clearly shown by Antonio Téllez. The British Special Branch (although the Government has no mandate to support Franco's regime by police action and no Western government has even dared to invite Franco on a State visit because of popular distaste for his police methods) are as deeply involved in the conspiracy against the people of Europe, and against Spanish anti-fascism, as any other secret political police force. Those who take a stand against fascism and oppression have no 'country' behind them.

For years, the Spanish authorities have attempted to get the international police forces to put pressure on active opponents of the Franco regime living abroad. Yet so great is the detestation in which ordinary people hold the Franco regime that in countries where public opinion is of some consequence this has to be done by conspiracy and intrigue rather than by open laws. Though the last Wilson Government was not, openly at any rate, prepared to grant this demand, Scotland Yard still gave it their support, ignoring Government policy. The late Conservative Government gave them every possible facility. The policy of sending arms to Spain has been revived. And nobody can know better than myself how opponents of the Franco regime can be harassed with raids, pressure on employers, intimidation of friends, the 'leaking' of information to the press, the framing of charges and the planting of incriminating evidence ... and I was born in Scotland! What would it have been like if I had been born in Spain and had to ask permission to come and go? What was my crime? That of having subscribed to the concept of class war and, of course, showing solidarity with political prisoners, the victims of fascism.

There are, of course, many of 'advanced' political ideas who find such activities acceptable in South-East Asia, Africa and South America, but throw up their hands in horror at the idea of urban guerrilla warfare on the home front. For the 'revolutionary' socialist, Northern Ireland is the nearest such activities can exist without becoming 'élitist' and 'vanguardist'! As Sabaté and others found out in the academic and apathetic atmosphere of the endless meetings of the Spanish exiles, discussion and agenda are too often used as a cover for cowardice and inertia.

Urban guerrillas are not the 'vanguard' of the revolution and this is amply illustrated in the life of Sabaté. They are the rearguard and know only too well that the army of the revolution can only be the workers themselves. The most they can do is cover [against] the attacks made on the people in retreat. Governments today are well aware of the dangers inherent in a class-divided society, and the contradictions of capitalism. It was brought home to them suddenly by the events of Paris in May 1968. Until then many politicians subscribed to the 'conspiracy theory' of history – that all situations are engineered artificially by a small group of highly motivated individuals (no doubt because they themselves rose to power that way, working for their own ends). Arrogance blinded them to the fact that revolutionary situations and revolutionaries spring from popular discontent and a none-too-cleverly disguised class justice – to them, revolutionaries lived and operated in a social vacuum which had no bearing on the day-to-day lives of ordinary people. What they forgot was that all ordinary people are potential revolutionaries.

I translated this book in prison while awaiting trial. It has since been revised by the author and is more detailed and complete than the Spanish and Italian editions. I would like to take the opportunity to thank Brenda, who (apart from typing the finished version) in my sixteen months wait, on remand in Brixton, kept me as cheerful and comfortable as possible, visiting me every day and helping to prepare my defence. Also my old friend and collaborator, Albert Meltzer, for his active solidarity before, during and since the trial which enabled me to finish this book. Another colleague in the International Black Cross, my old friend Miguel Garcia Garcia, helped me over the more difficult points in this translation. His personal knowledge of the period is immense, and no doubt he will follow his book, *Franco's prisoner*, with its references to the men of the Resistance, with some of his experiences with such figures as Massana, the

Sabaté brothers,[3] José Lluis Facerias, Wenceslao Giménez,[4] Juan Busquets[5] and others.

Introduction to *Sabaté: guerrilla extraordinary* by Antonio Téllez (Davis-Poynter, 1974).

---

3.   Spanish anarchists and guerrillas, José (1910–1949), Francisco ('El Quico', 1915–1960), Manuel (1927–1950). All were killed by the Francoist state.
4.   Wenceslao Giménez Orive, 'Wences', (1921–1950) Spanish anarchist and guerrilla. He worked with Facerias before forming the Los Maños group. He killed himself after being wounded in a police ambush. See *Los Maños: the lads from Aragon; the story of an anti-Franco action group* (Christie-books ebook 2013; Kate Sharpley Library pamphlet 2014).
5.   See the tribute by Stuart on page 166.

Introduction to *Man! An anthology of anarchist ideas, essays, poetry and commentaries*

Marcus Graham (Shmuel Marcus, 1893–1985) was a Jewish Ru-
manian immigrant to the USA, where he joined the anarchist
movement. He edited the *Anarchist Soviet Bulletin* (1919–1920) and
its successor, *Free Society* (1920–1922); he was briefly involved
with the anarchist journal *The Road to Freedom* from 1924 to
1925. An uncompromising figure, he became close to the militant
Italian-American followers of Luigi Galleani (1861–1931) grouped
around the newspaper *L'Adunata dei Refrattari*. His association
with the International Group of San Francisco led to his editorship
of *Man!* (1933–1940) which Kenyon Zimmer described as 'the finest
and most popular English-language anarchist publication of the
era'.[1] He successfully resisted attempts to deport him in 1919, 1936
and 1940.

For Stuart, propaganda by word or deed are not 'separate
paths' or carried out by two different sorts of anarchist. What people do depends on the conditions they face, and all those who
resist are his kindred spirits.

Marcus Graham is, at eighty-one, an indefatigable anarchist prop-
agandist, one of that strange breed that has never received its due
acknowledgement in the history of the class struggle.

They are not as other men and women; they are not at all
as other editors, publishers, speakers and writers; they are not
even always like other anarchists. They share their passionate

---

1.   Kenyon Zimmer, *Immigrants against the state: Yiddish and Italian anar-
     chism in America* (Urbana: University of Illinois Press, 2015), p. 187.

devotion to the cause of freedom with others, but theirs is a devouring, insatiable urge to communicate, to proselytise, to tell how it is.

Journalists of lesser talent spend the week from bar to bar on high salaries and expense accounts, writing a story, or perhaps a paragraph or two ... these others sit in a little room – often their living room – surrounded by papers, books, all in indescribable confusion – writing away, night after night, capable of producing whole newspapers on their own, not only preparing it for the printer but even if need be running it off as well. They spend their lives in poverty, though often skilled workers on good wages; for everything they have goes on 'literature'. When the situation becomes difficult they will go out to rob a bank to raise the money for a printing press, and from a small handpress in the cellar they will bring out leaflets, newspapers, books and pamphlets alongside forged passes, documents and all the other needs of the activist in a totalitarian regime.

They are not paid organisation editors, writers who live on their royalties as the worker does on his wages, those who have the benefit of collective money to bring out their works, or the advantage of an established publishing house. Those have their place in society, no doubt and even in the libertarian movement, but these others tirelessly bring out publications, write articles and envelopes and raise funds sometimes from their friends, but mostly out of their own pockets.

To take a few of whom I know personally and many of whom I know only from hearsay, as I did Marcus Graham when I first read this book in manuscript; of veteran Willi Huppertz[2] in the Ruhr, who took his books and his mimeograph down to

---

2. Reinhold Wilhelm Huppertz, (1904–1978), German anarchist. A short biography by Nick Heath is at https://libcom.org/history/huppertz -willy-1904-1978.

the cellar in Nazi times, whom I met at the Carrara Anarchist
Congress in 1968; of Pa Chin,[3] publishing the complete works of
Kropotkin in Chinese at the height of the Japanese invasion; of
my fellow prisoner in Madrid, unquestionably senior in the time
he served (twenty years), Miguel Garcia, setting up by hand on
an antiquated machine in the back of a Barcelona shop after the
Francoist victory; of Franco Leggio[4] in Ragusa, Sicily; of Victor
Garcia[5] in Venezuela; of Frank Leech[6] back home in Glasgow,
dedicating years of his life to bringing out pamphlets on a press
that would now be (and perhaps was then) a collector's piece and
speaking every Sunday on Glasgow Green to hundreds of workers; J.W. (Chummy) Fleming,[7] one time 'Last of the Mohicans'
of Australian Anarchism, single handed carrying on a public
rostrum at Yarra Bank, Melbourne, week after week, and holding a one-man anarchist demonstration every May-Day – to die,
while still active, in his nineties, just before the libertarian revival
on that continent; M.P.T. Acharaya,[8] lone voice of anarchism
in another great continent year after year bringing out leaflets
and books from a tiny flat in Bombay, and who incidentally was

3. Now transliterated Ba Jin (1904–2005), Chinese anarchist and writer.
    There is a short biography on the Kate Sharpley Library website: https://
    www.katesharpleylibrary.net/4xgxxt.
4. Franco Leggio (1921–2006), Italian anarchist. See the tribute by Stuart
    on page 143. A short biography by Pippo Gurrieri is on the Kate Sharpley
    Library website: https://www.katesharpleylibrary.net/vmcwp8.
5. Victor Garcia (1919–1991), Spanish anarchist. See the tribute by Stuart on
    page 172.
6. Frank Leech (1900–1953), British anarchist. A biography of him by
    Nick Heath is on Libcom.org: https://libcom.org/history/leech
    -frank-1900-1953.
7. Chummy Fleming (1863–1950).
8. M.P.T. Acharaya (1887–1954), Indian anarchist. A biography of him
    by Nick Heath is on Libcom.org: https://libcom.org/history/acharya
    -mpt-1887-1951. See also *We are anarchists*, a collection of his writings ed-
    ited by Ole Birk Laursen (AK Press, 2019).

a great friend both of Marcus Graham and of my old friend in London, Albert Meltzer, himself yet another of these tireless propagandists, working long hours in the print industry (and with a writing talent beyond anyone in Fleet Street) and spending almost all his hard earned wages running a duplicator, offset or a hall, publishing books, pamphlets and magazines, prolifically writing and undertaking every imaginable task for the idea of anarchism from addressing a few people in a draughty room to plunging into yet one more struggle against heavy and sometimes hopeless odds, as do they all.

These people do not write the history books, which are penned by academics with an eye to what academic flourished at a particular time and endowed his thesis to theories tested in the flames of struggle by working people and welded into theory by these propagandists, apostles of the idea of anarchism. For the academic they are sectarians, even eccentrics, too harsh for his taste, they lack the necessary academic degrees to judge the lessons of history.

Marcus Graham is typical of this strange, unknown, unappreciated tribe. How typical is shown by the casual reference in his autobiographical introduction to the fact that while earning what was very good pay at the time, he was able to bring out his *Anthology of revolutionary poetry*,[9] paying for its publication with the money that he had earned with the sweat of his brow. It did not occur to him to save for his old age, as it does to the vast majority of other people. There are more distinguished gentlemen who can produce scholarly anthologies of revolt while receiving government money at a pleasant university in ivy covered cloisters, discussing their selections over a glass of sherry. But would such an anthology compare for inspiration and range with that

---

9. *An anthology of revolutionary poetry* was published in 1929 (copyright Sh. Marcus), printed by the Active Press.

produced by the tailor's cutter from the East End in his spare time? Something is lacking when the academics write of revolt ... some writers in *MAN!* unashamedly, but not religiously, call it soul.

The publication *MAN!* from which the essays in this book are taken appeared at regular monthly intervals from January 1933 until April 1940. It covered a wide range of subjects, cultural as well as political, from an anarchist point of view. In some ways the articles are unmistakably of their time and place; at other times one has the feeling of indestructible force that drives these men and women on, who have this urge to proclaim the idea, and who cannot be crushed whatever the repression; when the blow of a Hitler or a Stalin or a Franco falls on the working people, there is always someone who has escaped the net and is somewhere looking around for a few reams of paper, or if need be paint and brush, and wields it with the same devastating effect as deadlier weapons, sometimes at the same time, too, such as Mateo Morral who threw the bomb at the hated Alfonso XIII of Spain.[10] Men and women of this calibre will always be found in all countries and all times until social, political and economic injustice has been eradicated from the annals of mankind and a free society based on worker's control, mutual aid and co-operation built in its place.

The articles preserved here for posterity discuss anarchism from many angles and present fascinating biographical glimpses of people and movements, part of a great onward struggle to crush capitalism and the State. From these articles and my collaboration with Marcus Graham and his contemporaries in the States, and elsewhere, I personally derive a great inspiration. I was not born

---

10. Mateu Morral (1880–1906) Spanish anarchist and librarian at Ferrer's Modern School. His attempted assassination of Alfonso XIII of Spain failed but killed numerous bystanders. He killed himself rather than be arrested.

when they were written. I can reasonably hope to be alive when those hopes and ambitions and struggles for ANARCHY reach their fulfilment.

STUART CHRISTIE
Cienfuegos Press
December 1974

From *Man! An anthology of anarchist ideas, essays, poetry and commentaries* (Cienfuegos Press, 1974).

Review of *Anarchism* by George Woodcock

George Woodcock came to anarchism from the pacifist movement during the Second World War. He was closely involved with Freedom Press, which published his book *Anarchy or chaos* in 1944. He left the anarchist movement to pursue his literary career and in 1949 moved to Canada. In the first edition of *Anarchism: a history of libertarian ideas and movements* in 1962 he declared that his departure was a contributory factor in the 'death' of anarchism. His later writings on anarchism, proposing a non-revolutionary, intellectual and exclusively pacifist anarchism, made him a divisive figure within the British anarchist movement and elsewhere.

This is an updated version of Woodcock's 1962 'obituary' on anarchism in which he wrote the anarchist movement off as totally finished and defeated and includes a postscript in which he insists that he was right all the time but that a 'new' anarchism has arisen, which he ascribes to some minor literary ventures, including his own, some lesser intellectual figures (his own friends, some totally obscure) and the pacifist movement which is his real love.

On the British movement his ignorance is so appalling he thinks of the anarchist movement – from the Universities (where he thinks it abounds) to the Angry Brigade – deriving its 'inspiration' not merely from Freedom Press but from its largely unknown secretary[1] in particular. He is wildly inaccurate about its composition or history.

Theoretically he accepts the anarchist critique of the State so long as it is confined to theory, and those who have written philosophically upon the absence of government earn his

---

1.   Vernon Richards.

benign approval. With his sectarian pacifist attitude activist anarchism earns his firm hostility and is still clearly marked down as 'defeated'.

From *Time Out* No. 273, 6–12 June 1975

Obituary [for Franco]:
When the Machine Stops

While Stuart did, in retrospect, believe that failing to assassinate Franco was the best possible result, he never lost his loathing for the murderous dictator. Stuart described Francoism as 'an unbroken chain of mass murder, terror, repression, and unimaginable suffering inflicted on the many by criminal and avaricious opportunists operating under the cloak of a religious and moral crusade led by a megalomaniac general'.[1]]

Francisco Franco de Bahamonde has rotted and died – as generals normally die – in bed. The archetype of the tyrant general, he never won or even fought a battle unless it was against his own people. In his youth he was guilty of colonial repression. He fought the Saharan wars against the subjects of the State rather than against foreign enemies. His career of murder and repression against the people of Spain began in 1934 when he was brought in by the perfidious Spanish Republican Government to shoot down the workers on strike. It was he who brought in the Moorish soldiers to suppress the Asturian miners. His most 'distinguished' conquests took place between 1936 and 1939, when he rose against his employers and betrayed his oath, to ally himself with his country's enemies. He continued this war against the people of Spain until the last drop of watery blood came to a final standstill in his cursed body. He maintained rule by military occupation to a degree unheard of except by foreign domination. The massacres, tortures and repression which followed the war established him firmly in power, but they left scars so horrible and so deep that the

---

1.   Stuart Christie, *General Franco made me a 'terrorist'*, p. i.

suggestion of their renewal – because of the shooting or garrotting of opponents – has left Spain in turmoil.

Drawing by Marco on cover of *Black Flag*, v. 4, no. 5 (November/
December 1975) celebrating the death of Franco.
Digitised by The Sparrows' Nest.

Bahamonde suffered the fate of all dictators in that he could not relax his grip on the regime: if he attempted to liberalise in any way the people would take advantage of the laxity to overthrow him. Yet at the same time he could not tighten the repression, for it was already tightened to bursting point. He could not tolerate a successor for that successor would have ousted him at the first opportunity. It is for this reason that the puppet Juan Carlos[2] has been manoeuvred and compromised by his total subservience to the wishes of the *Caudillo*. There is no man of power to take Franco's place. If there were, the Right would have already put him forward to be groomed as successor, and to 'groom' another dictator means to impose fear, and fear in turn cannot be imposed without severe repression. The Spaniards will not take another repression. They will either resist or they will leave it a ghost country as they have created ghost towns with the economic migration.

As Franco decayed and rotted on the death-bed he could see his empire decaying too. Perhaps in a last vision of dreadful clarity he saw his achievement without illusion for what it really is: a period of death and disaster, catastrophe and ruin, fear and agony brought upon a people for no other reason than that they failed to free themselves from Army rule. Or perhaps the shroud of the Virgin of Pilar and the holy water and the incantations and the rest of the mumbo jumbo are intended to drown out those visions?

Bahamonde's epitaph was spoken by Miguel de Unamuno[3] long ago when the philosopher declared – in the presence of dona Carmen Polo de Franco[4] and of the notorious General Millán

---

2. Juan Carlos, grandson of Alfonso XIII, was selected as Franco's successor and oversaw the 'transition' to 'democratic' capitalism.
3. Miguel de Unamuno (1864–1936) Spanish writer and academic. *Unamuno's last lecture* by Luis Portillo was published by Simian in 1971 in a pamphlet also containing 'Spanish prisoners and what can be done' by Miguel Garcia and 'The Catalan Manifesto'.
4. Wife of Franco (1900–1988).

Astray[5] who exceeded Franco in villainy: YOU HAVE CON-QUERED. BUT YOU WILL NOT CONVINCE. Millán Astray's favourite saying was 'Long Live Death', and Death has been the major achievement of Franco and his cohorts. Now it takes him too.

From *Freedom: Anarchist Fortnightly*, vol.36, nos. 46–47, 22 November 1975.

---

5.   José Millán Astray (1879–1954) of the Spanish Legion.

Review of *The Angry Brigade* by Gordon Carr

Gordon Carr's 1975 book on the Angry Brigade received a partial welcome from Stuart. If Carr overplayed the importance of Situationism, he at least understood the libertarian socialist background to the events. Since then, although the Angry Brigade have appeared in fiction several times, Carr's history has not been superseded. Stuart was to edit and publish an expanded edition in 2003.

Gordon Carr, the BBC producer of the documentary of the same name, felt dissatisfied with the visual presentation of the politically and jurisprudentially complex story behind Britain's best known libertarian action group, *The Angry Brigade*, so he set himself the task of writing what will no doubt become the standard work on this subject... that is, this side of the revolution.

The book is an excellent summary of the background to and the development of the Angry Brigade and the trial of the *Stoke Newington Eight*, the eight people presented by the police and the D.P.P.[1] as the hard core of the Angry Brigade. Despite Gordon Carr's obsession (passed on I may add from the *mysterious Special Branch sergeant* who detected and isolated the Situationist inspiration in the AB communiques who we can now reveal as Roy Creamer – now Inspector – Scotland Yard's eclectic dialectician) with Situationism as the main historical influence on the AB, which is totally baseless so far as the Stoke Newington Eight are concerned but which could, perhaps, be inferred from the language of the AB communiques which had more to do with poetry

---

1.   Director of Public Prosecutions.

than explanation, it is reasonably politically fair to those of us who stood trial, understanding the libertarian beliefs of the defendants and the more wordy communiques of the AB itself.

Press conference at the offices of *Time Out* on 10 December 1972, after the acquittal of four of the Stoke Newington Eight defendants in the so called 'Angry Brigade' trial. Front row-L-R: Kate McLean, Angie Weir and Stuart Christie with Brenda Christie. Back row centre in sheepskin is Chris Broad (sadly deceased), a member of the Stoke Newington Eight Defence Group. Third from left is Stuart's lawyer, Benedict Birnberg. From the Phil Ruff photo album on the Kate Sharpley Library website.

However, it must be borne in mind that Gordon Carr is somewhat limited in that, he has reached the conclusion that all those who were found guilty should have been, and all who were acquitted were innocent. Complete objectivity could not thus be obtained within the boundaries of the laws of libel. One defendant (myself) was alleged to have had explosives in his car and the jury, after almost six months carefully listening to the case, decided this was not true. The only possible inference from this decision can be that the police put them there; but while this can be said, it cannot be said that something similar might have happened to those found guilty. (The reverse also applies. The police would be quick to say, in fact did say this at a press conference immediately after the trial, but qualifying it with an 'off the record boys').

Also, such a record can never be fully objective because by detaching a section from the whole and examining it under a microscope one may learn a lot about the section, but it is misleading rather than helpful. If in discussing the conduct of troops in battle the only references made concerned those who rushed over the top and charged the enemy, it would give a John Wayne atmosphere to military history. But these people would never have done it if they had been 'isolated' or 'elitist' as such an examination would show them to be. There were others there, some doing a lot more, some doing a lot less, some remaining patiently in the front line for years, some running away at the first sniff of NITRAMITE 19C...[2] they all have to be considered as part of the battle without which there was no battle. To examine (as in effect Gordon Carr is doing) a few people in a foxhole on the Stoke Newington front, however meticulous it sets out to be, can never be very illuminating if one even forgets to mention there was a war on at the time.

The contrast between the police who knew and said from the first that it was a political trial, and the judiciary who fell over themselves backwards to assure us that it was nothing of the sort as there were no political offenders in England, only political police (and even *they* were called Special Branch), degenerated into

2.   The blasting explosive allegedly used by the Angry Brigade.

a farce at times, but a farce for real in which the playwright could not insert in the programme *TEN YEARS LATER*. During the interval people have gone to prison for ten years and are suffering the monotonous rigours and passive violence of English jails.

Those who wish to learn from the mistakes of others would be wise to read this book.

From *Cienfuegos Press Review of Anarchist Literature 1976* (*Cienfuegos Press Anarchist Review*, no 1.)

Two editorials from *The Free-Winged Eagle*

Stuart and Brenda moved to Orkney in 1976. While their work with Cienfuegos Press is well known, they also found time to produce a local alternative paper, *The Free-Winged Eagle*. The title comes from a poem by the Mexican anarchist, Ricardo Flores Magón (Cienfuegos had published *Land and liberty: anarchist influences in the Mexican Revolution*, a compilation of Flores Magón's articles by Dave Poole in 1977). Here Stuart switches seamlessly from celebrating a rebel from the past to discussing the current challenges facing Orkney, notably the threat of uranium mining. His aim is not to recruit people to the idea of anarchism, but to encourage local autonomy as a step in the right direction.

Editorial from issue 1 (Winter/Spring, 1979)

'We cannot break our chains with weak desire,
With whines and supplicating cries.
'Tis not by crawling meekly in the mire
The free-winged eagle learns to mount the skies.'

The above words were written by someone from the darkness of his prison cell, after many years of persecution. We cannot help but admire the spirit contained in those lines, that even from a prison cell one may show one's resistance to arbitrary authority, and challenge the obscurantism of those who defend the State. We therefore call this publication FREE-WINGED EAGLE, with the knowledge that our forefathers fought and died for Freedom, and the certain hope that the generations to come shall experience that Freedom.

We want to hear from you. This publication is a forum of every activity that is going on in Orkney. Don't wait for some political leader to predict a shift in public opinion – write to us now and let's all hear your views and ideas. With this idea firmly in mind, we would like to think the Letters Pages will become one of the most important parts of the publication. You are invited to send in articles on any subject you like, though preference will be given to issues directly relevant to Orkney; and anything in support of any political party, bureaucratic body, or obscurantist organisation will find its way straight to the waste-paper basket. Reviews, poetry, illustrations etc., will also be considered welcome. What better way to spend a cold winter's night than sitting by the peat-fire's glow with a jug of home-brew, writing the odd page or two for the *Free-Winged Eagle*!

We feel, obviously, that there is a need for an alternative press in Orkney, but any means of communication cannot survive if it is not used, and this publication is a living organism of which you are a part, and whose growth depends on you. We cannot exist as a slick magazine, catering to passive consumers of preconceived ideas, no matter how fashionably radical those ideas may appear to be. Life is real, and if the 'good guys' aren't always so 'good,' then that is how we shall tell it!

There isn't much more to say, but you may be wondering when the next issue will be out. Soon, we hope! Publication will be irregular, but from a practical point of view a quarterly appearance would be the ideal. Meanwhile, write to:– Free-Winged Eagle, Over the Water, Sanday, Orkney KW17 2BL.

FAREWELL!!

We cannot break our chains with weak desire,
With whines and supplicating cries.
'Tis not by crawling meekly in the mire
The free-winged eagle learns to mount the skies.

The gladiator, victor in the fight,
On whom the hard-contested laurels fall,
Goes not in the arena pale with fright
But steps forth fearlessly, defying all.

O victory, O victory, dear and fair,
Thou crownest him who does his best,
Who, perishing, still unafraid to bear,
Goes down to dust, thy image in his breast.

Farewell, O comrades, I scorn life as a slave!
I begged no tyrant for my life, though sweet it was;
Though chained, I go unconquered to my grave,
Dying for my own birth-right – and the world's.
Ricardo Flores Magón

Ricardo Flores Magón, born in 1874,[1] founded the Mexican Liberal Party[2] in 1905, which organised two unsuccessful rebellions against the government in 1906 and 1908. Prior to this he had been imprisoned several times by the authorities for editing opposition newspapers. With the revolution of 1910, Magon saw the error of his reformist ways,[3] and devoted the rest of his life to the anarchist cause.

Through his influence large areas of land were expropriated by the labourers and worked in common by them under the banner of *Tierra y Libertad*, LAND AND LIBERTY.

During the years of struggle which followed, he opposed

---

1. Ricardo Flores Magón was born in 1873. 1874 as his date of birth appears in *Land and liberty: anarchist influences in the Mexican Revolution*.
2. Mexican Liberal Party (Partido Liberal Mexicano, PLM).
3. Ricardo became an anarchist during his exile in the United States. The PLM only announced its anarchist position in 1911, once the Mexican revolution was under way.

successive so-called 'revolutionary governments', resisting both the old and new dictatorships with equal vigour. During a period of exile in the U.S., he is suppressed by the authorities under spying laws, and in 1918 is sentenced to 20 years forced hospitality in Leavenworth Prison, Kansas. It only took 4 years to murder him however, as he died on November 22, 1922.

Thanks to Jean Weir,[4] Catania, Sicily:– who helped out when all seemed lost!

Special thanks to all who helped in one way or another.

Editorial from Issue two (Autumn 1979)

Here we are at last with the second issue of the *Free-Winged Eagle*, and we apologise for the extended period of rumination we took before going to press, but the first issue brought a whole concatenation of problems, some of which took a great deal of thinking over and sorting out. The first and main problem came about when we were informed over the telephone by Mr. Edwin Work of 'The Leonards', Orkney's main newsagents and distributors to nearly all other newsagents in Kirkwall and Stromness, that he was withdrawing our publication from sale because he considered it to be too radical, and thought that some of its contents might be offensive to certain important persons.

The great restrictions on circulation thus imposed brought about two more problems. Unfortunately, it is impossible to produce any kind of paper without money. We may despise money, but meanwhile we have to learn to live with it, or in our case, without it! Limited readership has resulted in a low level of feedback, which is the lifeline of any community press. Nevertheless, the response we have had has been encouraging. Our first issue was received with moderate critical acclaim in local newspapers,

---

4. British anarchist, writer and publisher. She was one of those acquitted in the Suárez case.

but the Radio Orkney reviewer could only contemptuously dismiss us as some sort of bandits armed with ungrammatical invective, in the manner of the politically illiterate US journalists who, reporting on the Mexican revolution at the beginning of this century, referred to the peasants who rose against the dictator, Diaz, as 'bandits'. The tyrant Diaz was one of the cruellest men in history, who kept the peasants in the most devious form of slavery, debt peonage, yet the revolt was portrayed as bandits rising against legal authority, and the mythology is continued to this day by Hollywood movies. Incidentally, it is not so long since debt peonage was practised in many parts of Orkney, through wages being paid 6 months in arrears.

Second issue of *The Free-Winged Eagle* from the Kate Sharpley Library.

Anyway, revolutionary change is not what is needed in Orkney and, contrary to what many people thought, we were not offering a model for a new dispensation. What is needed in Orkney is the revolutionary will to resist change – the will to defend ourselves from Oil, Uranium, and all the many other facets of the national and multi-national colonisation of Orkney. We have been asked to spell out our aims more clearly. Orkney, we have been told, is a relatively happy and peaceful community, and that any attempts to change this would be met with opposition. We are glad to hear this, because it is precisely for the sake of the harmony of the community that we say Freight Subsidies, Oil Pollution, and, yes, even Uranium Mining are but diversions which sidetrack us from the *real* problem which Orkney will undoubtedly have to resolve before the end of this century. That is the struggle between autocracy and freedom: between bureaucracy and municipal and community independence: between centralisation and the republican federalistic principle.

We believe that any liberating movement must unavoidably involve some violence. That is not to say we 'believe' in violence. Violence is repugnant to us, but faced with the choice of, say, being 'evacuated' for uranium mining, or of taking up the gun to fight for the land that has been tilled by countless generations of Orkneymen, which would *you* do? Would you join the ranks of the self-righteous 'non-violent' brigade and choose to live on your knees, or would you fight for your birthright to live and die free, here in Orkney? In the end, this is the choice which Orkney men and women will ultimately be faced with. We have no doubt that the conclusion of this editorial will be widely criticised and condemned – that is the price we pay for attempting to spell out the truth.

If Orkney is to enter the next century as a LIVING COMMUNITY, then we must start organising now, in a movement for an AUTONOMOUS ORKNEY, with republican federalism as its immediate goal.

* * * * * *

In future issues of this paper we hope to bring you many notes and articles on the organisation and operation of both 'official' and clandestine attempts to achieve regional autonomy in various parts of the world, and hopefully in Orkney too. We would be interested hear from our autonomist brethren in Shetland, where ideas about self-government are well established. We would also like to have pieces in the Orkney dialect, short stories and poems, as well as the usual wide variety of articles and comment that reflect the rich and vibrant culture of a living community. We offer our pages as the meeting place and focal point for all those with the common interest of self-government for Orkney, community socialism and the federalist idea. But to do *all* of this we are very much dependent on our readers for feedback, and we must develop a good network of contacts and communications between reader and paper, and between readers themselves. Please let us hear your views and ideas. It's easy to write an article or even a letter once you get started – even if you've never written anything more ambitious than a shopping list before.

Write to: Free-Winged Eagle, Over-the-Water, Sanday. Orkney KW17 2B1. [...]

Although publication is irregular, we offer a subscription rate of £1 for 3 issues (if we can keep going that long). Back Numbers: just think – in 20 years time copies of our issue number one might be considered a rare piece of Orkney ephemera, changing hands at prices up to £30!! Get yours now for only 30p + 10p post.

The Blunt End of the Wedge

The 'Persons Unknown' case of 1978–1979 began with allegations that British anarchists wanted to 'overthrow society' and lurid headlines about bomb plots. Albert Meltzer recorded in his autobiography 'The charges were so ludicrous there were fits of laughter from the well of the court, so that when it came to "conspiring with persons unknown", though not unusual phraseology, it caused such merriment the magistrate had to threaten to clear the court.'[1] By the time of the trial, the charges had been changed to conspiracy to rob. The four defendants who had pleaded not guilty, Iris Mills, Ronan Bennett, Vince Stevenson and Trevor Dawton, were acquitted. This provoked Judge Alan King-Hamilton to show his disapproval by lecturing the jury and reading out Stewart Carr's 'confession'.[2] Here Stuart doesn't focus on the acquittals, but on the dangers of political show trials, and the threat to trial by jury.

We have just witnessed the first of the political show trials of the '80s. There will certainly be others – and what proportion of them will be before freely-selected juries? Before any kind of jury? With anti-libertarianism becoming the rallying cry of the extremists of the right and centre, the state is creating an ugly balance to the unifying anti-nazism of the left. Its methods are rather different, however. Such is its vigilance that it can find conspiracies when nothing has happened.

Crime is manufactured from the fantasies and prejudices of the police and judiciary and attributed to anyone who seems politically appropriate. A few state props and a jury 'randomly'

---

1. Meltzer, *I couldn't paint golden angels*, p. 280.
2. Described by Stuart below as 'an unsupported statement made by a fifth defendant leaned on by the police to plead guilty'.

selected from a controlled list and the conjuring-show can begin. 'Were it not for the tireless work of the police (applause) those in the dock would almost certainly have (insert chosen nightmare)'. An anarchist believes in the end of society as we know it, X is an anarchist. The jury only has to complete the syllogism to convict, and cheer the sleight-of-hand.

Ronan Bennett,[3] the prime target of police and security officers in the 'Persons Unknown' trial, was the most vulnerable and likely of victims. Having spent 18 months in Long Kesh, Bennett was finally acquitted on appeal for the murder of a Belfast policeman. Knowing he would have a short life span if he were to remain in Northern Ireland, with the UDA[4] sworn to kill him, he was obliged to leave home and move to England.

Like a growing number of other Irish prisoners, Bennett had become interested in anarchism while in his British concentration camp and had been corresponding with Iris Mills of the Anarchist Black Cross. Having established a close friendship with Mills, Bennett went to live with her and her husband, Graham Rua, in Huddersfield. Aware of his growing involvement with the Anarchist Black Cross, the local police, under instruction from London, kept the Huddersfield address under close surveillance. Obsessed with the doomsday-vision of the Irish situation spilling over to infect the heart of the monster, with the British and European anarchist movements combining forces with the more radical sections of the Irish Republican movement – particularly the Irish National Liberation Army with whom they believed Bennett to have very close contacts – the police moved in and arrested everyone living in the Huddersfield house. They also raided the homes of all known associates in the area. Bennett and Mills were both charged under the all-purpose 'Prevention of Terrorism' Act.

---

3. Ronan Bennett would go on to become a successful writer.
4. Ulster Defence Association, Loyalist armed group.

Self-confessed individuals

Unable to produce any evidence to satisfy the court that Bennett was a danger to society, or that he should be sent back to Northern Ireland (other than the fact that he was Irish and, like a good part of the population in Northern Ireland, had anti-Establishment politics) Bennett was released from custody much to the astonishment and anger of the police who engineered the arrest. Was he not an anarchist? Had not he and Mills admitted it? Later, all the papers, including the supposedly unbiased *Guardian*, were to use the police phrase 'self-confessed' anarchists as though no further proof of guilt was required.

Having made it quite clear to Bennett they believed his earlier acquittal on the murder charge to have been a travesty of justice, the police told him that one way or another they were going to 'get him'. Next time the case against him was to be prepared with more attention to detail.

The case against Bennett, Mills and the other defendants in the 'Persons Unknown' trial was co-ordinated and planned by Scotland Yard's chief anarchist-spotter Inspector Roy Cremer; who last surfaced in the Angry Brigade investigation (a case, incidentally, in which I argued I was planted with explosives by the same squad). This time Cremer was assisted by West German GSG-9[5] agents operating in London. When Bennett and Mills were arrested again in London, the charge was more specific, than the earlier PTA one – 'conspiracy to cause explosions'. After all, what else would 'self-confessed' anarchists be doing with flour, sugar, weedkiller and electric wiring among their many household possessions?

As in every conspiracy show trial since time immemorial one arrest leads to another, and another, and another, until the state

---

5.   GSG-9 (Grenzschutzgruppe 9): elite West German police 'anti-terrorist' unit.

believes it has a sufficient number of people its the dock to allow the jury – if there is one – to salve its conscience by acquitting those against whom the prosecution has presented minimal evidence other than that of association. The jury can then convict those portrayed as the main 'conspirators'. After all the police would never have brought the case in the first place if they hadn't been up to something – would they?

Iris Mills and Ronan Bennett, two of the 'Persons Unknown' trial defendants. From *Black Flag*, digitised by The Sparrows' Nest.

The Black Farce: Act II

As the committal proceedings dragged on and it became increasingly clear there was no evidence at all to back up the charge of 'causing' or 'conspiring to cause' explosions, the police quietly stopped feeding 'shock horror' announcements to a voracious press. The original much publicised charge which led many to believe that the defendants were found *in flagrante* having intercourse with the devil and plotting to overthrow society, was suddenly dropped and charges of robbery substituted. Money replaced 'idealism' as a motive.

In Act II of the black farce, an Austrian turned up out of the blue at Vince Stevenson's flat where Trevor Dawton, another of the accused, happened to be staying, and left a suitcase filled with guns and sufficient evidence to implicate everyone involved, including Dafydd Ladd, now on the run, who was under constant surveillance by West German agents in this country because of his involvement with the Red Army Fraction and 2nd June[6] defence groups in Germany, and Black Aid, the German political prisoners relief organisation based at Rising Free,[7] the left London bookshop. The prosecution case was that Rising Free provided the main link between all the defendants. A chilling thought for the many people and groups who use it as a meeting place and mailing address.

The case itself was a showpiece of the power of judges. This was demonstrated as much in the way the proceedings were handled as in the extraordinary and unprecedented decision to bring the jury back to court the day after they had delivered their verdict. Without actually telling them so, King-Hamilton could not have indicated more clearly that *he* at least thought the jury had

---

6.   A reference to the 2nd of June Movement (Bewegung 2. Juni), West German armed group, originally based in West Berlin.
7.   Rising Free was an anarchist bookshop in Islington.

reached the wrong verdict. It was strange indeed to see people who have given their lives to support such a humanitarian idea as anarchism, being subjected to interrogation by a tedious, pompous and ill-briefed lawyer who, having spent his adult life advancing his career in our capitalist society, argues that *their* motives are dubious, *their* principles unworthy, and *their* defence a pack of lies. Incidentally, every time the prosecution said someone was lying the defence was able to produce evidence to back up its case. The police claimed, for instance, that when arrested Bennett tried to escape. The defence produced a passing cab driver who witnessed the arrest, but for his civic pains he too was called a liar. Fortunately, the fare, a barrister, was able to corroborate his evidence.

Trial by water

This brought the prosecution case to its most farcical. Bring on the Holy Book and see if they flinch. Regarding the Almighty as a junior court functionary responsible for enforcing the Perjury Act, the Prosecution closely questioned many of the defence witnesses as to their belief in God. The judge had decided all anarchists must be atheists, and all atheists... The prosecution, one step on from seeing whether they float when immersed in water, also made the point that a woman who lived with a man without the benefit of holy matrimony was his 'mistress' and that all wives must take the opinion of their husbands who were thus responsible for their wives' views.

Of all the anarchist books ever published, the only one the prosecution turned to was the *Anarchist cookbook*, a publication which has nothing to do with anarchism and is a silly and highly dangerous 'guide' to the home manufacture of explosives. The prosecution seemed to be implying with this exhibit that its mere possession was irrefutable evidence of guilt. Presumably, one automatically agrees and acts on every book in one's possession.

I wonder what his reaction would have been had he known that as a bookseller I have been pestered for some considerable time by numerous police authorities, including Scotland Yard library, Bramshill Police College and various obscure sections of the Ministry of Defence to supply them with copies of this particular title. In fact, had it not been for this trial and the related publicity, and the earlier demand from government agencies, there would be little or no demand for the book and no copies available in the country. As it is we now have orders for over 200! Not even an anarchist witness likening the book to the *Protocols of the Elders of Zion*[8] managed to convince Mr. Justice King-Hamilton otherwise. But, other than adding to the paranoid fantasies of the state, what had all this to do with the charges before the court of armed robberies?

Ultimately, the state had to rely on its carefully-selected jury. Were they influenced by the bigotry of the gutter press? Were they swayed by the knowledge that they too had come under the scrutiny of the state's police before being called for jury service, been closely examined by a Kafkaesque committee, and could just as easily be the next victims? Did the judge's anti-anarchist bias and obvious hostility towards the prisoners combine with the heavy-handed, ill-mannered and laborious prosecution case to swing them in favour of the defence? Were they sufficiently impressed by the defendants, and in particular Ronan Bennett's obvious sincerity and eloquent conduct of his own case?

Class justice
Whatever the answers, one way or another the jury finally decided the innocence of the accused. As an anarchist and comrade of the defendants their guilt or innocence was never of importance to me. My sentiments on the question of robbing supermarkets is

---

8.   Antisemitic propaganda tract.

best summed up in a quote from Élisée Reclus,[9] the anarchist geographer: 'Personally, however I may feel about this or that action or individual, I shall never add my voice to the hateful clamour of men who mobilise armies, police-forces, magistrates, clergy and laws to preserve their privileges.' It's a quote we should bear in mind every time the media exhorts us to hate the Blunts[10] of this world, the IRA, Claimants Unions, British Leyland workers, the Iranians,[11] etc.

What was always of crucial importance in this case was that the two principal defendants, Iris Mills and Ronan Bennett, had obviously been selected as victims long before any of the robberies with which they were eventually charged had taken place. The other defendants were woven into the 'conspiracy' merely as make-weight through their politics and association with Bennett and Mills.

Faced with the machinations of the state police, the ignorance and bigotry of an old man long due for retirement, and an unsupported statement made by a fifth defendant leaned on by the police to plead guilty, it was wrongly thought the defendants stood little chance.

Class justice of such an obvious nature is not easily ignored. With this decision by the jury to acquit all the defendants in the

---

9. Élisée Reclus (1830–1905) French anarchist, writer and geographer. The quote comes from a letter dated 25 December 1893 from Reclus to English Christian socialist writer (and ex-pupil of his) Richard Heath (1831–1912). From page 263 of Eliseo Reclus, *Correspondencia (de 1850 a 1905)* (Buenos Aires: Ediciones Iman, 1943), p. 263. A translation of the rest of the letter is on the Kate Sharpley Library website: https://www.katesharpleylibrary.net/5tb443.

10. Sir Anthony Blunt (1907–1983) confessed to spying for the Soviet Union in 1963. This was made public and he was stripped of his knighthood in 1979.

11. The Shah of Iran was overthrown in 1979, which was followed by the establishment of an Islamic Republic.

face of what was almost a direct order to convict by the judge, the jury have asserted their right to oppose the political use of the courts and police against dissidents and those who oppose the power of the state to control their lives.

When the jury vetting scandal broke Sam Silkin,[12] self-styled socialist supporter of jury vetting in politically sensitive cases, said in its defence that it was either that or the abolition of juries altogether, to be replaced no doubt by something similar to the Diplock courts in Northern Ireland. The decision to acquit by a vetted jury in this case has proved that vetting does not work. Doubtless, as you read these lines, the political and legal establishment are discussing how best to sugar the pill of non-jury, trials in future 'sensitive' cases.

The writing is on the wall.

This article was written for both *Time Out* and *Black Flag* by Stuart Christie.

From *Black Flag*, Vol.5, no. 13 (January 1980). It was reprinted with minor changes as 'British Anarchists Found Not Guilty' in North American anarchist newspaper *Fifth Estate*, no. 301 (26 February 1980): www.fifthestate.org/archive/301-february-26-1980/british-anarchists-found-not-guilty.

---

12.   Sam Silkin (1918–1988) Labour Party politician. As Attorney General he was not simply a 'supporter' of jury vetting, but in charge of it.

Freedom is a fiction:
Stuart Christie looks at
how radical publishers are
surviving the recession

Here Stuart discusses the technological changes which led to the diverse radical press of the sixties and seventies, and how financial and legal worries limit the circulation of radical ideas. He is clear about the value of the international network Cienfuegos Press created. He also emphasises how calls for repression of their work provide free publicity for the radical publisher.

In his first great novel *Notre Dame de Paris* Victor Hugo[1] proposed the theory that until the fifteenth century architecture was the principal register of mankind: 'That all ideas of any complexity which arose in the world became a building; every popular idea, just like every religious law, had its monuments; that the human race, in fact, inscribed in stone every one of its important thoughts.'

Perhaps Hugo's priest, who voiced the fear that 'the book will destroy the building' (meaning here specifically his church) would today look at the small offset litho press and then at the establishment which has, in many respects, taken on the mantle of the old church, and would make the same remark. Radical publishing has flourished with the advent of offset litho printing and although it may not 'destroy the building' it has certainly served to weaken the authoritarian infrastructure of establishment

---

1. Victor Hugo (1802–1885) French novelist. The book, first published in 1831, is better known in English as *The hunchback of Notre Dame*.

publishing and helped to expose its conscious and unconscious biases.

Since the political upheavals of the late 1960s and early 1970s the Left has become increasingly fragmented; ideological and organizational dominance has slipped away from the traditional vanguardist parties towards smaller decentralized radical groups each increasingly better equipped to put forward its particular point of view through books, pamphlets and newspapers.

The shifting of centres, fostered by the revolution in publishing technology, has served to foster a more searching and radical exploration of values; a less authoritarian and more completely self-managed spirit is expressed not least in the healthy network of community based bookshops servicing the needs of neighbourhoods and in the proliferation of radical publishing houses, each with its own particular historical, geographical, political or social priorities.

All these owe their continued success, despite the very deep recession in the commercial book trade, to the feeling of more and more people that they are outside the decision making processes of everyday life and to their desire to redress that balance by searching for new values on which to build a more satisfying and non-coercive society.

The small radical publishers have a growing share of the market, competing with ease with the larger corporate publishing houses, the university presses and the state-controlled publishing houses of the Eastern bloc and China which churn out Marxist-Leninist tracts to an extent not exceeded by the Bible Societies of the nineteenth century.

One thing long known by radical publishers is that we live not in a free society, but rather in a society in which freedom is tolerated until it seems to threaten the power and privileges of those who control and depend directly on the state and the economy. Free enterprise and the open, competitive market are, ideologically speaking, notoriously relative and this applies most crucially to the radical publisher. Freedom of expression is, of course, less a fiction to those who can afford the expensive luxury of a libel action or whose books and magazines are acceptable to the larger distributors.

Although radical publishers must at least aspire to profitability, few indeed can distribute excess profits among their directors or shareholders. Once any bills are paid, any money left is usually ploughed straight back in to consolidate and expand the publishing programme, for people involved in radical publishing are concerned to get their ideas across to as large a section of the community as possible.

Does radical publishing really threaten the status quo? The establishment seems to view it as a present but minor irritant, but also as a great potential danger in a time of crisis. Field-Marshall Lord Carver wrote in his prefatory endorsement of General Frank Kitson's *Low intensity operations*[2]: 'If a genuine and serious grievance arose, such as might result from a significant drop in the standard of living, all those who dissipate their protest over a wide variety of causes might concentrate their efforts and produce a situation which it was beyond the powers of the police to handle. Should this happen the army would be required to restore the position rapidly. Fumbling at this juncture might have grave consequences, even to the extent of undermining confidence in the whole system of Government.' There is little doubt that, in such a situation, the radical presses would be seen as one of the sources of disruption, focusing and concentrating dissent as they do.

One thing that has undoubtedly helped Cienfuegos Press, for which I work, and whose priority is the social and political

---

2. *Low intensity operations: subversion, insurgency and peacekeeping* was published in 1971, and seen by anarchists as an important and threatening book. Cienfuegos published an analysis, *High intensity subversion* by 'Ronin' in 1981.

philosophy of anarchism, is the considerable adverse publicity we have attracted over the past few years; we now have more readers than ever, and other houses have benefited from the same inverse law of notoriety.

Each radical publishing house has its own priorities and its own peculiar problems. Ours arise from our anarchism itself. Our stated aims are to promote the widest possible circulation of the ideas and history of anarchism and self-management; to oppose all authoritarian systems and ideologies and to explore viable libertarian alternatives to the problems of our society.

A brief account of our development may give some insight into the structure, finances and possible future of radical publishing houses. Named after Camilo Cienfuegos,[3] the Cuban libertarian revolutionary whose murder by Raoul Castro signalled the political about-turn by his brother Fidel that finally established the Cuban Communist Party in power, the press was formed in 1974 by myself and my wife following the 'Angry Brigade' trial in which I was acquitted after spending 16 months on remand in Brixton prison.

Our list began with two books: *Sabaté, guerrilla extraordinary* and *Man! An anthology of anarchist ideas, essays, poetry and commentaries*. These two books were financed by money I received from post-trial interviews, translation fees, and donations from sympathisers; this is by no means an unusual means of funding in radical publishing. To raise additional capital by debenture we became a limited company in 1975, and in 1976 moved to our present location in Orkney to avoid constant surveillance from the Special Branch, the almost inevitable concomitant of any radical activity and especially radical publishing.

The furore that followed our publication of *Towards a citizens' militia: anarchist alternatives to NATO and the Warsaw*

---

3.   Camilo Cienfuegos (1932–1959).

Pact[4] was a case in point, and, while remarkable, by no means unusual. The introduction made it clear that the book was not intended as a do-it-yourself guide to military revolution – a ludicrous concept for anarchists anyway – but a guide on how to organise resistance to a foreign invasion, Soviet or other, or to a military coup d'etat.

The outcry was that the book should be banned and Cienfuegos closed down. This, and the case of a young Italian student living in Brixton[5] at the height of the riots who was raided, arrested and sentenced to deportation on the strength (this was the evidence offered) of Cienfuegos books found in her flat, highlight that focusing of repressive attention on the radical press which follows any such upheaval.

Why is this kind of reaction so virulent? Surely there can be no democratic objection to showing that there is an alternative to statism, an alternative to capitalism and consumerism that is not Marxism-Leninism and vice versa?

In the recent Brixton case we can safely assume that the police and court would have found little to object to had they found essays on monetarism or on the role of the proletariat in a controlled economy, or even (such as have been circulated apparently freely by neo-fascist terror groups) the relative merits of Zyklon B gas as against repatriation. What concerned the court here and led to the outcry over *Towards a citizens' militia* was not the information in the book, which was available from many other respectable sources, but the fact that it was being directed to the general public.

---

4. First of May Group, *Towards a citizens' militia: anarchist alternatives to NATO and the Warsaw Pact* (Sanday: Cienfuegos, 1980).

5. Patricia Giambi. She was imprisoned but won her appeal against deportation. For details see the appendix to *We want to riot, not to work* published by the Riot Not To Work Collective, 1982. Available on libcom.org (https://libcom.org/history/1981-the-brixton-riots) and has been reprinted by Past Tense.

The very idea of a *popular* defence alternative was anathema to those right thinking guardians who had just spent £13 billion allegedly trying to do the same job. What they and those who think like them do find objectionable and threatening is the non-authoritarian philosophy and the anti-authoritarian attitudes which this alternative implies.

Apart from the many commercial and-left-wing bookshops who were scared away from handling *Towards a citizens' militia* by the media and political outcry against us, we also lost our radical alternative trade distributors; their refusal to handle the book, on advice from both Scottish and English lawyers, exemplifies a particularly insidious and potent form of censorship. We withdrew all our titles from their lists.

More seriously, however, was the effect on one of our regular printers and binders; they refused outright to handle anything further from us since, as they admitted quite frankly, they felt they would be laying themselves open to police and state persecution. While it is no great problem to organize a distribution network and print small pamphlets and booklets, there are no actual anarchist (or closely sympathetic) printers and binders in the world who are equipped either to handle our larger books (over 200 pages) or provide us with normal credit facilities.

I imagine most radical publishing houses are badly undercapitalized to begin with. One of our strengths is that we are a subscription-based publishing project, and we coordinate a multinational network of participating sympathizers from as far afield as New Zealand and Alaska, Hawaii, Finland, Cape Town and Buenos Aires. Most of these participants, like Michael Moorcock and Noam Chomsky, regularly contribute their professional skills, labour, material and ideas to the project as well as money. Since 1974 we have been able to publish almost 40 titles in this way.

In spite of the fact that our turnover has doubled every year for the past few years we are finding it very difficult to keep pace with production costs, which have escalated in the same period, and the credit squeeze.

Ironically, our size and flexibility have enabled us to weather the storm rather better than the larger commercial houses, which are now being hit hard by the recession and are announcing redundancies every week.

Probably the most important things on our side are our very low overheads (other than transportation costs) compared with what similar publishers in inner city areas would have to pay, and our committed and loyal group of around 600 subscribers, with our further two thousand more or less regular international mail-order customers.

Cuts in library buying have not affected us greatly, but, as with the majority of houses, we have had to limit the number of hardback editions and concentrate on larger format paperbacks. While success or failure does not depend on the vagaries of the market place or the current economic climate the radical presses must give serious thought to the best means of avoiding compromising political aims while remaining viable.

Cienfuegos Press advert by Richard Warren. From *Black Flag* vol. 6, no. 12 (June/July 1982). Digitised by The Sparrows' Nest.

Although titles sell out fairly quickly – a print run of 3,000 copies would last a year, more or less – we usually invest our limited resources in new titles and allow old ones to go out of print.

One unexpected bonus arising from this is the intrinsic rarity of short-run books. Many of our titles are now sought after as collectors' pieces, such as Flavio Costantini's *Art of anarchy* and the first four issues of the *Cienfuegos Press Anarchist Review*. While this arrangement does help to keep turnover up, it also means that unless we catch the imagination of some philanthropic libertarian millionaire (if such a creature exists) or come up with a cult best-seller, all our minor classics are doomed to a limited circulation of around 3,000 anarchists and secret policemen. This is a problem all the small radical presses inevitably face.

Ideally all radical publishers should have their own typesetting, printing and finishing facilities. This, of course, is no longer a pipe dream. Only then will they be able to escape the political whims, fears and prejudices of the state and marketplace on which they remain (ironically) dependent. One problem fairly unique to us is our geographical remoteness. Operating from the secluded North Isles of Scotland has its advantages, but again escalating costs add considerably to the budget.

One unforeseen cost we have had to bear came when almost the entire edition of one of our periodic Reviews was lost in a lorry fire while in transit from the printers. To a commercial publisher, this would probably represent only a tiny loss in proportion to his total run. To the small independent press it is disastrous, a complete loss.

To counter this and similar disasters we are setting up co-publishing and distribution arrangements with supporters in Canada, the United States, Australia, New Zealand, Scandinavia and Southern Europe and, again, economic strictures may lead to increased intellectual vitality.

One interesting development the radical book trade has been

the birth of the Federation of Radical Booksellers, through which most radical and community bookshops and publishers throughout the country exchange ideas, improve mutual efficiency and establish solidarity in the face of a concerted campaign by the neo-fascist right.

The most recent project of the FRB is the Radical Bookclub which should get off the ground this autumn. Anyone can join through a participating bookshop and then buy any number of titles on offer at a discount; Victor Gollancz's Left Book Club of the 1930s similarly used bookshops as the main method of distributing their titles. Such a scheme gives the bookseller normal trade discount so there is no conflict of interest and thus works to everyone's benefit and satisfaction. The only condition applied by the publisher is that the bookclub takes a minimum stock of 500 copies of each title.

What is the future for radical publishing? I think it will continue to grow in proportion to the desire we have to control our own lives and destinies, and the growing antipathy towards power politics and the competitive values of consumerism.

The author is a founder of the Cienfuegos Press.

Originally published in *The Times Higher Education Supplement* 16 October 1981, issued as a leaflet by the Friends of Cienfuegos Press for the Socialist Book Fair 1981.

Organise and survive

Stuart approaches the topic of defence without the state with mischievous humour, mixing the unlikely (Trotskyist Freemasons) with the merely unproven. Historical examples like the Makhnovist partisans during the Russian Civil War, the workers' militias of the Spanish Civil War, but also the Home Guard of the Second World War are used to suggest that anarchism is a practical alternative to the 'warfare state'.

Has our political way of life become increasingly surrealistic, or is it perhaps that increased communication has lighted up what was previously obscure and therefore unbelievable? The British secret services appear to have been run by Moscow for the past 30 odd years, Government Ministers have given serious consideration to the idea of assassinating troublesome Opposition spokesmen, there have been at least two military coups prepared against a British Government when the more paranoid among our ruling class feared bloody revolution on the streets of Britain, stories are circulating that MI5 successfully blackmailed a Prime Minister into resigning office,[1] that Lord Carrington[2] is really the head of the KGB,[3] and that the SDP[4] is the brainchild of the Trilateral Commission.[5]

A little while ago, Cienfuegos published *Towards a citizens'*

---

1.   Harold Wilson (1916–1995), who was twice Labour Prime Minster (1964–1970 and 1974–1976).
2.   Lord Carrington (1919–2018) was an aristocrat and Conservative politician.
3.   The Soviet Union's security service.
4.   Social Democratic Party, founded 1981.
5.   A 'discussion forum' best known for the 1975 report *The crisis of democracy: report on the governability of democracies*.

militia: anarchist alternatives To NATO and the Warsaw Pact and the immediate hysterical reaction from the authoritarian right, left and centre, even before it was out, highlighted this political paranoia and appears to have delivered a karate chop to a very sensitive constitutional nerve centre. The motley collection of politicians, police and army types who expressed concern about this title were all agreed on one thing – the book should be banned, our publishing house closed down, and yours truly thrown into the deepest dungeon in the Kingdom and the key thrown out of the Space Shuttle. The very idea of a *popular* volunteer defence force was anathema and should be strangled at birth.

I have an explanation for this extraordinarily virulent reaction. If the State does not control the army and police it becomes redundant, its power and authority crumble, Dracula-like, to dust, and its very reason for being goes up the chimney in a puff of smoke. Anatole France[6] defined it more succinctly: 'To disarm the strong and arm the weak would be to change the social order which it is my job to preserve. Justice is the means by which established injustices are sanctioned.'

Last year the government spent £13,000,000,000 of our money in furthering the illusion that this green and pleasant land of ours could be successfully defended against the 'enemy' both internal and external. The catalogue of threats which assail us daily through the media, – real, potential, imaginary and fantastic – in innumerable permutations, is extensive – ranging from the everyday fear of Soviet expansionism from the East, the Damocelan sword of nuclear Armageddon, Bolshevik and Trotskyist subversion of our secret services and school playgrounds, to paedophiles in the Foreign Office, homosexuals in the seats of power and cattle

---

6. Anatole France (1844–1924), French writer. The quote comes from 'Crainquebille' in *Crainquebille, Putois, Riquet and other profitable tales* (Translation by Winifred Stephens, London, John Lane, 1915.)

mutilators in the Min. of Ag. & Fisheries. The Golden Rule of all successful secret policemen is: paranoid fears *are* self-fulfilling and paranoids *do* have many enemies. Who needs such friends?

Against this background it is not unreasonable that the average thinking citizen should postulate the Discordian[7] theorem that *National Security is the chief cause of national insecurity*. The realisation that *the worst is possible* should provoke us to seriously consider our options. By *worst is possible* I mean anything from some Foreign Devil or home grown nutcase – noticeable the latter is the least likely and causes the most alarm – dropping the property-respecting Neutron Bomb to all-out nuclear or biological warfare, invasion, bloody revolution, military coup, or just the plain old collapse of 'society-as-we-know-it', whether due to super-inflation, genetic degeneration, famine, or the infiltration of 33rd Degree Freemasonry by the Militant Tendency,[8] or whatever.

History has shown that given such a not-so-hypothetical situation, a substantial majority of the population would follow the path of least resistance, willing to serve any master with the minimum of fuss and bother. However, for those of us who maintain against all trends a psychological attachment to the idea of freedom, there is little alternative but to resist to survive. If we are to survive with dignity and retain some of the more positive values of civilised society then we should start thinking about it now. Contingency planning should not be looked upon as exclusive

---

7. Discordianism is a parody religion. Discordian ideas informed *The Illuminatus! trilogy* by Robert Shea and Robert Anton Wilson, nominated as the 'Cienfuegos Press Book of the Year' (*Black Flag*, v.4 no. 13, February 1977, p. 14). In the same issue Albert Meltzer described it as 'a riproaring, mind-blowing spoof'.

8. The Militant Tendency was a Trotskyist group which infiltrated the Labour Party from its foundation in 1964 until it abandoned the tactic of entryism in 1991.

to government departments and military. How better to prepare than falling back on the alleged and much lauded Conservative tenet of rejecting dependency on the State – which after all won't exist after doomsday – and opting for self-reliance?

Just suppose, for the sake of argument, that due to an 'ongoing Polish situation',[9] the Russians/Americans have landed on the Kent coast or, heaven forbid, a cabal of eccentric and disaffected army and police officers led by a senior member of the Royal Family and a Press Baron[10] decided to impose *temporary* controls tomorrow at 4am in order to safeguard 'Freedom'. Having lived for many centuries in a society rooted in obedience to authority it is not unreasonable to assume that by midday people would be clapping the conquerors in the streets... by three we'd have citizens loading other citizens on to three ton lorries... on the nine o'clock news there would be a panel of well-known personalities oozing assurances that all is for the best and that it is our constitutional duty to accept the new order... and by 10.30 the following morning we would have respected members of the bench setting the seal of legality on the new regime by packing the opposition off to re-training centres at Wembley Stadium or the Orcadian uranium mines, with a worse fate reserved for the more recalcitrant of the three million unfortunate enough to be listed on the Central Register.

The idea of a popular citizens' defence force is not new, but to avoid any possible confusion I should make it clear I am not talking about a political gang-system defending sectarian interests such as those which have developed in Northern Ireland, or the private armies of the madcap would-be gauleiters who rose to

---

9. A reference to unrest following the 'Polish Autumn' of 1980 when working class protests against the Communist regime led to the founding of the *Solidarity* union.

10. A reference to people alleged to have been involved in the 1968 plot against Harold Wilson.

prominence in the mid-70's at the instigation of the professional 'terrorists' who earn their living peddling apocalyptic scare stories totally at odds with reality in the hope of raising tensions to a sufficiently intolerable level – the strategy of Chile, Indonesia, Italy, Afghanistan, Poland, etc.

No, the type of defence force I envisage is one which represents the community, and although the more recent examples have been short lived, mainly due to the fact they were popular movements and presented a direct challenge to State and Party authority, they have proved themselves to be workable, effective and the only genuinely democratic solution to the problem of community defence.

Cartoon by Richard Warren as printed in *Cienfuegos Press Anarchist Review* no. 6. Digitised by Libcom.org.

In the Ukraine, in 1919, the local peasantry, in revolt against both the Czarist armies and the new and already repressive Soviet State, called for the egalitarian mobilisation of the local population with villages and towns voluntarily providing soldiers to defend their communities and workplaces. The Makhnovist Insurrectionary Army of the Ukraine was thus organised successfully for three years on three basic principles, *voluntary enlistment*, an *electoral principle* whereby all officers and commanders were elected by all units, and *self-discipline* whereby rules for discipline were drawn up by soldier committees and generally approved by all units. These rules were rigorously observed on the basis of individual responsibility and awareness of the possible results of ill-discipline on fellow soldiers.

In Spain, after the national army proved to be the enemy, large areas of Spain organised spontaneously on the basis of workers' militia committees. These volunteer militia units were hastily created by the labour organisations and were thrown directly into battle against Franco's highly trained and seasoned regular troops backed by an Axis forces, but they did provide sufficient breathing space for what remained of the Republican army to decide which side it was on.

The Spanish militia units made many mistakes, hardly surprising as they were amateurs against professionals. However, one person who learned much from Spain was Captain Tom Wintringham[11] who was involved at the time of Dunkirk in setting up a totally unauthorised volunteer defence force. This spontaneous and popular movement put the wind up the British Government to such an extent that they hastily absorbed these Local Defence Volunteers into the Home Guard under the safe control of Westminster, in much the same way as the Communists and

---

11.　Tom Wintringham (1898–1949). British Communist who fought in the International Brigade in Spanish Civil War.

Republicans had done with the workers' militias in Republican Spain.

Given the present uncertainty in political life and the escalating degree of suspicion and paranoia in national and international affairs it is not implausible that due to a failure in communication we could suddenly find ourselves facing anything from human extinction to a 'pre-emptive' military coup on the Chilean or Afghan model. The question now facing us is how best to confront the problem of defence in the face of aggression within a democratic framework and sidestep present genocidal reliance on nuclear weapons at the same time. With a Citizens' Militia based on the *Community* Council and workplace we have the *only* realistic and viable defence alternative to the spiralling nuclear arms race with its inevitable outcome for all mankind. It also provides the only effective democratic solution to totalitarian aggression, be it of the right, left or centre. I'd also like to think that such a popular movement would stimulate our collective imagination sufficiently to remove once and for all the self-imposed blinkers obscuring the fact that it is ourselves alone, not politicians, civil servants, soldiers or policemen, who bear responsibility for the quality of our lives and those of our children from whom this world of ours is borrowed.

From *Cienfuegos Press Anarchist Review* no. 6 (summer 1982)

Author's preface to *We, the Anarchists!*

Stuart's study of the FAI, the Iberian Anarchist Federation, is an in-depth analysis and not a simple celebration. He looks critically at how a network of affinity groups dedicated to the revolutionary idea ended up putting the brakes on the revolution during the Spanish Civil War. He makes clear his lack of interest in building an organisation for its own sake, and his fear of ideas becoming institutionalised.

> *With the crowd of commonplace chatterers, we are already past praying for: no reproach is too bitter for us, no epithet too insulting. Public speakers on social and political subjects find that abuse of anarchists is an unfailing passport to popular favour. Every conceivable crime is laid to our charge, and opinion, too indolent to learn the truth, is easily persuaded that anarchy is but another name for wickedness and chaos. Overwhelmed with opprobrium and held up to hatred, we are treated on the principle that the surest way of hanging a dog is to give it a bad name.*[1]

Élisée Reclus

Since the official birth of organised anarchism at the Saint Imier Congress of 1872, no anarchist organisation has been held up to greater opprobrium or subjected to such gross misrepresentation than the Federación Anarquista Iberica, better known by its initials – FAI. Although the above lines by anarchist geographer Élisée Reclus predated the FAI by almost 50 years, they might well have been written as that organisation's epitaph.

---

1.   Élisée Reclus (1830–1905) French anarchist, writer and geographer. The quote comes from *An anarchist on anarchy* (reprinted from the *Contemporary Review* by Benjamin Tucker, 1884).

The hostility of extreme right wing commentators to revolutionary working class movements is hardly surprising and need not detain us long. The following quote is included merely as an example of how authoritarian commentators attempted to calibrate popular attitudes in such a way as to present the FAI, the rallying point for the defenders of the anarchist constitution of the Confederación Nacional del Trabajo (CNT), the Spanish anarcho-syndicalist union, as the agent of disharmony and the conspiratorial epicentre of mindless violence.

'The other (great corporation) unites the men who profess anarcho-syndicalist doctrines, styling itself the Confederación Nacional de Trabajadores (National Confederation of Workers) [*sic*]. It is for brevity's sake designated as CNT. Its ruling committee, the FAI (Federación Anarquista Iberica – Iberian Anarchist Federation) bears a name which strikes terror into the heart of most Spaniards. If "ruthless" be the qualification fitted for the UGT, "bloodthirsty" does not sufficiently describe the FAI. The members of both of these associations are recruited by methods most closely resembling coercion than persuasion, the flourish of a pistol being one of the most frequent. They are inscribed on the rolls without the slightest regard to their trade. One and the other furnish gunmen for social crimes, voters for the elections and militiamen for the front. These three seem the only activities of the UGT, the CNT and the FAI. To belong to any of these three justify vehement suspicion of criminality: membership of the last makes it certain.'[2]

Present day attitudes toward the FAI have been and continue to be formed, in the main, by the works of liberal and Marxist historians. More sophisticated than Arnold Lunn, these views, as the

2.   Arnold Lunn, *Spanish rehearsal*, London, 1937, p. 272 [Original note by SC. Lunn is quoting from an article by Francoist diplomat Alfonso Merry del Val y Zulueta in *The Nineteenth Century and After*, No. 721 (March 1937).]

American commentator Noam Chomsky has noted, continue to be supported 'by ideological conviction rather than history or investigation of the phenomena of social life.'[3]

This study developed out of a sense of irritation that the same myths and distortions about the millenarian or manipulative role of the FAI in its symbiotic relationship with the CNT continue to circulate unchallenged. I was equally concerned to establish that indolent and intelligent commentators alike have sought to demonise the FAI – and Spanish anarchism in general – by cynically or unintentionally distorting the available historical evidence. Whether to reinforce their own political prejudices, refute their enemies, or plain ignorance or malice is immaterial; what is intriguing is that apparently diligent historians should adapt and perpetuate wild hearsay assertions such as those propagated by Arnold Lunn, making no attempt to distinguish between fact and fantasy, is more than a simple infraction of the rules of historical hypothesis. Their failure to apply the rules of evidence in the case against the FAI not only undermines that case, but it also raises serious questions as to their intellectual and moral honesty.

In order to fully comprehend the role and function of the FAI it is first of all essential to understand three things:

1. That anarchism caught the imagination of a substantial section of the Spanish working classes because it reflected and articulated the values, lifestyles and social relationships that existed at the base of Spanish society.

2. That the predominant ideological influence within the major Spanish labour organisations between 1869 and 1939 was anarchism.

3. That the 'conscious minority' of rank and file militants who

---

3.　Noam Chomsky, 'Objectivity and liberal scholarship' in *American power and the new mandarins*, (New York: Pantheon, 1969), p.76 [original note by SC].

built up and sustained their unions through lengthy periods of relentless and often bloody repression were anarchists who sought, as an immediate objective through social revolution and the introduction of Libertarian Communism, a just and equitable classless and stateless society, moral objectives which brought them into conflict not only with the state and employers but also with their own union leadership whose immediate objectives were material.

There are two dimensions to this book. The first is descriptive and historical: it outlines the evolution of the organised anarchist movement in Spain and its relationship with the wider labour movement. At the same time it provides some insight into the main ideas which made the Spanish labour movement one of the most revolutionary of modern times. The second is analytical and tries to address from an anarchist perspective what for me is the particularly relevant problem of understanding change in the contemporary world; how can ideals survive the process of institutionalisation? If this is not feasible, at least to be able to identify the turning points so that we may be able to counter the process.

In tracing the history of the CNT and the FAI it is clear that anarchist organisations, like all other organisations and civilisations before them, are subject to a process of rise and fall. Once they achieve their specific objectives even the most committed libertarian and directly democratic organisations quickly degenerate. From being social instruments set up to meet real social needs they become transformed into self-perpetuating institutions with lives and purposes of their own, distinct to and in tension with the objectives which called them into being in the first place.

My main contention is simple: briefly, it is that as the Primo de Rivera dictatorship[4] began to founder in 1927 a struggle broke out between the non-anarchist leadership and anarchist base

---

4. Miguel Primo de Rivera (1870–1930) was dictator of Spain from 1923 to 1930.

of the anarcho-syndicalist Confederación Nacional del Trabajo (CNT). The leaders, that is, the members of the Regional and National Committees of the CNT, having become intermediaries between labour and capital, openly challenged the ideological objectives of the 'conscious minority' by seeking to overturn the federally structured anti-capitalist and anti-statist constitution of the CNT in order to compete with the socialist Unión General de Trabajadores (UGT) for hegemony over the Spanish working class. In their view the workers' cause would only be advanced when all workers belonged to their union, something that could only be achieved by operating within the legal parameters of the capitalist and statist system.

To the 'conscious minority' of anarchists this threatened to transform the CNT from a revolutionary weapon which could eliminate the misery of everyday life into a reformist labour union which served only to perpetuate and legitimise the exploitation of man by man. The anarchist militants who constituted the base of the CNT responded by founding the Federación Anarquista Iberica, an ad hoc federally structured association whose function was to reaffirm the revolutionary nature of anarchism and to provide a rallying point for the defence of the anti-political principles and immediate Libertarian Communist objectives of the CNT. By 1932 the reformist threat had been eliminated – democratically! – and the working class anarchists who had spoken in the name of the FAI (although many of these like Garcia Oliver and Durruti, had never been affiliated to the FAI) reverted to everyday union activity at Local Federation level or to conspiratorial revolutionary activity in the Confederal Defence Committee.

Instead of disbanding, however, or confining itself to acting as a liaison secretariat between autonomous agitational or propaganda groups, the FAI was taken over in mid-1933 by a group of rootless intellectuals and economic planners under the leadership of Diego Abad de Santillán,[5] a man for whom abstract theories took precedence over workers' practical experiences. With the coming of the Spanish Civil War three years later, the FAI had abandoned all pretence of being a revolutionary organ. Like the institutionalised CNT leadership it had helped out in 1930–1932, the FAI had become, in its turn, a structure of vested interests serving to apply the brakes to the spontaneous revolutionary activity of the rank and file and repress the new generation of revolutionary activists among the Libertarian Youth and the 'Friends of Durruti' group. 'Anti-fascist unity' and state power were promoted at the expense of anarchist principles while the hegemony of the CNT-FAI leadership was imposed over the local revolutionary committees and the general assemblies. Its principal aim had become to perpetuate itself, even at the expense of the revolutionary anarchist principles which had inspired it: the instrumental means had become the organisational end.

From *We, the Anarchists!: A study of the Iberian Anarchist Federation (FAI) 1927–1937*. The Meltzer Press and Jura Media, 2000 (p.ii–iv).

---

5.   Diego Abad de Santillán (1897–1983) (pen name of Baudilio Sinesio García Fernández), Spanish anarchist and writer.

Part 2

Biographical tributes and obituaries by Stuart

Albert Meltzer, anarchist

Albert Meltzer was one of the most enduring and respected torch-bearers of the international anarchist movement in the second half of the twentieth century. His sixty-year commitment to the vision and practice of anarchism survived both the collapse of the Revolution and Civil War in Spain and the Second World War; he helped fuel the libertarian impetus of the 1960s and 1970s and steer it through the reactionary challenges of the Thatcherite 1980s and post-Cold War 1990s.

Albert Meltzer & Stuart Christie, Birmingham 1981. From the Phil Ruff photo album on the Kate Sharpley Library website.

Fortunately, before he died, Albert managed to finish his autobiography, *I couldn't paint golden angels*, a pungent, no-punches pulled, Schvejkian[1] account of a radical twentieth century enemy of humbug and injustice. A life-long trade union activist, he fought Mosley's Blackshirts in the battle of Cable Street, played an active role in supporting the anarchist communes and militias in the Spanish Revolution and the pre-war German anti-Nazi resistance, was a key player in the Cairo Mutiny [after] the Second World War, helped rebuild the post-war anti-Franco resistance in Spain and the international anarchist movement. His achievements include *Cuddon's Cosmopolitan Review*, an occasional satirical review first published in 1965 and named after Ambrose Cuddon, possibly the first consciously anarchist publisher in the modern sense, the founding of the Anarchist Black Cross, a prisoners' aid and ginger group and the paper which grew out of it – *Black Flag*.

However, perhaps Albert's most enduring legacy is the Kate Sharpley Library, probably the most comprehensive anarchist archive in Britain.[2]

Born in 1920 into a mixed marriage in the London of Orwell's *Down and Out* in which there were few homes for heroes, but many heroes fit only for homes, Albert was soon enrolled into political life as a private in the awkward squad. His decision to go down the road of revolutionary politics came, he claimed, in 1935 at the age of 15 – as a direct result of taking boxing lessons. Boxing was considered a 'common' sport, frowned upon by the governors of his Edmonton school and the prospective Labour MP for the area, the virulently anti-boxing Dr Edith Summerskill. Perhaps it was the boxer's legs and footwork he acquired

1. A reference to the anti-authoritarian protagonist of *The good soldier Švejk* by Jaroslav Hašek (1883–1923).
2. The KSL is now based in the US, with collective members around the world.

as a youth which gave him his lifelong ability to bear his considerable bulk. It certainly induced a lifetime's habit of shrewd assessment of his own and opponents' respective strengths and weaknesses.

The streetwise, pugilistic but bookish schoolboy attended his first anarchist meeting in 1935 where he first drew attention to himself by contradicting the speaker, Emma Goldman, by his defence of boxing. He soon made friends with the ageing anarchist militants of a previous generation and became a regular and dynamic participant in public meetings. The anarchist-led resistance to the Franco uprising in Spain in 1936 gave a major boost to the movement in Britain and Albert's activities ranged from organising solidarity appeals, to producing propaganda, working with Captain J. R. White[3] to organise illegal arms shipments from Hamburg to the CNT in Spain and acting as a contact for the Spanish anarchist intelligence services in Britain.

Albert's early working career ranged from fairground promoter, a theatre-hand and occasional film extra. Albert appeared briefly in Leslie Howard's *Pimpernel Smith*, an anti-Nazi film that did not follow the line of victory but rather of revolution in Europe. The plot called for communist prisoners, but by the time Howard came to make it, in 1940, Stalin had invaded Finland, and the script was changed to anarchist prisoners. Howard decided that none of the actors playing the anarchists seemed real and insisted that real anarchists, including Albert, be used as extras in the concentration camp scenes. One consequence of this

---

3.   J. R. White (1879–1946) British (and Irish) anarchist. He joined the anarchist movement during the Spanish Civil War. He had earlier served with the British army in the Boer War and helped to drill the Irish Citizen Army in 1913. Cienfuegos Press reprinted his pamphlet *The meaning of anarchism* in 1981 with an introduction 'From Loyalism to Anarchism' by Albert Meltzer. His *Misfit: an autobiography* (1930) was republished by Livewire Publications in 2005.

meeting was Howard's introduction to Hilda Monte, a prominent but unsung hero of the German anarchist resistance to Hitler, which may have contributed to his subsequent death en route to Lisbon.[4]

Albert's later working years were spent mainly as a second-hand bookseller and, finally, as a Fleet Street copytaker. His last employer was, strangely enough, *The Daily Telegraph*.

While by nature a remarkably gentle, generous and gracious soul, Albert's championship of anarchism as a revolutionary working class movement brought him into direct and sustained conflict with the neo-liberals who came to dominate the movement in the late 1940s. Just as people are drawn to totalitarian movements like fascism and communism because of their implicit violence and ideological certainties, many otherwise politically incompatible people were drawn to anarchism because of its militant tolerance. Albert was vehemently opposed to the re-packaging and marketing of anarchism as a broad church for academia-oriented quietists and single-issue pressure groups. It was ironical that one of this group, the late Professor George Woodcock, should publicly dismiss anarchism as a spent historical force in 1962, blissfully unaware of the post-Butskellite[5] storm which was about to break and the influence anarchist and libertarian ideas would have on this and generations yet to come. It was his championship of class-struggle anarchism, coupled with his scepticism of the student-led New Left in the 1960s which earned Albert his reputation for sectarianism. Paradoxically, as friend and *Black Flag* cartoonist Phil Ruff points out in his introduction to Albert's autobiography, it was the discovery of class struggle anarchism through the 'sectarianism' of *Black Flag* under Albert's editorship

---

4. Hilda Monte is the pen name of Jewish German socialist and anti-Nazi activist Hilde Meisel (1914–1945).

5. A reference to the end of the social consensus where Rab Butler (Conservative) and Hugh Gaitskell (Labour) followed similar policies.

that convinced so many anarchists of his and subsequent generations to become active in the movement. The dynamic and logic
of Albert's so-called sectarianism continued to bring countless
young people into the anarchist movement then and for a further
thirty years until his untimely stroke in April 1996.

It is difficult to write a public appreciation of such an inscru-
tably private man. Albert Meltzer seemed often like a member of
a tug-of-war team; you never quite knew if he was there simply to
make up numbers or if he was the anchor-man of the whole operation. To Albert, all privilege was the enemy of human freedom;
not just the privileges of capitalists, kings, bureaucrats and politicians but also the petty aspirations of opportunists and careerists
among the rebels themselves. Much of what he contributed to the
lives of those who knew him must go unrecorded, but he will be
remembered and talked about fondly for many years to come by
those of us whose lives he touched.

Albert Meltzer, anarchist, born London, January 7, 1920; died,
Weston-Super-Mare, North Somerset, May 7, 1996.

From *Black Flag*, no. 208, June 1996. An edited version of this obituary
was published in *The Guardian* under the title 'Anarchy's torchbearer' on
8 May 1996.

Robert 'Bobby' Lynn, Glasgow anarchist and community activist

Born in the Calton, in the heart of Glasgow, in 1924 Robert Lynn (about whom Matt McGinn[1] wrote one of his wonderful songs – 'Bobby Lynn's Shebeen'[2] – in Ross Street) was educated at St. Mungo's Academy. Leaving school at 14 years of age he took up a shipyard engineering apprenticeship in Yarrows and became actively involved in the class struggle to improve wages and conditions there – a battle that had to be fought and refought in ensuing years. During the war years he was swept up in the maelstrom of political activity in the British shipyard and engineering industries. In 1944 the Tyneside strike – which saw Jock Haston and Roy Tearse[3] imprisoned – quickly spread to the Clyde where many shipyards, including Yarrows where Bobby worked, were brought to a halt.

During WWII, the influential shop stewards' committees were dominated by the Communist Party, but their policy of subordinating workers' interests to those of the Soviet Union drew a withering fire from anarchists, Trotskyists and other anti-Stalinist socialists alike, an experience that had a profound effect on Robert, and it was then he began to nurture Bakuninist ideas and the industrial strategy of syndicalism.

In post-war Glasgow Robert's influence in shipbuilding became increasingly irritating to both employers and CP-led union officials, and he was 'blacklisted' with the complicity of both.

---

1. Matt McGinn (1928–1977) Scottish socialist and folk singer.
2. A shebeen is an unlicensed drinking establishment.
3. James Ritchie (Jock) Haston (1912–1986), and Roy Tearse (1919–1986) were both members of the (Trotskyist) Revolutionary Communist Party (RCP).

Unable to work he joined the Merchant Navy as an engineering officer and spent some years seeing the world and its peoples, devouring libraries and absorbing the ideas of syndicalism and Stirnerism (Max Stirner's Conscious Egoist).[4]

Returning to Glasgow in the early fifties he threw himself into politics, marriage and trade union activity. He was an active member of the Glasgow Anarchist Group, which at the time consisted of Frank Leech,[5] Jimmy Raeside and Eddie Shaw, well-respected names in local and international anarchist circles. As George Woodcock said: 'The Glasgow Anarchist Group is the only group in the world where the egocentric philosophies of Max Stirner took root and were given popular expression.'[6] The anarchists held a workers' open forum in Renfrew Street, Glasgow where anarchists, members of the SPGB,[7] nationalists and Trotskyists debated – sometimes physically. In an open air arena ordinary working class men and women discussed, passionately, the ideas of Feuerbach,[8] Clara Zetkin,[9] Bakunin, Kropotkin and many, many others. Robert Lynn revelled in this, what he called the University of Life.

In the late fifties, with the death of Leech and the departure abroad of of Raeside and Shaw, the Glasgow Anarchist Group disintegrated and the task of reorganisation was left to Robert. This he did by immersing himself in his local community of

---

4.   Max Stirner (pen name of Johann Kaspar Schmidt, 1806–1856), German individualist anarchist and writer.

5.   Frank Leech (1900–1953), British anarchist. A biography of him by Nick Heath is on Libcom.org: https://libcom.org/history/leech-frank-1900-1953.

6.   Woodcock mentions meeting 'anarchist working men in Glasgow' who looked on Stirner's *The ego and his own* as 'a belated gospel' in *Anarchism: a history of libertarian ideas and movements* (p. 91 of the 1975 edition).

7.   Socialist Party of Great Britain, founded in 1904.

8.   Ludwig Feuerbach (1804–1872), German philosopher.

9.   Clara (Klara) Zetkin (1857–1933) German socialist and communist.

the Calton. He and Jean, his constant companion, became well-known, well-respected and to many – myself included – well-loved characters.

Robert returned to industry and worked at Howden's engineering plant in Glasgow's South Side where he promoted his ideas of syndicalism and libertarianism. Sadly, thanks to trade union officials who immediately recognised the threat to their power, Robert's views did not meet with any great success. However it was the Glasgow Anarchist Group of the sixties and early seventies which proved the most fruitful for Robert's ideas; a massive blossoming of literature and direct action exploded on the scene. The publication of pamphlets such as *Practical Anarchy* and *Why Vote?*, all bearing Robert's signature, appeared and were avidly read by many people who, being disillusioned with political parties of all shades, were becoming increasingly attracted to the ideas of anarchism. Robert initiated a great number of events, especially the Glasgow Anarchist Summer School which attracted libertarian socialists from all over Britain.

His death (on August 16 1996) was a shock to his family (Jean and daughters Jean, Joan and Betty), his many friends and comrades, and even to his political opponents. He was generous to a fault and although he did not suffer fools gladly he rarely had a bad word to say about anyone, even the worst of us. Loved deeply, missed sadly.

Edited versions of this obituary appeared in the *Glasgow Herald*, 29 August 1996 and ('Robert Lynn: A Scots world of anarchy') *The Guardian* on 10 September 1996.

Goliardo Fiaschi, anarchist

Goliardo Fiaschi, anarchist, born August 21 1930; died (aged 69) July 29 2000, was one of the youngest of the generation of anti-fascist partisans who resisted Mussolini's Fascist regime in Italy and Franco's dictatorship in Spain.

In 1943, the young Italian anarchist, Goliardo Fiaschi, falsified his birth certificate – to make himself appear older than his 13 years – and joined the wartime Italian partisans. Armed with a captured rifle almost as big as himself, he accompanied the women who regularly crossed the Apennines on foot carrying food from Parma, Reggio or Modena, some 150 miles away, back to the starving inhabitants of his Tuscan birthplace, Massa di Carrara. In 1944, he was adopted as a mascot by the Costrignano Brigade, and, in that role, entered Modena as standard-bearer on its liberation in April 1945. The natives of Carrara, the Carrarense, are reputedly descendants of Phoenician slaves who quarried marble for Rome. The city is also the cradle of Italian anarchism and a

historical centre of rebellion. The fascist years in Italy, from 1922 onwards, were particularly bitter in Carrara. The city itself was twice liberated from the Nazis by anarchist partisans prior to the arrival of allied troops.

Goliardo Fiaschi. Photo from Stuart Christie. Stuart said 'Goliardo left me his "Carrara" necktie (the Foulard he's wearing in the photograph) in his will.'

After the liberation, Fiaschi returned to the quarries, where he had worked alongside his father and uncle from the age of eight. By the early 1950s, he was involved with the Spanish refugee committee and became friendly with José Lluis Facerias, a Spanish anarchist veteran of the Ascaso column in the Spanish Civil War, who had been freed from a Francoist jail in 1945 and had lived illegally in Carrara since 1952, making regular guerrilla forays into Franco's Spain. In August 1957, the two men crossed the Pyrenees (with bicycles) to embark on a new guerrilla struggle against Francoism. They were betrayed and detected within a fortnight; Fiaschi was arrested in a forest hideout and Facerias murdered in a security services ambush in the Barcelona suburbs. After beatings and torture, Fiaschi was brought before a military court in August 1958, where he was sentenced to 20 years and one day in jail. For more than a decade, in 40 Spanish prisons, Fiaschi sent thousands of postcards, decorated with precisely detailed paintings, to friends and acquaintances. I met him first in one of those jails, and I was to receive those cards throughout the 35 years of our friendship, the last of which arrived only a few weeks before his death. With amnesties, he was released in 1966 and deported to Italy where he was immediately arrested and taken off to serve a 10-year prison sentence – passed in absentia, without his knowledge, and without any notification of the charges and without representation in court. This conviction was for his alleged involvement in a 1957 bank robbery in Monferrato with Facerias. Following an international campaign, he was released from prison in March 1974 after serving 17 years behind bars.[1]

Fiaschi became a key figure in the Carrarense anarchist movement. He ran a bookshop and cultural circle, and was a prime mover in the occupation of the Germinal Centre located, embarrassingly for the city fathers, in the most prestigious building in

---

1. See 'Goliardo Fiaschi' by Antonio Téllez in *KSL: Bulletin of the Kate Sharpley Library* No. 24 (October 2000).

Carrara's main square. Occupied by anarchist partisans during the liberation in 1945, the building was the defiant focus of anarchist activity until 1990, when the local authority finally wrested it back.

After the 1999 May Day celebrations in Carrara, which he had always helped organise, Fiaschi announced that he was terminally ill and was preparing to end his life. Persuaded to shelve this plan, instead he went into hospital saying: 'There was a time when suicide would have been the right thing. I could have left my body to science and for the advancement of medicine. Now, I must surrender myself alive, so they can study me. I realise they will carry out all sorts of experiments on me, but, since my death is inevitable anyway, I will try to be equal to the task.' Brought home after 14 months in a cancer ward, Fiaschi died the following day. His coffin was borne around Carrara on the shoulders of friends, followed by a band, and anarchists from all over Italy carrying red and black flags. His remains were laid to rest beside those of Gino Lucetti[2] and Stefano Vatteroni,[3] both would-be assassins of Mussolini, and of Giuseppe Pinelli, defenestrated from police headquarters in Milan in 1969.

Such was the esteem in which Goliardo Fiaschi was held that even the ranks of Tuscany, in the person of the mayor of Carrara, could scarce forbear to cheer with a farewell eulogy, which ended with the words: 'Thanks, Goliardo!'

An edited version of this obituary appeared in *The Guardian*, 16 August 2000.

---

2. Gino Lucetti was an Italian anarchist (1900–1943). He was sentenced to thirty years in prison for his attempt. He was killed in a bombardment, shortly after his liberation by allied forces. A short biography by Pietro de Piero is on the Kate Sharpley Library website (https://www.katesharpleylibrary.net/cnp6dn). Stuart published a biography, *Gino Lucetti and his attempt to assassinate Benito Mussolini (Il Duce) 11 September 1926* by Riccardo Lucetti as an ebook.

3. Stefano Vatteroni, Italian anarchist (1897–1965), was imprisoned for helping to fund and plan Lucetti's attack.

Walter Morrison, Glasgow 'Eskimo', community activist and former soldier who rejected war

The milieu in which the anti-nuclear Scottish Committee of 100 flourished no longer exists, its activists having long since adopted other agendas. However, its brief flowering will always be associated with the dynamic figure of Walter Morrison, who seemingly at birth had signed up for life as a private extraordinaire in the Awkward Squad.[1]

Morrison, who died in his eightieth year, fought courageously against the wrongs in society, proudly wore the badges of non-violence and libertarian socialism, and spoke his mind fearlessly no matter where he was or in whose company.

Angered by the Clydebank blitz in 1940, the 16-year-old Morrison lied about his age and joined the army. He wanted to fight fascism, but in less than a week, he found little difference between this enemy and the bullying attitudes and practices within the British army. From then on Morrison's war was fought on two fronts. Considered a difficult case, he was shunted from the Royal Scots Guards to the Black Watch, then on to the Parachute Regiment. During a visit by King George VI, the king politely asked him how

---

1. The term Glasgow 'Eskimo' comes from a protest against Polaris nuclear weapons that included attempts to board the submarines which carried them from canoes. 'The US naval commander, Captain Lanin, [...] derided them as "only a bunch of Eskimos". That name was immediately adopted by the demonstrators as a badge of honour and passed into legend with the song, "The Glesca Eskimos" written by Morris Blythman.' [p.124 of *My granny made me an anarchist*]. Sadly Lanin's chosen phrase is a slur for the Inuit people.

he was being treated, to which the good soldier Morrison replied: 'Terrible.' He was sent to India on the first available troop ship.

Morrison's pacifism grew from his army experiences in India. During the Gandhi demonstrations in 1942,[2] the troops were briefed that they would be facing women and children protestors. The 18-year-old asked what they would be expected to do if they refused to halt. 'Open fire,' was the curt answer. Walter promptly stood up and said he would be the first to open fire: he would personally shoot any soldier who turned their gun on a woman or a child, and he would then shoot the officer who gave the order. His feet scarcely touched the ground on the way to the glasshouse.

Morrison was placed in solitary confinement and singled out for sadistic treatment. He told his superiors that unless the NCO responsible backed off, he would kill the next man who entered his cell. Morrison won the case but was wracked with guilt over the moral quandary that he would have had to kill the first person – friend or enemy – who entered his cell. It was that incident which started him on his lifelong commitment to non-violence.

Although charged on a number of occasions with incitement to mutiny, he never faced a full court-martial; his sentences were always confinement to barracks, 30-days loss of pay or downgradement. He ended his army career and returned to Glasgow in 1946, without a war pension. (Walter's army experiences are told in Peter Grafton's book, *You, you and you: The people out of step with WWII*, Pluto, 1981.)

The arrival of the US Polaris submarine fleet in the Holy Loch in 1960 turned Glasgow into ground zero for any Soviet pre-emptive nuclear missile strike. Morrison was involved from the start in the campaign to stop US Polaris missiles being based in the Holy Loch. He became a leading light of the Scottish Committee of 100 and was in the thick of all the demonstrations from

---

2.   The pro-independence 'Quit India' movement of August 1942.

the day the submarines arrived. A man of deeds as well as words, Morrison was drawn to the more libertarian and action-oriented Scottish Committee of 100, rather than the passive, celebrity-and-politician-dominated CND.[3] The personal example Morrison set to others, coupled with his fame as a rebel, gave him considerable status among the young militants on the committee. My memories are of him standing single-handedly in Glasgow streets and at demonstrations around Scotland, surrounded by menacing and hostile opponents while arguing his case against the bomb. His tenacity and fortitude in going out in all weathers to demonstrate in the most hostile locations, often alone, was truly inspiring.

Protest was a family affair around the Morrison household. Walter's wife, Agnes Lygate, whom he married in 1953, and neighbour in Govan, Eleanor Hind, wife of writer Archie Hind, both early feminists, were founders of Women Against the Bomb and Youth against the Bomb. Betty Campbell, his later partner, was his constant support in the Corkerhill Community Council to which Morrison dedicated his life from 1976 to 2002.

On one occasion Morrison was setting up his tent on the foreshore of the Holy Loch, near Ardnadam pier which serviced the Polaris submarines and their support ships – it being illegal to camp on the land – when he was called over by someone waving to him from a large American car by the roadside. In the rear of the car were three men who addressed him by name, two from the Ministry of Defence's 'Psychological Warfare Group' in Dundee and the third an American of uncertain military or security provenance. They proceeded to warn Walter and his friends that they were out to get the so-called Scots Against War, a group who at the time were involved in publishing official secrets plus carrying out sabotage and other forms of direct action against military installations throughout Scotland. One of the MoD men pointed to

---

3.   Campaign for Nuclear Disarmament, founded in 1957.

the dark waters of the loch and told Walter that he was involved in a dangerous business and that it would be so easy for people like him to disappear, never to be found. Walter was a hard man, but this personal threat was something quite new and alarming to him.

A week after I was arrested in Spain in 1964, having been caught playing a part in a plot to assassinate the country's dictator, General Franco, Morrison hitched-hiked from Glasgow to London to hold a fast and a picket the Spanish embassy – having first telephoned Scotland Yard to ask permission. No sooner had he settled down on the pavement when a police van drew up and four policemen jumped out, bundled him into the van and drove to an unidentified London police station. Instead of being charged and taken to the police cells, he was escorted to what seemed like a large gym hall where three men sat at a table, one in police uniform and the other two in civvies. Morrison was then aggressively questioned about his relationship with me, about the Committee of 100 and again about the Scots Against War group, who had recently set fire to Ardnadam pier in the Holy Loch. Walter was an old hand at being arrested and locked up, but the sinister and surreal events of that night shook him up so badly that he resigned for a time from the Scottish Committee of 100.

After the Committee of 100 petered out a few years later, Morrison and Betty Campbell became pivotal figures in the Corkerhill Community Council, campaigning for improved housing, safer roads, play parks and improved social integration. Walter and his team brought international recognition to Corkerhill, a tiny housing scheme on the south side of Glasgow with just 1,300 tenants. It received a World Health Organisation award, the only community in the UK to qualify. When the award-winning community centre was closed after a long-running dispute with Glasgow City Council, Walter refused to bow out quietly, defiantly holding a flag-lowering ceremony as a final protest. On the last day, a large crowd turned out to see the flag of the WHO solemnly lowered over the centre. When the M77 carved through the south side of Glasgow, it was Corkerhill, led by Walter Morrison, who led the way organising resistance and winning major concessions.

Corkerhill was also the very first community in Glasgow to house the Vietnamese Boat People.

In 1998 when Morrison was at Buckingham Palace being awarded an MBE for his services to the Corkerhill community, the Queen's corgis had been running around the room unchecked and generally intimidating everyone. He said to HM: 'You know, Ma'am, if those dugs ran around like that in Corkerhill where I come from, I'd shoot the lot of them.' With a twinkle in his eye, of course.

He is survived by his partner Betty Campbell, his daughter Leigh and his son Grant.

Walter Morrison MBE, community activist, born March 20, 1924; died February 6, 2004.

An edited version of this obituary appeared in *The Guardian*, 27 March 2004.

Antonio Téllez Solà, the Herodotus of the anti-Franco maquis

Antonio Téllez Solà, who has died at his home in Perpignan aged 84, was one of the last survivors of the anarchist resistance which fought to overthrow the Franco dictatorship. He was also one of the first historians of the post civil war urban and rural guerrilla resistance to the fascist regime. In his actions and his writings, Téllez personified refusal to surrender to tyranny.

The son of a railway worker, he was born in Tarragona and was radicalised by the October 1934 insurrection in Asturias, which failed when the unions outside the mining region failed to give their support. On 19 July 1936, when the workers, this time united, held at bay the rebellion of most of the Spanish officer class against the infant left-wing Republic, Téllez was in Lérida where he joined the anarchist youth organisation, the Juventudes Libertarias,[1] immersing himself in the struggle to fight fascism and preserve the social revolution with which the union rank and file had answered the generals' attempted coup.

Téllez joined the army aged 18, in the final stages of the Republic's collapse, and saw action on various fronts until February 1939 when, with thousands of other anti-Francoist refugees, he was forced into exile in France. There he spent a year in the Septfonds concentration camp and then a further six months in the camp at Argelès-sur-Mer, two of many locations in which the French government interned the people who had held fascism at bay for almost three years. Escaping at the end of 1940, he joined a band of Spanish guerrillas operating in the Aveyron department,

---

1.   See FIJL in the glossary.

serving as part of the IX Brigade (French Forces of the Interior), resisting the occupation until Liberation in 1944.

In October 1944 Téllez took part in the ill-advised 10-day invasion of Francoist Spain by approximately 6,000 Spanish republican guerrillas of the CP-led Unión Nacional Española (UNE) via the Arán and Ronçal valleys in the Pyrenees, one of the first operations mounted by the maquis against the Franco regime. With the defeat of the UNE at the battle of Salardú, he moved to Toulouse where he set up clandestine arms dumps for the guerrilla campaign.

For two years Téllez served on the second peninsular committee of the Iberian Federation of Libertarian Youth (FIJL), carrying out clandestine liaison missions between the anarchist movement in France and Spain. Resigning from organisational activity in April 1946, he travelled undercover in Spain for three months establishing contacts with the guerrillas and what remained of the illegal anarchist movement. Téllez was unable to generate financial or organisational support for the Resistance due to the hostility of the Toulouse-based National Committee of the exiled anarcho-syndicalist union, the National Confederation of Labour (CNT) to armed struggle. Frustrated by oligarchic tensions and self-serving politicking, he moved to Paris where he worked as a reporter for Agence France Presse from 1960 until retirement in 1986, when he moved to Céret in the Pyrenees and then to Perpignan.

Antonio Téllez by Stuart Christie.
From the Stuart Christie photo album on
the Kate Sharpley Library website.

In Paris Téllez continued to contribute to the anarchist press, but from 1954 onwards it was clear that his life's work was to write the histories of the legendary names of the anarcho-syndicalist action groups: Francisco Sabaté Llopart, José Lluis Facerias, Wenceslao Giménez Orive,[2] Francisco Denis,[3] Raul Carballeira,[4] Marcelino Massana Bancells – and many more, from the mountains and sierras of Catalonia, Aragón, Asturias and Galicia in the north to the Levante and Extremadura in the west and east, to Andalucia in the south.

I met Téllez for the first time in Paris in 1973. While I was on remand in Brixton prison he had sent me a copy of his newly-published biography of Francisco Sabaté, which I translated from Spanish into English.[5] After my acquittal I visited him to discuss the book, which he was constantly updating and revising, as he did with all his work. We became firm friends. His archives were enormous and his apartment overlooking the Père Lachaise cemetery was stacked from floor to ceiling with boxes of files, documents and photograph albums. His accomplishments in a particularly difficult area of study were quite remarkable given that his subject matter was clandestine groups and secretive and highly individualistic militants who were activists rather than theorists, many of whom were outcasts from their own organisations.

---

2. Wenceslao Giménez Orive, 'Wences', (1921–1950) Spanish anarchist and guerrilla. He worked with Facerias before forming the Los Maños group. He killed himself after being wounded in a police ambush. See *Los Maños: the lads from Aragon; the story of an anti-Franco action group* (Christiebooks ebook 2013; Kate Sharpley Library pamphlet 2014).

3. Francisco Denís Diéz, 'El Catalá,' (1898–1949) Spanish anarchist and guerrilla guide, killed himself when arrested to avoid talking under torture.

4. Raul Carballeira Lacunza, 'El Argentino,' (1917–1948), Argentinean anarchist and member of the resistance to Francoism. He was killed in Barcelona trying to break out of a police cordon.

5. See Translator's Introduction on page 56.

I witnessed a good example of this in Paris, when I introduced Téllez to Octavio Alberola, the coordinator of Defensa Interior, the clandestine anarchist group responsible for organising assassination attempts on Franco between 1962 and 1965. The two men had never met and Alberola was taken aback when, from on top of his wardrobe, Téllez produced the original plans for the proposed 1963 assassination attempt on Franco at the Puente de los Franceses near the Oriente Palace in Madrid. We never did discover where he acquired them.

Téllez's published and unpublished output was phenomenal, covering the period from Franco's victory on 1 April 1939 to his death on 20 November 1975, and beyond. He had two main objectives: to record the lives of selfless men who would not compromise their ideals nor treat with a system they found villainous and vile, men who devoted their adult lives to freeing Spain from the last of the Axis dictators. His work has been a major contribution to the movement for the recovery of historical memory which is now playing such an important part in contemporary Spanish politics. Téllez's other objective was to demonstrate that the individual is never helpless; there is always the possibility of rebelling and defending an idea one considers just, even in the most unfavourable and adverse conditions.

Téllez is survived by his partner, Harmonía, and a son.

Antonio Téllez Solà, anarchist, guerrilla, historian, born January 18, 1921; died March 27, 2005.

From *KSL: Bulletin of the Kate Sharpley Library* No.42, May 2005. An edited version of this obituary appeared in *The Guardian*, May 10, 2005.

José Ignacio Martín-Artajo Saracho – Anarchist, diplomat, blasphemer, poet and man of letters

My first meeting with the dynamic and generous-spirited writer José Martín-Artajo (Pepe) was in London in the early part of 1968. It was a year after he broke completely with his bourgeois past and walked out of his career as a Francoist diplomat, following the US-led colonels' coup in Greece in April 1967. He had been first secretary at the Spanish Embassy in Athens. At the same time he separated from his German wife, Christa von Petersdorff, a psychoanalyst and translator of the works of Freud into French. Christa and Pepe met while she was researching her PhD on the comparative myth of 'Don Juan' in France, Italy and Spain. After the split she always said, with a smile, that she had 'known Don Juan personally'.

After leaving Greece José Martín-Artajo moved to Coolhurst Road in London's Crouch End (where I was living at the time) with his then partner, the ethnomusicologist and broadcaster Lucy Durán. Lucy, whom he had met in Athens, was the daughter of Republican civil war general Gustavo Durán Martínez.

The son of Alberto Martín-Artajo, right-wing Catholic, pro-monarchist and Franco's Foreign Minister from 1945 until 1957, José Martín-Artajo came from 'impeccable' Francoist, Integrist Catholic stock (an uncle became a Jesuit), and was a rebel from early youth. In the early 1950s he was arrested by the Gestapo-trained Brigada Politico Social for anti-Francoist activities, but instead of going to jail his father had him 'sectioned' on grounds of mental illness, a common ploy among the well-placed Francoist elite with dissident children, a device they shared with their opposite numbers in the Soviet Union and elsewhere, including the US according to Kurt Vonnegut's novel *God Bless You, Mr Rosewater*,[1] in which the young son of a wealthy bourgeois family wishes to become a firefighter – 'Where's the profit in THAT?'

In his London years (1967–76), José Martín-Artajo (Pepe) became closely involved with the work of the Anarchist Black Cross, the Centro Ibérico, and latterly, in Paris, through Octavio Alberola, with Pepe Martínez of the libertarian Spanish-language publishing house Ruedo Ibérico.

In 1976, having put him in touch with my old comrade and cell-mate, the recently released Luis Andrés Edo, secretary general of the CNT and editor of *Solidaridad Obrera*, José Martín-Artajo returned to Spain after 9 years of exile where he threw himself into the task of helping rebuild the CNT and the Spanish Libertarian Movement. According to Federica Montseny, Martín-Artajo 'fell into the wrong hands' in London, Paris and Barcelona (she was referring to among others Miguel García, Albert Meltzer and myself in London, Octavio Alberola in Paris, and Luis Andrés in Barcelona).

In December 1979, the director of the International Institute of Social History in Amsterdam (IISG), Rudolf de Jong, refused to accept the credentials of José Martín-Artajo, Luis Andrés and Victor León as official representatives of the CNT, sent to negotiate the return of the union's archives (the 'Amsterdam Boxes'), which had been deposited there since the end of the Spanish Civil War. De Jong's obduracy led to the three comrades occupying the IISG main hall and CNT lawyer Pep Castells being sent to join them with a letter confirming their authority from newly elected CNT secretary general José Bondía. Even so, de Jong still refused to authorise the archives' release and it wasn't until the eve of

---

1.   *God Bless You, Mr Rosewater* was published in 1965.

the Xmas holidays (22 December), following a serious shouting match (in German) between Martín-Artajo and the IISG director, that an agreement was reached. The archives were returned to the CNT in Spain the following year.

In 1980, the prestigious publishing house Ediciones Júcar published his novel, *Tigre Jack, La vuelta de Ulises, El pecado del espíritu: prosas atroces*. Pepe also edited the military memoirs of Lucy's father, Gustavo Durán, *Una enseñanza de la guerra española: glorias y miserias de la improvisación de un ejército* ...

His other published works of fiction include *Fiesta a oscuras* (Ediciones Era, Mexico, 1975), a critical attack on the repressive Catholic and bourgeois society in which he grew up, and *Historia de la misteriosa desaparición de Porfiria Santillana, fragona española en país superdesarrollado* (Joaquín Mortiz, Mexico, 1970). There was also another novel based on his time as consul in Frankfurt.

José Martín-Artajo at the Conway Hall, London, 1976. Photo by Phil Ruff.

Incidentally, it was also José Martín-Artajo who, entirely out of his own salary and savings, generously, selflessly (and quietly), funded and maintained Miguel García García's famous hostelry and international anarchist social centre, the Bar La Fragua in Barcelona's carrer Cadena.

In those early post-Francoist years, Artajo's connections with the so-called 'Apaches' of the CNT and the international activists of the movement made him vulnerable to provocations, one of which was an unsuccessful attempt by Antonio Navarro, a police agent infiltrated into the FAI (Iberian Anarchist Federation) to implicate him in an arms-smuggling operation.

The first time I returned to Spain, in 1981, with my 3-year-old daughter Branwen, Pepe was waiting for us with his diplomatic credential at the airport arrivals lounge – just in case the police decided to detain me. Fortunately they didn't

In 1984 Spain's first socialist government wanted him out of the way and sent him off as cultural attaché to their embassy in Caracas and later, in 1990, to Brasilia. It was a difficult decision for him to accept the posting, which he did only after lengthy discussions with close comrades, including Luis Andrés Edo and Octavio Alberola, who appreciated how useful he could be to the movement in such a position. However, once installed in the Caracas embassy he became an important conduit and helped at least 5 wanted comrades escape to safety in South America. They entered the country through Colombia, which at the time required only a 'weekend-pass', where José Martín-Artajo arranged for the pass to be changed to a visa, which allowed them to move on, with the help of comrades, and establish themselves in Brazil, Bolivia or Nicaragua.

José Martín-Artajo spent the later years of his life in Massanes, Gerona (with his second wife, Marisa Ares, and his son Josta, born in 1992) writing and translating Chinese literature and poetry into Spanish. He has left many unpublished manuscripts. He also has a daughter, Iris, by his first wife, Christa von Petersdorff.

Throughout this time he worked closely with Edo, who was with him when he died.

José Ignacio Martín-Artajo Saracho – b. 1932, Madrid; d. 14 April 2005, Gerona.

From *KSL: Bulletin of the Kate Sharpley Library* No.80, October 2014.

Franco Leggio – the intractable Sicilian (1921–2006)

Franco was a veteran of the Sicilian-Italian anarchist and anti-Francoist resistance movements and one of the protagonists of the short-lived insurrectionary Ragusa Commune of 1945.[1] Short and wiry, he cut a striking figure with his long greying hair, olive complexion and slightly Asiatic appearance, a look that was enhanced by a Genghis Khan moustache that would have made Jack Palance green with envy. Franco – then in his late forties, a well-known and popular figure in Ragusa, was a native Sicilian, a people considered by Neapolitans to be the oldest and most intractable people on earth, 'older than the Roman Empire and the Caesars, older even than the Etruscans or Minoans, so old that their ways and ideas were incomprehensible to anyone but the Devil himself.'[2]

I first met Franco Leggio in Carrara in 1968, an extraordinary man from a mining family in Ragusa whose working life began in the Sicilian sulphur mines in the early 1930s, during the Mussolini dictatorship. Politicised by the coverage of the Spanish Civil War, by the end of the decade Franco had become an anarchist and, with some of his friends – Ciccio Dipasquale, Pino Catanese and Mario Perna – he formed a local, revolutionary anti-fascist group.

Franco played his own small part in Mussolini's downfall. During the war he served in the Italian navy, patrolling the Mediterranean, ostensibly looking for Allied shipping. So unsuccessful were they in locating and sinking enemy ships – probably

---

1. Commune of Ragusa (January 1945) was the culmination of the Non si parte/Don't go revolt which began in December 1944. See *Rebellious spirit: Maria Occhipinti and the Ragusa anti-draft revolt of 1945*, Kate Sharpley Library, 2008.
2. From Robert Anton Wilson's 1982 novel *The earth will shake*.

deliberately so – that the German high command finally felt obliged to put their own officers on board Mussolini's ships to shadow Italian officers and gunners. Franco's strategy was inspired by the 'Good Soldier Svejk', the anti-militarist character created by Czech anarchist Jaroslav Hašek. With his German naval officer overseers beside or behind him, Franco turned into the idiot of the gunnery deck, deliberately mishearing or misunderstanding their instructions and orders. Among his achievements he counted the loss of three ships – all his own. Whenever an Allied vessel was located the German officer would give target commands, in pidgin Italian, which gunner Leggio deliberately misconstrued, fixing the exasperated Teuton with an amiable smile and a sweet and pleasant manner. By the time the angry German had pushed Franco out of the way to do his job for him, the Allied ship would have either disappeared or blown their ship out of the water. As I said, Franco ended up in the Mediterranean three times. It gave the lie to the Italians' 'acquired reputation' of cowardice. Most simply did not want to serve fascism – nor for that matter probably any other 'ism.' When forced, many did their best to do as little fighting and as much sabotage as possible.

Brenda Christie and Franco Leggio, Ragusa, 1973 by Stuart Christie. From the Stuart Christie photo album on the Kate Sharpley Library website.

It may also have been these bouts in the sea that contributed to Franco's tuberculosis, which led to him being confined,
in 1944, to the Ragusa sanatorium. In December 1944, the (now
pro-Allied) Italian government began redrafting Italian workers
to fight against the German fascist army in the north, but Italians
had already suffered over 20 years of fascism and five years of war
and occupation and enough was enough. Draftees, recently returned from the war, found a new set of call up cards landing on
their door-steps and the defiant watchwords 'no go' turned into
'no go, and no going back'. Determined to play his part, Franco
slipped out of the sanatorium to lead the local 'non si parte' ('we
won't go') revolt against the return of draftees to the navy. In January 1945, in the district of Ragusa known to locals as 'Russia',
Communist Party militant, Maria Occhipinti,[3] was called out
onto the street by neighbours as the carabinieri were rounding
up local 'draft dodgers' and bundling them into trucks. As it was
about to be driven away Maria, who was 5 months pregnant at
the time, threw herself in front of the wheels saying 'you can kill
me but you shall not pass'. As more and more people surrounded
the truck, the authorities were forced to release the draftees, although according to some, the crowd helped them to escape,
rather than the police surrendering to *force majeure*. According
to Meno Occhipinti, 'the next day during an argument between
a sexton and an army officer about why the draft was happening
again, the officer lobbed a grenade at him – and blew him up'.
This was the catalyst for what became known as 'the Commune
of Ragusa,' with anarchists such as Franco Leggio, Mario Perna,
dissident communists like Erasmo Santangelo and rank and file
leftists such as Maria Occhipinti leading an armed uprising which
resulted in Ragusa declaring itself a free city – and holding off the

---

3.   Maria Occhipinti (1921–1996) Sicilian communist then anarchist, femi-
     nist and writer. Her memoir *Una donna di Ragusa* was published in 1993.

combined Allied and Italian armed forces for over a week. This was at a time when the whole of Sicily was in a state of critical political turmoil, with the armed separatist (pro-union with America) bands under the control of the mafia-protected Salvatore Giuliano in the West and Concetto Gallo in Catania province in the East. Hundreds of arrests followed and Franco was arrested, serving 18 months in prison.

After his release, Franco returned to the mines and, in 1949, he played a leading role in an epic two-month occupation of the sulphur mines in an attempt to fight lay-offs. Forced to leave Ragusa after the failure of the occupation, Franco worked his way across Italy and, in France, he worked on building sites with Cipriano Mera,[4] the 'bricklayer general' who had led one of the most formidable anarchist columns of the Spanish Civil War and who won the only Republican victory at the Battle of Guadalajara in 1937.

During this period Franco was collaborating closely with the Spanish anarchist guerrilla José Lluis Facerias and in fact narrowly avoided capture in the 1957 Barcelona shoot-out in which Facerias was killed and Goliardo Fiaschi was arrested. In 1960 he founded the publishing house La Fiaccola – which was the inspiration for my own publishing ventures from 1973 onward – and throughout the 1960s Franco worked closely with the clandestine anarchist resistance organisation Defensa Interior and, later, the First of May Group. He did not return to Ragusa until 1969, after the murder (defenestration) of anarchist Giuseppe Pinelli and the Piazza Fontana bombing carried out by Italian neo-fascists and Italian secret service agents. In 1982 Franco's involvement in the trial of another Italian anarchist, Giovanni Marini,[5] led to him serving a further

---

4.   Cipriano Mera (1897–1975) Spanish anarchist, writer and member of Defensa Interior. A short biography by Julián Vadillo Muñoz is on the Kate Sharpley Library website: https://www.katesharpleylibrary.net/kwh83j.

5.   Giovanni Marini (1942–2001) Italian anarchist. Marini killed a member

six months in Ragusa jail. He was also at the forefront of the struggle against the installation of US cruise missiles at Comiso in Sicily in 1983.

---

of the fascist MSI (Movimento Sociale Italiano) in self-defence when he and another comrade were attacked in Salerno in 1972. He was sentenced to twelve years in 1974, and released in 1979. A biography by Nick Heath is on Libcom.org: https://libcom.org/history/articles/1942-2001-giovanni-marini.

Luis Andrés Edo: Anarchist activist whose life was dedicated to the 'Idea' and the struggle for liberty

With the death of Luis Andrés Edo, aged 83, in Barcelona, the anarchist movement has lost an outstanding militant and original thinker, and I have lost a comrade-in-arms, a former cell-mate – and an irreplaceable friend. The son of a Guardia Civil, Luis was born in the *benemérita* barracks in Caspe (Zaragoza) in 1925, but the family moved to Barcelona the following year when his father, Román, was transferred to a new *cuartel* (barracks) in the Sants district of Barcelona, where the young boy grew up, educated by nuns, monks and priests. Later, after the social revolution of July 19 1936, the ten-year old Luis became not only a 'child of the barricades', but also a 'son of the CENU' (el Consell de l'Escola Nova Unificada), the successor rationalist schools to the Modern School launched by Francisco Ferrer i Guàrdia in 1901 (and forced to close in 1906). The education he received there and on the streets of revolutionary Barcelona was to prove life-changing. Luis's working life began in 1939, at the age of 14, cleaning machinery and odd-jobbing with Spain's National Railway company, RENFE, where he was apprenticed two years later as a locomotive engineer and, in 1941, aged 16, he affiliated to the underground anarcho-syndicalist labour union, the National Confederation of Labour (CNT). He remained with RENFE until 1946 when, after completing his apprenticeship at the age of 21, he was arrested and spent a short time in prison accused of 'stealing potatoes' from trains as part of the CNT's 'food redistribution' campaign during those years of terrible hunger. On his release he became a glassworker, manufacturing thermometers, a job that was to cause him serious and enduring health problems from ingesting mercury and hydrofluoric acid.

Luis was called up in October 1947 to do his National Service, but by December he had had enough of Franco's army and deserted, crossing clandestinely into France, still dressed in his military uniform. In 1952 he returned to Barcelona following a serious crackdown by the French authorities on the activities of the CNT in exile. This was the result of a bungled armed robbery in Lyon the previous year in which three people were killed and nine others injured.[1] Luis was not involved in the Lyon robbery, but the French police went out of their way to make life intolerable for all Spanish anarchist exiles at the time. Back in Spain Luis was arrested on desertion charges in August 1952 and was not freed until October 1953 when he was returned to the ranks – promptly deserting again early in 1954. Re-arrested, he served a further six months in the dungeons of the notorious Castillo de Figueres, a military prison in Gerona, after which, like so many others, he went into permanent exile in France where he threw himself whole-heartedly into the libertarian anti-Francoist resistance movement. In Paris in 1955, Luis became closely involved with Laureano Cerrada Santos,[2] another former RENFE employee and a key figure in the WWII anti-Nazi Resistance and escape and evasion networks. Cerrada was also a master forger and an influential figure in France's criminal demi-monde, especially the Parisian and Marseilles *milieux*, and was, undoubtedly, one of the most problematic, enigmatic and mysterious figures of the Spanish anarchist diaspora. It was Cerrada who, in 1947, had purchased a powerful US Navy Vedette speedboat used by the CNT's defence

1.   The robbery took place on 18 January 1951 in Rue Duguesclin. Two guards died and one of the suspects later either killed himself or was 'suicided'.

2.   Laureano Cerrada Santos (1902–1976) Spanish anarchist.

committee to transport arms, propaganda and militants from France into Spain; he also bought the plane used in the aerial attack on Franco's yacht in San Sebastian in September 1948.[3] After the fallout from the Lyon robbery in 1951, however, Cerrada was expelled and ostracised by the official CNT for 'bringing the organisation into disrepute' because of his 'criminal connections'. Cerrada had, in fact, been in custody in France on forgery charges for a month prior to the Lyon robbery. That cut no ice with the CNT National Committee in exile in Toulouse who wanted rid of all the 'Apache' elements in the organisation who threatened the legality of their comfortable existence in France.

In Paris, Luis's involvement with the Juventudes Libertarias, the Spanish anarchist youth organisation also brought him into contact with most of the other well-known 'faces' of the anti-Franco Resistance, men such as 'Quico' Sabaté, the near-legendary urban guerrilla, and José Pascual Palacios[4] of the CNT's Defence Commission, the man responsible for coordinating all the action groups operating in Spain and described by Barcelona police chief Eduardo Quintela as Spain's 'Public enemy number one'. It was Luis who organised a meeting between 'el Quico' and the former Communist Party army general, 'El Campesino'[5] at the latter's request in 1959, shortly before Sabaté's death at the hands of the Francoist security services. During this time in Paris he worked at the Alhambra Maurice Chevalier Theatre as assistant scene painter to Rafael Aguilera,[6] the famous Andalusian artist

---

3. For more on this abortive attack see *The assassination attempt on Franco from the air, 1948* by Antonio Téllez (London: Kate Sharpley Library, 2006).

4. José Pascual Palacios (1916–1970) Spanish anarchist, loosely connected with Defensa Interior.

5. 'El Campesino' (Valentín R. González) was a Communist who went into exile in the Soviet Union in 1939. He was later imprisoned in the Gulag and was a critic of the Communist Party after he escaped to the West.

6. Rafael Aguilera (1903–1998).

from Ronda. What few people knew, however, was that Aguilera – a hero of the Spanish Civil War and the Resistance who had been imprisoned by the Nazis – was also responsible for maintaining an important arms deposit in Paris for the CNT Defence Commission. One of these caches was in his workshop in the attic of the Alhambra. When there was no work to be done in the theatre, Edo and Lucio Urtubia,[7] a close friend and a protégé of Quico Sabaté, would clean and oil these weapons. On one dramatic occasion Lucio was conscientiously cleaning an old Mauser pistol when it went off in his hand, almost blowing Luis's brains out. By the early 1960s Luis was secretary of the Alianza Obrera (CNT-UGT-STV),[8] propaganda secretary of the National Committee of the CNT, secretary of Paris Local Federation of the CNT, secretary general of the Peninsular Committee of the FIJL in Exile, and was closely involved with, among others, Octavio Alberola, García Oliver and Cipriano Mera in the setting up of Defensa Interior, the clandestine section of the Spanish Libertarian Movement in Exile (MLE). The function of Defensa Interior was to plan and implement subversive actions targeting the Francoist regime and to assassinate Franco himself; it was in this role that I first encountered Luis in Paris in 1964, prior to setting off for Madrid with plastic explosives intended for that very purpose.

My next encounter with Luis was two years later, in Carabanchel Prison in Madrid as a result of a betrayal by a police agent, Inocencio Martínez. He and four other comrades were arrested in October 1966 by Franco's secret police, the Brigada Político-Social (BPS) and accused of planning to kidnap the head of the US armed forces in Spain, Rear Admiral Norman Gillette

---

7.   Lucio Urtubia, Spanish anarchist (1931–2020). See the tribute by Stuart on page 193.

8.   ASO (Alianza Sindical Obrera) a collaboration of the Anarchist, Socialist and Basque union federations. It was organised from within Spain and not supported by the exiled CNT.

and, allegedly, the exiled Argentinean politician Juan Perón. He was also accused of complicity in the Rome kidnapping, six months earlier, of Monsignor Marcos Ussiá, the 40-year old Spanish ecclesiastical attaché to the Vatican. These actions were carried out under the auspices of the First of May Group, the autonomous international anarchist action group, which succeeded Defensa Interior following its dissolution by the CNT-FAI's Toulouse leadership subsequent to my arrest in 1964.

Luís Andrés Edo in 1983. From the Stuart Christie photo album on the Kate Sharpley Library website.

Luis and I shared a cell in the infamous sixth gallery of Carabanchel, the political wing. I had just turned twenty at the time and in fact it was he who first taught me how to shave. During that time we became close friends as well as comrades. I often recall, with pleasure, the lengthy discussions we had each evening after lock-up until 'lights-out' in which we seemed to cover every conceivable subject under the sun. Many of these strands of thought he dedicated to fine onion paper in minuscule hand which we later smuggled out of prison. Some of these theses appeared forty years later in his collection of theoretical essays *La Corriente*. Certainly, for an inexperienced and naïve youth such as myself, Luis, with his charisma and strong personality was the ideal teacher, mentor, and role model. They were interesting and educational times indeed and involved two escape attempts which were organised by Luis with help from an action group from Paris. The discovery of the plan, just before his trial, led to our separation and my transfer to the penitentiary of Alcalá de Henares in the summer of 1967. Tried by a civil Public Order Tribunal, something unusual in itself for anarchists who, like myself, were normally charged under military law with 'Banditry and Terrorism' and tried by a drumhead court-martial, Luis was sentenced to three years imprisonment for illegal association (membership of the Juventudes Libertarias), six years for illegal possession of arms, and a 25,000 peseta fine for possessing false identity documents. The sentence would have been considerably harsher had he been tried by a 'Council of War'. Luis was released from Jaén prison in 1972, having run the gamut of many of Franco's maximum security penitentiaries – including Soria and Segovia in which he organised escape committees and mounted a number of hunger strikes and mutinies, for which he spent months in the punishment cells. Arrested again in 1974 on charges of illegal association with the anarchist action groups of the GARI (Grupos de Acción Revolucionaria Internacionalista) and with complicity in the Paris kidnapping of Spanish banker Baltasar Suárez, Luis received a five-year prison sentence in February 1975 of which he served a little over two years, being released in 1976 under a royal amnesty during the post-Francoist transition, in spite of having led the first major mutiny during his time in Barcelona's Model Prison. It was a particularly painful period of imprisonment as he was separated from his partner, Rosita, and his two small children, Helios and Violeta who remained in Paris.

With Franco dead but his cohorts still in the driving seats of power, Luis played a key role in the CNT's re-construction in Catalonia and was one of the organisers of the 'Montjuic Meeting', the first legal public gathering of the CNT since 1939 – an event which attracted 300,000 people, most of them a new generation of young libertarians. He was also a prime mover in organising the 'Libertarian Days', the Jornadas Libertarias, a week-long international anarchist festival which followed the Montjuic meeting and, for five extraordinary days in July, turned Barcelona into an international showcase for – and celebration – of anarchism.

But the transition period between 1976 and 1981 was also a time of major provocations by the rump of the Francoist power elite, the Búnker, desperate to hang on to their power and privileges, and avoid being brought to justice for their reign of criminality and terror. They and their new social-democratic partners were also anxious to discredit and neutralise the radical elements of the nascent CNT and the FAI – the so-called 'Apache sector'. Again it was Luis who was in the forefront of exposing the Spanish State's 'Strategy of Tension', which began in earnest in January 1977 with the massacre of five leftist lawyers in their offices in Atocha and leaving four others seriously injured, by the same Italian neo-fascists responsible for a similar terror campaign under way in Italy since 1968. These terrorists, and other parapoliticals of the SCOE (Servicio de Coordinación, Organización y Enlace), operated under the control of Rodolfo Martín Villa, Adolfo Suárez's fascist minister of the interior and his notorious police commissioner, Roberto Conesa Escudero. The hands of Martin Villa and Escudero were also to be seen in the Scala fire of 15 January 1978 in which four people died, and the blame for which was laid at the door of the CNT.

Luis was arrested again in 1980 and charged with '*formación terrorista*' (organising a terrorist group) – conveniently shortly before the trial of the accused in the Scala case – with the prosecutor asking for a sentence of twenty years, but he was released on provisional liberty in August 1981 after the attempted Tejero coup.[9] The case against Luis was finally dropped in 1984 due to lack of evidence.

In the subsequent twenty-five years – right up until the moment of his death, and in spite of a seriously debilitating seven-year illness – Luis was supported throughout by his soulmate and partner, Doris Ensinger,[10] with whom he shared his life after finally separating from his first partner, Rosita, in 1981. Luis and Rosita had effectively separated in 1976 when he refused to return to Paris at such a pivotal moment in Spain's history, while she and the children refused to live in Barcelona. Luis and Doris began their relationship in 1978, living together as a couple from the day he was released from prison in August 1981.

Luis Andrés Edo remained always both an untiring activist and an intellectual dynamo of the international libertarian movement, constantly provoking thought and developing new anti-authoritarian ideas. His was the voice – the conscience if you like – of what he was proud to call 'the Apache sector', defending the anarchist principles of the CNT and fighting untiringly for the restoration of the union's property and assets seized by the Francoists in 1939, and for justice for the victims of Francoism,

---

9.   23 February 1981.
10.   Doris Ensinger, German anarchist and writer (1944–2020).

particularly the cases of Delgado and Granado[11] the two young anarchists garrotted in 1963 for a crime of which they were innocent. And for at least two generations of young Spanish anarchists who came into contact with him, Luis Andrés Edo was undoubtedly the inspirational role model of the post-Francoist era. He was, to the clandestine libertarian anti-Francoist movement, what Jean Moulin[12] was to the French Resistance.

In 2002 Luis published *La Corriente*, (originally entitled *El pensamiento antiautoritario*) an anthology of his prison essays in which he explores his ideas on thought and action. And in 2006 he published his autobiographical memoirs: *La CNT en la encrucijada: aventuras de un heterodoxo* (*The CNT at the crossroads: adventures of a maverick*) in which he traces the trajectory of his extraordinary life as a militant.

Although Luis Andrés's death has left those whose lives he touched with a massive sense of regret and loss, he has also left present and future generations a valuable legacy, his memory and his example – *Écrasez l'Infâme!*[13]

Luis is survived by his partner, Doris Ensinger, and his two children, Helios and Violeta.

Luis Andrés Edo, anarcho-syndicalist, born 7 November 1925; died 14 February 2009.

An edited version of this obituary was published in the *Independent*: 'Luís Andrés Edo: Anarchist who fought the repressions of Franco's Spain', 24 March 2009.

---

11. See the glossary and the tribute to Antonio Martín Bellido on page 182.
12. Jean Moulin (1899–1943) was a central figure in the French resistance. Captured and tortured by the Gestapo, he died en route to Germany.
13. The injunction to destroy abuses by Voltaire (1694–1778), French writer and philosopher.

Remembering Miguel García

My first meeting with Miguel García García took place in the mid-1960s in *la primera galleria* of Madrid's Carabanchel Prison. He was in transit to another penitentiary and was in what was known as *periodo* – a fortnight of sanitary isolation, ostensibly to prevent or limit the spread of disease. I was the practice nurse (*practicante*) for the 7th Gallery, a position that gave me the run of most of the prison and allowed me to liaise with comrades in different wings, especially with isolated transit prisoners or prisoners in solitary confinement. Miguel passed through Carabanchel on a number of occasions over the years, going backwards and forwards between penitentiaries and Yeserias, Spain's main prison hospital in Madrid.

Miguel and I struck up a close relationship, one that was to endure for a decade and a half until his death in 1981. What particularly impressed me about him on our first meeting was his undoubted strength of character – forged by his experiences in the Resistance as an urban guerrilla and *falsificador* (forger), and in Franco's prisons – and the extraordinary quality of his spoken English, a language he had acquired entirely from English-speaking prisoners. No other political prisoners I came across during my three years imprisonment in Franco's jails had Miguel's mastery of language, or his skills as a communicator. Our conversations centred on how to expose the repressive nature of the Francoist regime and raise the profile of Franco's political prisoners in the international media, something I was in a position to do given my relatively privileged position as a foreign political prisoner and the access I had to the outside world through my by then extensive network of friendly functionaries in Carabanchel itself.

In 1967, following receipt of a personal pardon from Franco, I was released from prison and, on my return to Great Britain, I became involved with the resuscitated Anarchist Black Cross, an anarchist prisoners' aid organisation. The focus of our activities was international, but Franco's prisoners were, naturally, because of my history and the continuing and intensifying repression in Spain, top of our agenda. The case of Miguel García García, one of the Anarchist Black Cross's most prominent correspondents, was one that we regularly pursued with the international press and through diplomatic channels.

Released in 1969, after serving twenty years of a thirty-year sentence (commuted from death), Miguel came to live with me in London. It took him a little time to acclimatise to the profound social and technological changes that had taken place in the world since his arrest as a young man in the Barcelona of 1949, changes that were even more profound in the 'tolerant' and 'permissive' London society of 1969. In fact, so great was the trauma that he literally was unable to speak for some months. The shock of his release had triggered a paralysis in some of the muscles in his throat, and, through Octavio Alberola then living under effective house arrest in Liege, we arranged for him to see a consultant in Belgium about his condition. The time with Octavio was well-spent and brought him up-to-date with what was happening within the European movement and the role of the International Revolutionary Solidarity Movement, which operated under the banner of the Grupo Primero de Mayo, [First of May Group] a continuation of the clandestine anarchist Defensa Interior (DI), which had been tasked with the assassination of Franco.

The First of May Group had recently emerged from the sabotaged (by Germinal Esgleas[1] and Vicente Llansola[2]) ruins of

---

1. Germinal Esgleas (Josep Esgleas i Jaume, 1903–1981), Spanish anarchist and General Secretary of the CNT in exile. Member of Defensa Interior. Partner of Federica Montseny.
2. Vicente Llansola Renau (1915–1996), Spanish anarchist and CNT member. Member of Defensa Interior.

Defensa Interior (DI) as an international, anti-capitalist, anti-imperialist revolutionary organisation, structured to carry out spectacular direct actions. It took its name from the first operation carried out on 1 May 1966 when members of the group kidnapped the ecclesiastical adviser to the Spanish Embassy to the Vatican, Monsignor Marcos Ussia.[3] Soon the group began taking in a much broader area of attack targeting, in particular, the US and European governments for their complicity in the imperialist war in Vietnam.

Back in London, mainly with the moral and financial support of comrade Albert Meltzer, my co-editor of *Black Flag* and the driving force behind the revived Anarchist Black Cross (ABC), Miguel entered into a dynamic new phase of his life as the International Secretary of the ABC and a pivotal figure in the libertarian resistance to the Franco regime. With Albert he embarked on lengthy speaking tours of England, Scotland, Wales, Northern Ireland, West and East Germany, France, Belgium, Denmark and Italy, talking to a new generation of radicalised young Europeans about anarchism, international solidarity and, of course, the need to confront tyranny with practical cooperation and direct action.

It could be said that the result of one of Miguel's early talks – in a crowded meeting room at the offices of Freedom Press in London's Whitechapel High Street in February 1970, shortly after his arrival in Britain – was to give rise to the so-called Angry Brigade, Britain's first urban guerrilla group. Miguel's voice was still weak so I had to do much of the talking for him, but as the evening wore on and the story of his adventures and deprivations at the hands of the Francoist authorities unfolded, that and the fact that his revolutionary spirit and determination remained

---

3. His kidnapping was the first action of the First of May Group (the kidnapping was announced to the press on the first of May, the traditional anarchist and socialist date for protest and solidarity). Monsignor Ussia was held from the 29 April to the 11 May, 1966. He was released unharmed.

clearly undiminished, it was clear he had made a deep emotional impression on the fifty or so young people in the audience. Here, in front of them, in person, was someone who had been in direct confrontation with a fascist state, who had been totally involved in resistance struggles, and who had paid a heavy penalty. Nor was it a purely historical struggle. Franco remained in power and a new internationally coordinated anarchist action group, the First of May Group, was carrying on that struggle.

At Freedom Press that February night in 1970, the significance, the importance of the First of May Group, and the tradition it – and Miguel – sprang from, was not lost on the people crammed into the small room to hear Miguel García's story. Among those present were some of the core activists later convicted in the historic 'Angry Brigade' trial: John Barker, Hilary Creek, Jim Greenfield and Anna Mendelson.

Miguel Garcia in the kitchen at Centro Iberico, London 1975. From the Phil Ruff photo album on the Kate Sharpley Library website.

Miguel's flat in Upper Tollington Park, near North London's Finsbury Park, soon drew visiting anarchists from all over the world. It also began to attract police attention once Miguel launched (with Albert's help) the Centro Ibérico and International Libertarian Centre in London, a cosmopolitan venue that became a magnet for anarchists everywhere; it had been many years since there was such a thing as an international anarchist club in London, and its success was entirely due to Miguel's powerful personality.

In 1973 the Centro Ibérico moved to a large basement in Haverstock Hill to which came many extraordinary people, including survivors from innumerable political upheavals. Visitors included the Spanish militant and historian José Peirats[4] and Émilienne Durruti,[5] partner of Buenaventura Durruti. Another regular at the Centro Ibérico was ETA leader Pedro Ignacio Pérez Beotegui,[6] also known as 'Wilson', who was involved in the planning of the December 1973 assassination of Franco's protégé and deputy, prime Minister Carrero Blanco.

The new Centro was entirely Miguel's creation and he spent his whole time nurturing it, cutting himself off from any paid employment, even though he was well past what should have been retiring age anyway. Through Albert, however, he did extract a small pension from the British government.

Phil Ruff, the *Black Flag* cartoonist who shared Miguel's Upper Tollington Park flat after Albert moved to Lewisham, remembers accompanying Miguel on endless trips from Finsbury Park to Haverstock Hill, almost every night throughout the 1970s, to open up the Centro so that someone would be there *if* anyone

---

4. José Peirats, Spanish anarchist (1908–1989), author of *The CNT in the Spanish Revolution*.
5. Émilienne 'Mimi' Morin (1901–1991), French anarchist.
6. Pedro Ignacio Pérez Beotegui, Basque nationalist and member of ETA (1948–2008).

dropped in. Often it was just Phil and Miguel looking at the paint peel off the walls and having a drink, but if someone *did* drop by Miguel would immediately make them welcome, cook up a paella, and start weaving his magic. He was without doubt a great communicator and would have made a wonderful hostage negotiator. Everybody left the Centro feeling they were Miguel's best friend, and ready to slay dragons. He had a way of making you think that. He turned the basement into an internationally known place to go if you needed help in London; somewhere to find a welcome, food, a bed for the night, or a place to squat. He also brought people together from all over the world, becoming the birthplace for many affinity groups that were active in Central and South America, and Europe.

In 1970–71 Albert was working in Fleet Street as a telephone reporter/copy-taker for *The Daily Sketch*, a right-wing British national tabloid newspaper, and after much discussion and argument – and believe me Miguel could be extremely argumentative and pugnacious – Albert finally convinced Miguel to write his memoirs. And so it was that the typescript of what was to become *Franco's prisoner* was hammered out between Miguel and Albert and typed up in a disused back room of one of Britain's foremost Conservative populist newspapers – and paid for on the time of Associated Newspapers. The book, *Franco's prisoner*, was published in 1972 by the Rupert Hart-Davis publishing house.

As well as providing wide-ranging advice from abortion to legal aid to squatting, Miguel played a key role in many of the international defence campaigns run by the International Anarchist Black Cross at the time, including those of Julián Millán Hernández[7] and Salvador Puig Antich in Spain, and Noel and Marie

7. Julián Millán Hernández better known as Julio, Spanish anarchist born in 1935.

Murray, two members of the Dublin Anarchist Group sentenced to death[8] in Ireland for their alleged part in killing an off-duty Garda officer during a bank robbery in Dublin, in 1975.

Salvador Puig Antich had been a regular visitor who accompanied Albert and Miguel on some of their speaking tours around Britain. Returning to France in August 1973 to take part in a conference of young activists to set up the anarchist defence group known as the MIL (Movimiento Ibérico de Liberación), Salvador Puig Antich was involved a series of spectacular bank expropriations across Catalonia and Southern France. In September 1973, however, Puig Antich walked into a police ambush in Barcelona's Calle Gerona in which he was wounded and a Francoist policeman was shot dead. Puig Antich, 25, was garrotted in Barcelona's Modelo prison on 2 March 1974.

After the military coup in Argentina on 24 March 1976, Miguel persuaded a lot of people to 'lose' their passports so that comrades fleeing to escape the Junta could adopt a temporary identity change. In June 1976 he installed a printing press in the basement at Upper Tollington Park, on which he printed a number of anarchist books in Spanish, including *Anarquismo y lucha de clases* (the Spanish translation of *Floodgates of anarchy*, written by Albert Meltzer and myself) that he distributed in Spain. As well as printing identity documents, he also got together a group of young Spanish comrades in London to produce their own anarchist paper *Colectivo anarquista*.

In the late 1970s Miguel returned to his native Barcelona where, funded by the Spanish writer and former diplomat José Martín-Artajo,[9] anarchist son of Franco's foreign minister Alberto Martín-Artajo, he fulfilled one of his life's ambitions – to open his own bar. La Fragua, a former forge at No 15 Carrer de la Cadena in

---

8.   Their lives were saved by the international solidarity campaign.
9.   See the tribute to Martín-Artajo on page 138.

Barcelona's Raval District – not far from where *pistoleros* working for the Catalan employers' organisation gunned down the noted CNT leader Salvador Seguí[10] and his friend Francesc Comas[11] in 1923 – opened for business in 1979. As with the Centro Ibérico, La Fragua became a Mecca for anarchists and libertarians from all over the world, and an important meeting place for the anarchist activist groups of the so-called 'Apache sector' centred around Luis Andrés Edo in Barcelona.

Miguel's humanity was the most characteristic thing about him, that and his tenacity and ability to persevere and survive despite all odds. He was, without doubt, a pretty significant figure to the generation radicalised in the late 1960s and 1970s. Miguel had gone to prison fighting – and that was how he came out. He was untouched by the years of squabbling and in-fighting that characterised the life of the Spanish Libertarian Movement in exile. Miguel's answer for any dire situation was always the same – 'we must DO something!' His work with the Black Cross – providing practical aid to libertarian prisoners all over the world and making solidarity an effective springboard to militant action – influenced a new generation of anarchists not just in Spain but in many other parts of the world including Britain, France, Belgium, Italy and West Germany.

I was living on the northern island of Sanday, in Orkney, for much of the time Miguel was in Barcelona, but we met whenever we could. In 1980, Brenda, my partner, went to work with him at La Fragua for six months, at his invitation, to help improve the bar's menu. Miguel's culinary skills, acquired in Franco's prisons during times of great austerity, left much to be desired! It was on Sanday, one December evening in 1981, that I received an

10. Salvador Seguí i Rubinat, (1887–1923) secretary of the CNT National Committee. He was assassinated on 10 March 1923.

11. Fransesc Comas (aka 'Paronas') died of his wounds on 13 March 1923.

unexpected telephone call from Miguel who was back in London, in a nursing home, being treated for advanced TB. It was nice to hear from him and we chatted about this and that, but nothing in particular, and for that reason alone it was strange. Usually, when Miguel rang it was to arrange to do something or get something done. But on this occasion it was simply to talk, nothing else. He also spoke with Brenda, again about nothing in particular, and she promised to write him one of her long chatty letters the following day, which she did. Unfortunately, Miguel never received it. He died in the early hours of the following morning.

Miguel García García's life is a good pointer to what anarchism is in practice. Not a theory handed down by 'men of ideas', nor an ideological strategy, but the self-activity of ordinary people taking action in any way they can, in equality with others, to free up the social relationships that constitute our lives. Miguel García García may have lived a hard life, but it was a worthwhile life, and he was an inspiration to us all.

Introduction to the Spanish edition of *Franco's prisoner*. [*Prisionero de Franco: los anarquistas en la lucha contra la dictadura*, Anthropos, 2010. ISBN 9788476589793]. Published in *KSL: Bulletin of the Kate Sharpley Library* No. 65, February 2011.

Juan Busquets Vergés
(aka 'El Senzill')

Busquets, born in Barcelona on 25 July 1928, began his working life in 1944 as an apprentice at the Hispano-Suiza car plant in Barcelona and was first arrested, in 1946, by the Gestapo-trained Francoist Brigada Politico Social (BPS), during a strike organised by the anarcho-syndicalist labour union, the CNT (Confederación Nacional del Trabajo). In 1947 Busquets crossed into France, illegally, where he worked for a time as a miner in Cransac (Aveyron), where he made contact with the exiled Spanish Libertarian Movement (MLE – CNT-FAI).

The following year he joined the 18-strong anarchist guerrilla group led by Marcelino Massana Bancells (aka 'Pancho') and took part in a number of operations in Spain, dynamiting electricity pylons and railway lines, particularly around Terrassa, in the east central region of Catalonia. In the summer of 1949 Busquets joined the guerrilla group led by the Culebras brothers (Gregorio and Saturnino Culebras Saíz, aka 'Los Primos')[1] and crossed into Spain with them on 4 September 1949. The group was guided by Ramon Vila Capdevila (aka 'Caraquemada'), the last guerrilla to die in action in Franco's Spain (7 August 1963). Busquets was on his way to join up with the Barcelona-based anti-Francoist urban guerrilla group of José ('Pepe') Sabaté Llopart ('Pepe' was the oldest of the Sabaté brothers of whom the most famous was Francisco Sabaté Llopart, aka 'El Quico'). In addition

---

1.   Gregorio and Saturnino Culebras Saíz, Spanish anarchists and guerrillas. Gregorio (1910–1980); Saturnino (1920–1950) was shot on the 24 February 1950 alongside Manuel Sabaté. Both used the alias 'Primo' ('Cousin') which can also means 'fool' or 'idiot'.

to the Culebras brothers and Busquets, the group consisted of: José Conejos García,[2] Manuel Aced Ortell,[3] Helios Ziglioli,[4] and Manuel Sabaté Llopart,[5] the youngest of the Sabaté brothers.

The trip was ill-starred. After a number of incidents en route – shoot-outs with the Guardia Civil – the group finally reached the Catalan capital and met up in Clot, a district of Barcelona, with José ('Pepe') Sabaté Llopart's group to co-ordinate their actions and collect the arms and explosives they had cached in a nearby wood. On 18 October the group walked into a Civil Guard ambush in which some were killed and others wounded, but Busquets was arrested. Transferred to Barcelona's Model Prison on 16 November 1949, he was tried by a military 'Council of War' on 7 December and sentenced to death, a sentence that was later commuted to 30 years.

In 1956 Busquets was involved in an escape attempt from San Miguel de los Reyes with another anarchist writer and historian, Juan Gómez Casas,[6] but the escape went wrong as they were going over the prison wall and Busquets fell 30 feet, breaking his leg in the process. He managed to crawl to a ditch where he remained in agony, slipping in and out of consciousness until the guards found him the next morning. They then proceeded to batter him mercilessly around the face and hands with their rifle butts until he was senseless, breaking his nose and the bones of his hands as well as

---

2.   José Conejos García, Spanish anarchist and guerrilla, born 1911.

3.   Manuel Aced Ortell, 'El Francés,' French anarchist and guerrilla, born 1914.

4.   Elio Ziglioli (1927–1949) Italian anarchist and guerrilla. See 'Elio Ziglioli, an Italian in the anarchist guerrilla struggle: the story of a return' by Argimiro Ferrero on the Kate Sharpley Library website: https://www.katesharpleylibrary.net/hmgs7k.

5.   Manuel Sabaté Llopart, Spanish anarchist and guerrilla (1927–1950).

6.   Juan Gómez Casas, Spanish anarchist and writer (1921–2001). A short biography by Mitch Miller is on the Kate Sharpley Library website: https://www.katesharpleylibrary.net/ncjtth.

his leg, after which they left him in solitary confinement without medical treatment for two months.

It was in February 1966, in Carabanchel, that I first met Busquets. He was in transit, on his way back to Burgos from Yeserías, Franco's central prison hospital in Madrid, after yet more operations on his hand and leg. He sent word to me by one of the 'cabos' (trusties) that he was in the Seventh gallery and could I get in to see him. Fortunately, a friendly warder was on duty and I managed to get in that same afternoon for a chat. He remained in Carabanchel for a further three weeks, during which time I managed to see him almost every day. Busquets's *periodo* (solitary confinement) lasted only a week, instead of the usual ten days, because of his post-operative condition; as medical orderly I could draw on my good relationship with the doctor and *practicante* (practice nurse), impressing on them that Juan was an old friend and needed fresh air and exercise. They knew perfectly well what I was up to, but they saw me as *simpatico* and swung a reduced *periodo* for him anyway. We usually managed at least an hour's *paseo* every day, chatting and walking up and down, backwards and forwards across the patio, him limping and me strolling. One subject that particularly concerned us was how to improve communication between the different prisons, particularly with Burgos, the main holding prison for politicals. Busquets's regular visits to Yeserías involved complicated and tiring transit movements through the prisons of Francoist Spain. But this regular movement also meant he played a crucial role in the clandestine inter-prison communication network linking anarchist prisoners across Spain. He brought the latest news and gossip from Burgos about the situation with my co-defendant, Fernando Carballo Blanco, and the other comrades.

It was Busquets who arranged for me to receive a 500 peseta giro every month from the MLE-CNT Prisoners' Defence Committee in Toulouse. The names of the remitters were, in rotation,

George, Paul, John and Ringo, the only English names known to the political prisoners' support fund, all of which led to the rumour that I had been bankrolled by the Beatles, something which gave me considerable kudos among my fellow prisoners. Occasionally, I would bring along another old *cenetista*, Ramón, who had been on the general staff of the 5th Army Corps during the Civil War. Ramón, who was then inside for a 'common' offence, was the *encargado* (trusty) of the carpentry shop and was in the Fifth Gallery with me. When Busquets's transfer back to Burgos finally came through, both Ramón and I went to see him off, carrying his bedroll for him as far as the spiked gate at the entrance to the First Gallery, the furthest we were allowed to go.

Juan Busquets at Mas Tartás, the anarchist guerrilla base at Tartás de Osseja (Languedoc-Roussillon). The arrow indicates the guerrillas' crossing point into Spain. Photo by Antonio Téllez. From the Stuart Christie photo album on the Kate Sharpley Library website.

After my release in September 1967 I kept in contact with Busquets in Burgos (who was released in 1969 after serving exactly

20 years imprisonment). In the late autumn of 1971, after my arrest as a suspect in the so-called 'Angry Brigade' case, I was being held on remand in Brixton prison, going back and forth to Clerkenwell Court every day for three months, proving what a wonderful thing *habeas corpus* was. Every week the police said they were continuing their inquires, but we were too dangerous to let loose on bail. One day, after a remand hearing, I was in the cells at Clerkenwell Police Station/Magistrates' Court awaiting transfer to Brixton when Brenda, my partner, came to visit. With her she brought the dear friend I hadn't seen since Carabanchel – Busquets. The custody sergeant on duty at the end of the corridor took one look at him, with his lapis lazuli blue eyes, swarthy complexion, broken nose, scars, stocky build and dressed in a white trench coat with a turned-up collar – and panicked, assuming he was a Mediterranean gunman – which I suppose he was, or had been in his day – come to break me out and sounded the alarm. A group of Special Branch and Bomb Squad detectives quickly appeared at either end of the corridor. Those who were armed fiddled nervously with their holsters while I burbled on enthusiastically with my old friend through the hatch of the cell door. The detectives moved closer and closer to Brenda and Busquets until they were surrounded by eight detectives. Sgt. Roy Cremer, the senior Special Branch officer, asked Brenda who he was, and Juan, who spoke no English, assumed they wanted his ID card went for his inside pocket. As soon as he made this move the eight detectives dropped to the floor, thinking he was about to take them all out. But before anyone had a chance to shoot, Busquets was waving his French identity card and smiling broadly. Brenda said she hadn't laughed so much in years, neither had Busquets. Cremer noted his details and when Busquets returned to Toulouse the following day, his apartment was raided by the French police and as a result he spent two days in the local police station explaining his relationship with Christie, 'La Brigade de Colére' and 'Le Groupe

du Premier Mai'. I suppose it was difficult for them to understand that he felt sufficiently strongly to make that journey in a show of friendship and solidarity. If they had understood, perhaps they would not have been policemen.

Busquets was arrested again in May 1974, by the French police, on suspicion of involvement in the First of May Group kidnapping[7] of Francoist banker Ángel Baltasar Suárez, but he was later released without charge. In October 1976, during the state visit to France of Franco's successor, King Juan Carlos, he was again detained again by the French police – along with a dozen other anarchists – and flown on military transport to the Belle Ile where they were held until after the Spanish king had left the country. In 1998 he published his memoirs *Veinte años de prisión: los anarquistas en las carceles de Franco.*[8]

---

7. This was actually claimed by GARI, the Internationalist Revolutionary Action Groups.

8. *Veinte años de prisión* has been translated by Paul Sharkey and published by Stuart as *Sentenced to death under Franco*, Meltzer Press, 1996.

Victor Garcia

Tomás Germinal Gracia Ibars (1919–1991), better known by the pseudonym 'Victor Garcia', the most commonly used of his many pseudonyms (Germen, Santo Tomás de Aquino, Egófilo, G. G, Ibars, Quipo Amauta, Julian Fuentes), a founder of the Catalan Libertarian Youth (JJLL)[1] was one of the most prolific writer-propagandist-activists of the Spanish anarchist movement in the post Civil War period.

When his father died the family settled in Barcelona where he worked in the textile industry from the age of 12. At fourteen he joined the CNT, and, in 1936, Gracia's Libertarian Youth organisation; by August 1936 he was active in the 'Quixotes of the Ideal' affinity group along with Abel Paz,[2] Liberto Sarrau[3] and others. When the military attempted their *pronunciamento* (coup) in July 1936 he joined the Los Aguiluchos flying column, but deserted the front when the militias were forced to disband and militarisation was enforced towards the end of 1936. Subsequently, he was a bookkeeper at CNT-FAI headquarters in Barcelona, but following the Republican defeat at the battle of the Ebro in 1938 he joined the 26th Division (former Durruti Column) and was wounded in Tremp, after which he crossed the frontier and went into exile (and imprisonment) in the French concentration camps of Argelès-sur-Mer, Barcarès and Bram.

Arrested by the Germans in 1942 for suspected Resistance activities he was held in Vernet prison but escaped before he could

---

1. See FIJL in the glossary.
2. Abel Paz is the pen name of Diego Camacho (1921–2009), Spanish anarchist and writer. A short biography by Agustín Guillamón is on the Kate Sharpley Library website: https://www.katesharpleylibrary.net/v41q3n.
3. Liberto Sarrau, Spanish anarchist and writer (1920–2001).

be transferred to Dachau. After the Liberation, Germinal was appointed administrative secretary of the Paris-based Libertarian Youth organisation (FIJL), but soon resigned due to personal differences with other FIJL Committee members. Returning to Spain clandestinely in 1946 he worked for the underground Libertarian Youth (FIJL) organisation but was arrested that December. Released in July 1947 he was employed for a time in the building trade but in August 1948 was forced to return to France across the Pyrenees having escaped a police trap set for him.

Emigrating to Venezuela in December 1948 he remained there until 1954 when he embarked on a world tour which took him to Uruguay, Brazil, Argentina, Chile, Panama, Southeast Asia, Japan, China, India, Turkey, Egypt, Iraq, Israel, Cyprus, Greece, Italy, Germany, Holland and France, finally returning to Venezuela in 1961 to head the secretariat of the now re-united CNT-in-Exile (MLE), and to relaunch the FIJL journal *Ruta*.

Víctor García (Tomás Germinal Gracia Ibars), with partner Marisol and daughter, at Macchu Pichu. From the Stuart Christie photo album on the Kate Sharpley Library website.

Expelled from the CNT in 1966, Germinal moved first to France and then to Libya, and thence back to Caracas in 1969 to resume the editorship of *Ruta*. Germinal died in Castelnou, France, on 10 May 1991 after a long and painful illness. An inveterate traveller until his death, 'Victor' regularly sent me snapshots from his latest exotic destination along with fascinating news of the comrades and groups he had discovered and befriended on his travels. A remarkable, kind, and lovely man, he truly was the 'Marco Polo' of the post-war anarchist movement.

Flavio Costantini

More often than not it is the artist, writer or poet, rather than the historian or sociologist, who succeed in capturing the spirit of an age; in so doing, they make an important contribution to our understanding of society.

Flavio Costantini is such a person. Born in Rome in 1926, his earliest ventures into art were motivated more by intellectual frustration than by artistic masters. 'I started to draw because I read the Kafka[1] books... it was impossible to write like Kafka, so I began to draw'. Other writers followed, but it was the human condition as portrayed by Kafka which was to remain the dominant influence in Costantini's world.

Retiring from the navy in 1955, Costantini returned to Italy to begin a new career as a textile designer and commercial graphic artist. Fascinated by structures, Genoa, his chosen home base, provided him with an antidote to what had been for Costantini the Kafkaesque nightmare of New York.

The ancient Mediterranean port offered him visual inspiration in so many ways – the detail of an archway, a balustrade or the geometry of a piazza. Colour also came to play a more important part in Costantini's work. After a brief flirtation with oils in the early 1960s, tempera became the chosen medium.

The period between the early 1960s and mid 1970s coincided with a flood tide of intense democratic hopes for large numbers of people. Costantini had been a communist until 1962, but a month-long visit to Moscow caused him to reconsider his beliefs. In Moscow he saw 'an endless stream of tourist peasantry who

---

1.   Franz Kafka (1883–1924) Prague-born writer.

were strangely silent, neither sad nor happy, but were canalised in a disenchanted, unconscious pilgrimage ... The revolution had ended... In the squalid vertical squares of New York or in the equally squalid horizontal squares of Moscow, reaching beyond the languid reminiscences of old Europe, this was perhaps an alternative, an isolated but insistent voice, an ancient Utopia which, however, had nothing in common with the Fabian longings of HG Wells. Since then, since 1963, I have tried, within the scope of my possibilities, to publicise this uncompromising alternative.'

He reread a book he had disliked some years previously, *Memoirs of a revolutionary* by Victor Serge.[2] Serge's description of the heroic period of French anarchist activism which highlighted the end of the last century provided Costantini with a social theme which was to be his inspiration for the next two decades. He felt, like Serge, that although shot through with contradictions, the French anarchists were 'people who demanded, before anything else, harmony between words and deeds'. They were very often lonely and isolated individuals, sensitive in their own way, whose reaction to confusion and alienation was to act, to refuse to submit.

Costantini's work during these two decades is a documentation of this dramatic period in mankind's odyssey towards a free society based on the principles of social justice described by Bakunin over a century ago: 'It is the triumph of humanity, it is the conquest and accomplishment of the full freedom and full development, material, intellectual and moral, of every individual, by the absolute free and spontaneous organisation of economic and social solidarity as completely as possible between all human

---

2.   Belgian anarchist, then Bolshevik, then socialist, writer (1890–1947). *Memoires d'un revolutionnaire 1901–1941* was first published in French in 1951.

beings living on the earth.'³ Like a sun-illuminated stained glass window in a cathedral, the impact of Costantini's work is immediate. Events are captured without perspective and on a single plane in a startlingly innovative manner.

There is irony here, too: the faces of the policemen, for example, firing on strikers in Chicago, 1886, are those of four US presidents. Another tempera, depicting the capture of Ravachol,⁴ has Toulouse-Lautrec⁵ as the arresting officer.

Costantini's haunting faces, drawn directly from contemporary sources, provide an element of photographic realism which contrasts starkly with the decorative backdrop. Whether it is in the faces of the protagonists, the architectural or stylistic minutiae, there is a lovingly researched detail, harmony and structural perfection.

The ebbing of revolutionary hopes and expectations in the mid 1970s gave Costantini the sensation that he was witnessing the end of an era. He came to believe that the act of revolution, as a cathartic means of achieving the good society, was no longer possible without serious risk of sinking into a sea of anomie.

His disenchantment with the apparent hopelessness of the human condition in late capitalism is expressed in the final tempera in the revolutionary series with Kafkaesque symbolism. The painting depicts the room in which the Tsar and his family were murdered. The furniture has been removed and the room is empty: only the bullet-torn wallpaper indicates something irreversible has occurred. Most of the paintings in this series were reproduced in the now out of print *The art of anarchy*.

Perhaps with the intention of cushioning himself from the

3. Mikhail Bakunin, *Marxism, freedom and the state*, edited by Kenneth J. Kenafick (Freedom Press, 1950).

4. Ravachol is the pseudonym of François-Claudius Koenigstein (1859–1892), French anarchist.

5. Henri de Toulouse-Lautrec (1864–1901), French painter.

effect of this radical shift in his outlook, in 1980 Costantini began to immerse himself in a series of light-hearted portraits of the authors who had contributed most to his understanding of the world.

Each is accompanied by rebus-like objects associated with the subject, or which provide an important theme in their work. Thus, Kafka is shown with his beetle; Poe[6] with a bottle of Jack Daniel's whiskey; Stevenson[7] with a seagull, lifebelt and a kilted figure; Conrad[8] with a compass and a photograph of a steamer, and so on.

By the mid 1980s, another theme had emerged from this period of introspection, a more deeply allegorical one, also in the Kafkaesque tradition – the sinking of the *Titanic*. The year in which this criminal tragedy occurred, 1912, was a portentous and pivotal year, in the artist's view, in the history of the contemporary world.

The original scene-setting picture depicts the ship foundering of a peaceful evening with the great stern rising like a squat Leviathan and the lights from a 1000 empty portholes glittering on a calm sea. Even after the collision with the iceberg the passengers showed little concern for their safety – had it not, after all, been declared unsinkable – and continued to dance to the strains of numerous orchestras while others played poker.

Costantini is not a painter like all the rest; he is not prolific. His output these days may be two paintings a year, but in 1996, for example, he produced no work whatsoever. He earns a living out of his few and very select band of fans. His most recent commission has been to illustrate Dostoevsky's *Letters from the underworld* and these tempera paintings are currently being exhibited throughout Italy.

---

6.   Edgar Allen Poe (1809–1849), American writer.
7.   Robert Louis Stevenson (1850–1894), Scottish writer.
8.   Joseph Conrad (1857–1924) writer of Polish origin.

Apart from *The art of anarchy* (Cienfuegos Press, London, 1975), Flavio's inspired graphic insights have visually enhanced a number of literary classics in Italian, including *Il cavallino di fuoco* by Vladimir Mayakovsky (Emme Edizioni, [1969]), *The shadow line*, by Joseph Conrad (Edizioni Nuages, 1989) and Dostoevsky's *Letters from the underworld* (Edizioni Nuages, 1997). Flavio's work has been exhibited all over the world, including at the prestigious 1972 Xth Rome Quadriennale and the 1984 Venice Biennale exhibitions.

Stuart Christie, Honley 1975, with Flavio Costantini's poster of Ravachol on the wall. From the Phil Ruff photo album on the Kate Sharpley Library website.

Originally appeared in *Illustrators 50* (1976), published by the Association of Illustrators https://theaoi.com/ [Updated in May 2013 after Costantini's death.]

An Encounter in Carrara

It was in Carrara back in 1968 that Giuseppe Pinelli opened my eyes to the extraordinarily energetic art of Flavio Costantini who was at that time at work on his series '*The Anarchists*'. After seeing his powerful graphic representations of the execution of Ferrer[1] and of the events in Chicago on 3 May 1886,[2] I was so impressed that I wrote him immediately, asking him to design a manifesto for the newly created Anarchist Black Cross, of which Pinelli was the Italian secretary. Flavio promptly replied to me, sending me a picture of enormous figurative power that offered his own take on the 'Pyramid of Powers/we maintain all',[3] complete with a dying Kennedy at its base. It was the beginning of a long friendship, one that was to prove particularly fruitful for our publishing imprint, Cienfuegos Press, right from the moment when Flavio supplied us, free of charge, with the covers for virtually all of our books from 1972 onwards, including my own autobiography *The Christie file*, and allowed us to publish our own personal tribute to him and to his oeuvre, *The art of anarchy*, which in 1975 won the design award of the British National Book League. My greatest regret

---

1. Francesc Ferrer i Guàrdia (Francisco Ferrer y Guardia; 1859–1909), an-archist educator, was executed for supposedly being the 'mastermind' behind the 'Tragic Week' revolt of 1909.
2. The beating and shooting of workers who had stoned strikebreakers at the McCormick Reaper Works. Costantini's image appears on the cover of Voltairine de Cleyre's *The First Mayday: the Haymarket speeches 1895–1910* (Published by Cienfuegos Press, the Libertarian Book Club and Soil of Liberty, 1980).
3. This poster was reproduced in *Black Flag* in November 1974 (vol. 3, n.15). Catalogued as 'The great are only great because we are on our knees', on https://placard.ficedl.info/article3736.html and Center for the Study of Political Graphics (http://collection-politicalgraphics.org).

was that we had had to publish the book in black and white, simply because we could not afford to reproduce Flavio's images in colour, so as to display before the world his unmistakable warped perspectives and extraordinary range of colours. I am immensely proud of having known Flavio and of having enjoyed his friendship. 'May the soil lie lightly upon you, Flavio'.

Preface by Stuart Christie to *Flavio Costantini: l'anarchia molto cordialmente* by Roberto Farina (Milan: Le milieu, 2015)

Antonio Martín Bellido

I am sorry to announce the death this morning of my old friend and comrade Antonio Martín Bellido who died at 5.00 am, the same time 51 years ago as his two comrades, Joaquin Delgado and Francisco Granado, whose lives – and deaths – were so closely entwined with his own. His funeral will take place in a few days.

Antonio Martín Bellido was the son of a Madrid UGT (General Workers' Union) militant exiled in France where he lived, in Strasbourg, from the age of two. Having served his apprenticeship as an electrical engineer, he moved to Paris at the age of 19 where he joined the Iberian Federation of Libertarian Youth (FIJL). In 1962 he visited London with other young Spanish and French anarchists to take part in the annual anti-nuclear Aldermaston march, during which many enduring friendships were forged. That same year he joined the recently re-constituted MLE's (Libertarian Movement in Exile) clandestine planning section known as 'Defensa Interior' (DI), whose remit was (a) to organise and coordinate actions intended to destabilise and discredit the Franco regime internally and internationally, and (b) to assassinate General Franco. Among the anti-Francoist actions in which he participated that year were the explosions targeting the dictator's slave-built mausoleum at the Basilica de la Santa Cruz in the Valley of the Fallen (12 August 1962) and in St Peter's Square in Vatican City (23 September 1962) at the opening of the Vatican Council.

DI bombs were not intended to kill, only to draw international attention to the ongoing and growing repression and violent nature of the Franco regime. Small amounts of plastique were used in these devices, all of them timed to explode in the early hours of the morning. In fact, throughout the extensive, international, two-year DI bombing campaign against Francoist institutions, there was only one occasion – in the Dirección General de Seguridad [DGS], the HQ of Franco's secret police in Madrid's Puerta del Sol – when a few people were slightly injured as a result of a detonator mis-timing. During this period the DI organised two attempts on Franco at San Sebastian (18 June 1962), the Palacio de Ayete (19 August 1962).

Perhaps the most crucial actions for Antonio were those that occurred on 29 July 1963 at the Madrid HQs of the secret police (the Brigada Politico Social) and the Falangist Labour Front. It was the misfired bomb at police HQ that had the most serious consequences and the greatest lifelong impact on Antonio in terms of guilt. Unbeknown to him and his fellow DI comrade, Sergio Hernández, Octavio Alberola, the DI coordinator, had sent another comrade, Francisco Granado Gata, to Madrid in a specially modified car with weapons, explosives and a radio transmitter in preparation for a further attempt on Franco at the Palacio del Oriente during the annual presentation of new ambassadors to Franco's court. Unfortunately, there were no new ambassadors that July and the operation had to be cancelled, Francisco Granado withdrawn and the materiel passed over to another Madrid-based group led by a man called Jacinto Guerrero Lucas,[1] the protégé of former CNT Defence Secretary (and guerrilla combat groups organiser in Catalonia between 1949 and 1952) José Pascual Palacios.[2] Another FIJL/DI activist, Roberto Ariño, was sent to Madrid on 20 July to contact Granado, and advise him of the change of plan but missed his rendezvous with the latter. Eight days later an anxious Alberola sent trusted friend and comrade

---

1. Jacinto Guerrero Lucas, after spying on the anarchist movement was allegedly involved with the Spanish state's 'dirty war' against ETA. He was described as 'the Spy with Three Faces' by Xavier Montanyà.
2. José Pascual Palacios was a Spanish anarchist (1916–1970), loosely connected with Defensa Interior.

Joaquin Delgado to Madrid to contact Ariño and Granado and instruct them to return to France, after depositing the materiel in a Madrid safehouse for Guerrero's Madrid-based group to collect later. Ariño returned to France the same day, 28 July, but Delgado was unable to make contact with Francisco Granado until the following day, the day the fateful bombs planted by Antonio Martín and Sergio Hernández exploded prematurely in Security- and Falangist HQs. Sergio returned to France by train immediately after the explosion, but Antonio remained in Madrid for a week or so until the hue and cry had died down sufficiently for him to make his escape. On 31 July, as Delgado and Granado were preparing to leave Madrid, they were arrested by a Guardia Civil officer allegedly on the grounds they were 'acting suspiciously', a classic ploy used by police wishing to conceal the fact that they are acting on information received from informers or agents. Both men were arrested, tortured, charged with 'Banditry and Terrorism', tried by a summary (drumhead) court martial on 13 August 1963 and sentenced to death by *garrote vil*. The two innocent men were executed in Carabanchel prison at dawn on 17 August 1963. The BPS were fully aware they had no involvement in the actions of 29 July, but they did know that the cache of weapons and explosives they discovered were to have been used in an attempt on Franco. The question was, who was – or were – the traitor or traitors responsible for the deaths of Delgado and Granado? It was a question that was to haunt Antonio Martín for the rest of his life, as did his deep sense of guilt over his role in the crime for which they were judicially murdered. When he discovered the fate of the two comrades on his return to Paris, Antonio wanted to make a public statement admitting his responsibility, but was persuaded against doing so; it would have made no difference to the decision to execute Delgado and Granado, especially Delgado, a freemason and an influential figure in both the FIJL and the DI. General Eduardo Blanco, head of the security service (DGS), wanted scapegoats and they fitted the bill perfectly. Both men had been under surveillance throughout their stay in Madrid, their mission – to kill Franco – had been betrayed by Pascual's protégé, Jacinto Guerrero Lucas, a police agent who remained active within the ranks of the exiled libertarian movement until the end of the 1960s.

In 1968 – as secretary of the Paris branch of the FIJL – Martín was arrested and confined to Saint Brieuc for membership of an 'association of evildoers' (*malhechores*), a reference to the First of May Group, the successor action group to the DI. Throughout the rest of his life he remained a tireless supporter of the anti-Francoist activities of the FIJL and the CNT-in-Exile. Latterly, he played a key part in ensuring that the Spanish Republican and anarchist contribution to the Liberation of Paris by Leclerc's 2nd Armoured division, 'La Nueve' received the public recognition they deserved.

Antonio Martín Bellido at l'Escorial de Madrid (July 1963). Photo from Stuart Christie.

Finally, on 17 October 2009, after years of investigation, Antonio Martín succeeded in organising a videoed debate/confrontation in Madrid in the presence of Jacinto Guerrero Lucas and a number of the surviving comrades from his own Madrid group – his victims – who had been tortured and jailed in connection with various attacks mounted in 1962 and 1963 on sites of symbolic significance to Francoism.

Antonio Martín Bellido, Madrid 1938–Paris August 17, 2014.

From *KSL: Bulletin of the Kate Sharpley Library* No. 78-79, September 2014.

Txema Bofill

Txema Bofill, blogger, researcher, libertarian, newspaper columnist (his interviews were a regular feature in the newspaper *Catalunya*), educator (he earned a doctorate in education from his prison cell), activist and revolutionary, was born into a middle class family in La Bisbal del Empordá on 2 January 1953. By the age of ten he had entered a Catholic seminary, intending to become a missionary in Africa, but contact with an order of progressive-minded worker priests from Gerona left him with a political awareness that soon brought him into contact with Marxist groups. Studying medicine in Barcelona, he rotated through a spectrum of groups from Bandera Roja[1] to the PSUC[2] and various Trotskyist factions before he drifted into anarchist circles and he became a student agitator. From experience, he discovered that much can be achieved by just a few people. He was soon arrested for anti-Franco graffiti at Gerona University. After serving 3 or 4 months and refusing to do his military service, he left Spain for Toulouse, associating with the 'official' CNT before moving on to Paris and parting company with the CNT over the MIL group.

Along with a swathe of children of exiles he helped establish a MIL Prisoners' Solidarity Committee. After the MIL decided to disband he got involved with the Ediciones Mayo del '37 and an anarchist bookshop and press in Toulouse. He helped published

---

1. Organización Comunista de España (Bandera Roja), Communist Organization of Spain (Red Flag), May '68-influenced breakaway from the PSUC which re-entered that party after a few years. Covered a wide range of views.
2. Partit Socialista Unificat de Catalunya/ Partido Socialista Unificado de Cataluña, the Communist Party of Catalonia.

a magazine, *Basta*[3] and was part of a cooperative producing books and pamphlets. Attempts to smuggle such publications over the Pyrenees followed.

These activities brought him into contact with Jean-Marc Rouillan and other ex-MIL personnel, After the execution of the MIL's Salvador Puig Antich, Txema helped launch the GARI 'which was no longer an autonomous bunch of friends but a proper organisation, a network of groups.' The name GARI was an umbrella covering various groups operating in France, Belgium, Italy and Holland, groups ignored by the historians. As he was quick to point out, they aimed at rather more than a transition to democracy; a constitutional monarchy was less than they had hoped for. Txema was pulled in for questioning about GARI operations of which he knew nothing, operations mounted in, say, Belgium. Known by his nickname of Sapata (he had lost a shoe during one demonstration) he was then fingered as having been behind a hold-up, mounting a 23 day hunger strike in protest. He was eventually granted political prisoner status and released from custody in France under an amnesty. 'We were France's last political prisoners', since which time all prisoners have been treated as criminal prisoners.

From jail Txema asked libertarian academic René Lourau[4] to act as his thesis supervisor, because student status assured him of a student card, a residence permit and a grant as a political refugee in France. With Jean-Marc Rouillan hotly pursued by the police, Txema was threatened by four French policemen who had found his name in Rouillan's address book.

In 1978, with Franco dead, Txema returned to Spain, shuttling between France and Spain. The changes that has taken place in Spain failed to live up to his expectations and hopes. He became

---

3.   Issues are online at http://cras31.info/spip.php?article501.
4.   René Lourau was a French sociologist (1933–2000).

involved with the CNT in La Bisbal, writing articles exposing how the media were being used in the Scala case[5] to criminalise and discredit the CNT. During the 1970s he also visited Gaza and Israel and witnessed the injustices there for himself.

The 1980s saw Txema in Spain, the Canaries and France. In addition to that, he served some jail time in Sweden in connection with the travellers' cheque fraud generally associated with Lucio Urtubia. 'In two days [passing the forged cheques] I raked in 4 million [dollars].' At the time, Rouillan had settled in Barcelona and together they had planned to open a libertarian school. In 1988 Txema left for Nicaragua to see the revolutionary experiment there at first hand but left the country after things there degenerated.

In the 1990s he set off for Venezuela but finished up in Colombia, working for his own tour company and as a teacher in FARC-held[6] territory in Guainia. The widespread corruption that he witnessed 'everybody out there was working either for the narcos or for the FARC or the self-defence groups or whatever', plus his mother's failing health brought him back to Spain in 2001.

After that, he developed an association with the Ateneu Enciclopèdic Popular in Barcelona and with the anarcho-syndicalist CGT[7] which encouraged his interest in organising the unemployed. The release of the movie *Salvador* – a travesty of the life of Salvador Puig Antich, executed by garrotte for the alleged (and contested) killing of a police officer – led him to join a campaign against its production company, MediaPro and to exploit the controversy to revive interest in the fate of the imprisoned Jean-Marc Rouillan who had been all but forgotten. In 2014 he interviewed

5. 1978 firebomb attack on a Barcelona nightclub carried out by a police agent to discredit the newly-legalised CNT.

6. Fuerzas Armadas Revolucionarias de Colombia (Armed Revolutionary Forces of Colombia).

7. Confederación General del Trabajo, General Confederation of Labour.

Rouillan for *Catalunya* after Rouillan (whose C.V. covers the MIL, GARI, Action Directe and, more recently, the New Anticapitalism Party in France and who has served a quarter century in French prisons) was allowed to visit Spain while on parole from a French prison (and London in 2014 for the Anarchist Bookfair where he presented the film *¡G.A.R.I.!*)[8]

Txema was the first to admit that he had been a bit of a butterfly, having been less than an 'organisation' man but having been active 'in a variety of autonomous commandos driven by circumstances.' The outlook, as he described it in an interview in 2011, was disheartening, although he did see a glimmer of hope in the squatter movement. 'These are people who get on with it, carry out actions and somehow organise themselves from the bottom up.' As for the trade union movement, he regarded it as 'regrettably, fucked up. They have us well under control through the mass media, education is a shambles and it is all looking very bad. I am a pessimist, but I believe that one learns by doing. Even a few people can pull off things that count.'

Txema Bofill was killed in a crash between his car and a bus on 7 December 2015.

His blog (in Catalan) can be found at blocs.mesvilaweb.cat/txemabofill

With regard to Txema's involvement with Lucio and the Citibank fraud check out the film (with English subtitles) *Lucio* (2007, directed by José María Goenaga and Aitor Arregi).

---

8. *¡G.A.R.I.!* By Nicolas Réglat came out in 2013.

Jaime Pozas de Villena

Sad to announce the fatal heart attack yesterday (14 February 2017) of Jaime Pozas de Villena[1] (b. 1941), a veteran comrade of the clandestine anti-Francoist struggle: 'Los Ácratas', the Madrid student group influenced by professors Agustín Garcia Calvo,[2] and later the CNT-FAI-FIJL, the Grupo Primero de Mayo [First of May Group] and the Autonomous Action Groups.[3] A chemistry student at Madrid University, Pozas first fell into the clutches of Franco's secret police in February 1965, during that year's university disturbances when he was arraigned before Madrid's notorious Public Order Tribunal (TOP) along with professors García Calvo, José Luis López-Aranguren[4] and Enrique Tierno Galván.[5] We first met, briefly, during that short interlude in Carabanchel. Arrested again in January 1968 for illegal propaganda and public order offences (which included throwing a crucifix out of a classroom window – for which he was permanently expelled from the university) he was sentenced, in June 1969, to 6 years and a day.

---

1. His father, Jaime – from whom he was estranged – was a 'Falangist of the first hour'. Pozas was also the great-nephew of General Sebastián Pozas Perea, former Director-General of the Guardia Civil and commander of the Republic's Army of the Centre during the Spanish Civil War [original note by SC].

2. Agustín Garcia Calvo was a Spanish philologist, philosopher and writer (1926–2012). His *On how the student uprising is reabsorbed* was published by Simian, 1971.

3. Informal ad hoc groups that formed and dissolved for specific purposes and in some instances never 'claimed responsibility' for their actions.

4. José Luis López-Aranguren, Spanish academic, philosopher – and ex-nationalist (1909–1996).

5. Enrique Tierno Galván, Spanish academic and socialist politician (1918–1986).

During his time in Carabanchel and Soria prisons he came into contact with CNT militants, Luis Andrés Edo and Miguel García García, men who were important influences on both our lives.

On his release he moved to Sweden where he joined the anarcho-syndicalist SAC labour union,[6] but throughout his time in exile he maintained close links with the CNT-FAI and was a frequent visitor to London, working closely with the International Anarchist Black Cross/Centro Ibérico in Haverstock Hill, often travelling into Spain on organisational missions. By 1977, after Franco's death, he was a member of the first legalised National Committee of the CNT and, in 1978, as a consequence of the brutal murder (by prison guards following a failed escape attempt) in Carabanchel prison of his friend and comrade Agustin Rueda Sierra[7] he moved to London, working again with Miguel García García of the ABC.

---

6. Sveriges Arbetares Centralorganisation, founded in 1910.
7. Agustin Rueda Sierra, Spanish anarchist, CNT member and active in COPEL (Coordinadora de Presos Españoles en Lucha, Spanish Prisoners in Struggle Coordinating Body), (1952–14 March 1978).

Lucio Urtubia Jiménez, a legendary life

The life of Lucio Urtubia Jiménez (1931–2020), an anarchist from Navarre in northern Spain, is the stuff of legend. As an activist in 1950s Paris he counted André Breton and Albert Camus among his friends, worked with the legendary anarchist urban guerrilla Francisco Sabaté (*El Quico*) in attempting to bring down Franco's fascist regime, and carried out numerous bank robberies to fund the struggle to free Spain. But it was in 1977, after having his earlier scheme to destabilise the US economy by forging US dollars rejected by Che Guevara, he put his most infamous plan into action, successfully forging and circulating 20 million dollars of Citibank travellers cheques with the goal of funding urban guerrilla groups in Europe and Latin America, and bringing the bank to its knees in the process. In between he was involved in the kidnapping of Nazi war criminal Klaus Barbie from his hideout in Bolivia, aided the escape of Black Panthers from the US and not surprisingly was targeted by the CIA. Lucio defends his life's work thus: 'we are bricklayers, painters, electricians – we do not need the state for anything. The banks are the real crooks. They exploit you, take your money and cause all the wars.' Lucio, therefore, had no moral scruples about forging Citybank travellers' cheques. His motivation was not personal gain, but to dent confidence in this powerful financial institution.

Lucio is – and has been – many things to different people, of which I can give three good examples:

The first is the opinion of the noted Spanish theatre director, Albert Boadella, the founder of the Els Jonglars theatrical group whose escape from Spain in the late 1970s was organised by Lucio.

Boadella famously described him as 'A Quijote[1] who tilted, not at windmills, but at real giants...'

The second is that of Chief Superintendent Paul Barril of the French Police nationale who described Lucio as a criminal mastermind pulling the strings of an international criminal organisation of anarchists, like some latter-day Montecristo[2] – a Moriarty[3] of global terrorism with access to infinite funds from the international anarchist war chest and dedicated to promoting and funding terrorism and agitation against the established order around the world...

A third opinion is that the examining magistrate in the last and biggest of the criminal cases against Lucio – Louis Joinet – who scandalised *commissaire* Barril by praising Lucio saying he represented everything the magistrate would have loved to have been – Joinot, incidentally became the first Advocate General with the French Court of cassation – and has had Lucio round to dinner twice, first in Matignon, which is the French equivalent of 10 Downing Street, and more recently at the Elysee, the French equivalent of Buckingham Palace...

None of these opinions accurately capture the man, certainly not commissaire Barril's, which is bollocks – he was clearly grossly exaggerating Lucio's role as the most dangerous criminal he has ever met in order to enhance his own professional standing. As for Boadella's comparison of Lucio and Don Quijote, Quijote was a fruitcake and a loner who refused to recognise that the golden age of his dreams had passed – and failed. Lucio, however, is not

---

1. Aka Don Quixote, protagonist of the book (first published in 1605) by Miguel de Cervantes (1547–1616).
2. Montecristo, hero of *The Count of Monte Cristo* by Alexandre Dumas (1802–1870). Unjustly imprisoned, he escapes and uses a fabulous hoard to treasure to reward his friends and punish his enemies.
3. Professor Moriarty is described as 'the Napoleon of crime' in the Sherlock Holmes stories of Arthur Conan Doyle (1859–1930).

crazy, nor is he a loner and has always been able to tailor his actions to whatever the technological level of society required – and he was successful, for a time anyway.

Joinet's opinion of Lucio is, I would say, probably closest to recognising the essence of Lucio inasmuch as in him he sees a man of generous spirit who values freedom and justice above all else, even above his own life.

To get a better idea of his life I suggest you watch the biopic *Lucio*.[4]

---

4.   *Lucio: anarquista, atracador, falsificador pero sobre todo ... albañil* (Lucio: anarchist, bank robber, forger but above all ... bricklayer), directed by José María Goenaga and Aitor Arregi, was released in 2007.

Eulogy for Brenda Christie

Good morning everyone and thank you all for coming on this sad occasion to say goodbye to Bren, my wife, life partner, friend and comrade through fifty-one years of life's vicissitudes, caprices and blessings – the beloved mother of Branwen – and Nanna to grand-daughters Merri and Mo. Brenda was an intensely private person who – although engaging, sociable and witty – disliked being the focus of attention, but I've no doubt she would have been pleased to see everyone here, sharing this day with us.

A baby-boomer, born in Shoreditch in London in April 1949, Bren's formative years were spent in Gosport in Hampshire where her lovely dad, Bert, was a Chief Petty Officer, a 'Sparks' in the Royal Navy. She hoped to take up a career in journalism, but despite her sharp intelligence, enquiring intellect, love of literature and creative writing skills, the breakup of her parents' marriage and her tense relationship with her mother Eliza forced her to leave home at 15 and move to London where she became a copy typist, working in a variety of temporary jobs, including at the Treasury.

In 1967, her adventurous spirit took her to Milan where she worked for a time as companion to a glamorous American model, a job that introduced her to the *dolce vita* of Milan and Portofino, but it was a lifestyle that failed to satisfy her sense of moral integrity.

With news of the events of May 1968 in Paris and the radical political, musical and cultural turbulence that was taking place in Britain, largely provoked by the U.S. war in Vietnam, the feisty-spirited 19-year-old Brenda was drawn back to London to be part of the radical social and cultural revolution then taking place, which is where we got together on Bastille Day, 14 July 1968, shortly after my 22nd birthday.

We were together from then until the morning of her passing, just a month after she turned 70.

Those fifty-odd years of our lives together saw many adventures, good and not so good – laughter and tears – as happens in all relationships. But it's the treasured, shared and cheery memories that are the abiding ones.

On our first date in 1968 I took her to Jimmy's Greek Restaurant, a carpeted sewer in Soho's Frith Street which to me was excitingly cosmopolitan in character, but was also cheap with plentiful Mediterranean-style food. Brenda, however, was distinctly unimpressed, particularly when she spotted the column of cockroaches marching along the wainscoting by our heads. We made our excuses and left for the more salubrious Amalfi in Old Compton Street. From there we went on to the theatre; Unity Theatre in Somers Town to see *Little Malcolm and his struggle against the Eunuchs*[1] for which I had wangled complimentary tickets. I certainly knew how to treat a girl in those days.

After the performance we went back to my flat in Crouch End in North London where I further tried to impress Brenda with my skill in tossing a Spanish omelette, but my hand to eye coordination was skewed that night and it ended up splattered on the floor. Brenda, who was precariously balanced on a three-legged chair at the time, laughed so much she leaned back, lost her balance and ended up on her back on the floor with the remains of the omelette, legs akimbo, unladylike, flashing her knickers. Despite those early misadventures, and fortunately for me, Brenda shared my surreal sense of humour, and so began a tumultuous, lifelong, genuinely loving relationship.

Brenda was introduced originally to the Marxist-led International Socialists through her best friend Valerie Packham, and the pair were deeply involved in the staff and student occupation

---

1.   David Halliwell, *Little Malcolm and his struggle against the Eunuchs*.

of the Hornsey College of Art in Crouch End, which took place from May to July 1968.

Later, during the final years of the fascist dictatorship in Spain, she became increasingly committed to the anti-Francoist cause, working closely with the clandestine anarchist First of May Group, which brought her onto the radar of the Metropolitan Police Special Branch and the Security Service, MI5. That, of course, ran alongside her role as a co-founder of the anarchist publishing house Cienfuegos Press and her involvement with the Anarchist Black Cross and *Black Flag* magazine.

In the summer of 1971 I was framed and arrested on conspiracy and possession charges which led to me spending sixteen months on remand in Brixton Prison, which is when Brenda came into her own. While holding down a job as a temporary copy typist, not only did she visit me most days throughout those sixteen months, she brought me cooked meals all the way from Shoreditch to Brixton on public transport.

She also played a crucial and pivotal role in helping to organise and coordinate my ultimately successful defence – that the only incriminating evidence against me had been planted by former Flying Squad detectives, with their superiors' knowledge! – that and working late into the night typing up the barristers' notes during the eight-month Old Bailey trial, one of the longest in British legal history.

Her character and integrity won her the grudging respect of the senior police officers involved in the case. One of them, Commander Ernest Bond, brazenly admitted to her – in the presence of a Chief Superintendent – that they knew I'd been 'fitted up', but they could live with my possible acquittal. As far as they were concerned they'd succeeded in keeping me out of circulation for sixteen months.

It's at times such as those these that we come to really know people in ways of which others remain completely ignorant.

Brenda, to me, exemplified the Sufi and humanist ideal of 'faithful in loving friendship, kindness, compassion and solidarity'.

A few months after my acquittal, in May 1974, following the kidnapping in Paris by anti-fascists of a Francoist banker,[2] a Special Branch officer visited our flat in Wimbledon and advised us to move out of London. Whether or not this was friendly advice or an implicit threat we decided not to put to the test. As Falstaff says in Shakespeare's *King Henry the Fourth*, 'The better part of valour is discretion', and so we began our life Odyssey. I may not always have been her Odysseus, but she was certainly always my Penelope.

Our first house was a nineteenth century mill house in Honley, *Last of the summer wine*[3] country in West Yorkshire, in fact its exterior featured in a few episodes of that long-running series. As well as typesetting our books and journals, Brenda and a friend opened a competitively priced teashop called Touchwood, which became a popular eatery for local mill workers and long-distance lorry drivers on the Trans-Pennine A6024 between Huddersfield and Manchester. Their home-made pies and pasties were to die for. On Touchwood's last day, when we were preparing to leave Yorkshire for Sanday in Orkney, she and her partner Deanna gave all their regular customers free lunches. Many were in tears when they learned the teashop was closing down.

Our next home was the penultimate of the Northern Isles, Sanday in Orkney, where we lived for seven years with Bren's beloved dad, Bert. It was idyllic for a time, especially made glorious by the birth of our daughter, Branwen, albeit in fairly dramatic circumstances.

Our wonderful lady doctor had been struck down by cancer and she had been replaced by a series of locums straight out

2. See Suárez in the glossary.
3. *Last of the summer wine* is a British comedy series.

of the animated cartoon *Scooby Doo*. When the one arrived who was to deliver Branwen he had clearly been drinking, as had the taxi driver of the Commer van that doubled as the island ambulance. To aggravate the situation, the only bottle of oxygen on the island had been used up that morning trying to revive a suicide who had jumped off the end of the pier, having filled his pockets with stones.

I lay on the bed beside Brenda dripping chloroform onto a tea towel covering a flour sieve, both of us breathing the fumes intended to ease the pain of the birth contractions, which somehow the doctor's ineptness had caused to go out of synch. In the end we had to call for the local inter-island aeroplane to airlift her to hospital on the Orkney mainland. Even that was problematic as a heavy *haar*, a sea mist, had enveloped the islands so completely that the pilot had to fly in dangerously low, just above sea level. Even the lifeboat couldn't make it.

Stuart and Brenda Christie, Paris, 1974.
Photo by Antonio Téllez, from the Stuart Christie photo album
on the Kate Sharpley Library website.

That and a few other run-ins with incompetent locums, some of whom had already been struck off the Medical Register two or three times, proved to be the writing on the wall, especially given our now elderly Bert's deteriorating medical condition.

From Sanday we moved south again, to Cambridge where Brenda found a job as an editorial assistant with Cambridge University Press, working with the leading historian Albert Hourani and the noted Arabist Trevor Mostyn on a number of prestigious CUP titles such as the *Cambridge encyclopedia of the Middle East and North Africa*. Both men insisted Brenda was credited by name for her work on the encyclopedia, threatening to remove their names as authors and editors if the class-driven Press Syndics refused to comply, which they had done initially. To credit a lowly editorial assistant by name in such a distinguished publication was unheard of, and I doubt if it has happened since.

It was in Cambridge too that Brenda discovered what proved to be her true métier as a teacher, initially teaching Business Studies to 16- to 19-year-olds at Cambridge College of Further Education where her best friend Valerie was Senior Lecturer in charge of Secretarial Studies. Although to be honest she did think it was a thankless task trying to teach teenagers things they didn't particularly care about – and to be somewhere they didn't want to be.

However, after six years in Cambridge, Bert, Brenda's delightful dad, who'd lived with us since our Yorkshire days, passed away. It was time again to move on, this time to Hastings where we settled for twenty years, largely to ensure that Branwen, our daughter, could put down roots and enjoy some stability with regard to her education and friends.

Among her talents Branwen had a predilection for drama. But it turned out that the principal of the local after-school drama studio she attended was not only a drama queen, but a complete chancer to boot, one whose knowledge and understanding of Shakespeare and his time and plays was embarrassingly superficial.

Think Donald Trump meets Danny La Rue and you'll get some idea of the kind of person I'm talking about.

The bottom line was that Brenda ended up teaching Branwen herself, and was so successful that she swept the board at the local Music and Drama Festival, as well as other festivals in East Sussex, Kent and South London, putting to shame the competing local drama schools. Other mothers approached her to teach their children, which led to Brenda setting up her own Rude Mechanicals Drama Studio. This lasted for almost 10 years and won the hearts and minds of her pupils, whom she enthused with her love of Shakespeare – to say nothing of winning countless drama festivals across the South East.

Our final move was to Clacton. It seemed like a good idea at the time, but it coincided with a decline in Brenda's health. A heavy smoker for more than 50 years, she had increasing breathing and mobility difficulties, but these were eased by the entry into her life of her two darling granddaughters, Merri – born in 2014 – and Mo, in 2017. Their dynamic and irresistibly exuberant personalities boosted her spirits and recharged her morale enormously.

The end came much sooner than any of us expected. Hardly a month had passed between her biopsy and diagnosis of small-cell cancer, the first chemo session, and her death. It was sudden and unexpected – it came in the hour of the wolf, the hour between night and dawn.

What Branwen and I draw some small comfort from is the fact that it wasn't a long and painful process. She didn't suffer, she died at home, loved and cared for, not in a cheerless hospital ward or strange hospice room, and I was beside her, able to comfort her at the end. It was her time to go.

This morning we say goodbye to Brenda's body, but not to her spirit or to the love we had for her and she for us. She has joined what some African societies call the 'sasha', the recently departed, whose time on earth overlaps with people still alive. They do not die, they live on in the memories of the living, who can call them to mind, and bring them to life in stories and anecdote. Only when the last person to know an ancestor dies does that ancestor leave the 'sasha' for the 'zamani'; the generalised ancestors who are never forgotten, but are revered in memory.

Brenda was a feisty and spirited woman who found it difficult to pull her punches in her dealings with others. She didn't suffer fools gladly – or even badly, including me on occasions. But despite our sporadic harsh but soon forgotten and forgiven outbursts of frustration, words can never express my own and Branwen's profound gratitude to Brenda for bringing purpose, happiness and a sense of fulfilment to our lives – not least for her constant part in the general effort to alleviate the burden of the darker times we've shared.

Goodbye, dear.

Part 3

Tributes to Stuart

A Scot in Carabanchel
by Miguel Garcia

I was very interested to meet this young man who had come forward in our cause and given hope to the libertarian prisoners that they were not forgotten. Although he had a twenty years' sentence in front of him and he was a young man who liked life and action and pretty women, he was always bright and cheerful and kept up lively discussions with his comrades. For all his jokes he was indispensable in the infirmary, though his sole medical knowledge previously had been as an apprentice dental mechanic.

Stuart Christie, 1965, at Yeserías prison hospital in Madrid.

He received parcels from abroad, as his case had attracted worldwide attention, and shared his parcels with the 'commune' of libertarian prisoners in Carabanchel. His was the only source of aspirins, with which he supplied the entire prison and without which a medical orderly could not have given anything to a sick man. When later he was released, he understood the need for parcels to be kept up to prisoners and began an organization for helping the libertarian prisoners in Spain.[1] He even sat, while in jail, for his English examinations and gained several 'A' levels, one of them naturally in the Spanish language, which he had not understood before he came to Spain. [...]

He was still medical orderly during my stay and put me on the sick list so that we had the advantage of several days' conversation before I was on the way to Zaragoza. I discovered I did not speak English as fluently as I had thought. I had spoken French and Italian when I entered prison and throughout my years in jail I had been studying English. Now I found they pronounced their language in a completely strange way. I could read it, but conversation was beyond me. I left with an invitation to come to London 'any time it's convenient to you ... and the Director General [of Prisons].' [...]

I began to smuggle out letters in the way Christie has initiated, until one day the director of Soria Prison sent for me in a rage. I had had letters and communications published in influential foreign papers, which were also sold in Spain. He would punish me, he said. I would never get out of prison alive. I denied authorship.

'Who else could know so much?' he asked.

I shrugged my shoulders. 'Who else but Christie?' I said. It was safe to blame him, for after three years he had finally been released. 'Christie is in London, he writes whatever he pleases and

---

1. The Anarchist Black Cross.

if he chooses to do so, he uses my name. What can I do? Unfortunately God has punished the English for their heresies, and they do not have the benefits of our past glorious thirty years. We cannot ask the Lord Mayor of London to order out the army and imprison Mr Christie in the Tower for writing as he thinks, whether he uses my name or the Queen's.'

Christie's release had been presented as a special act of clemency following an appeal by Stuart's mother – as if she, and many thousands of mothers, including my own, had never thought of making such appeals before. The Spanish Press glamorized the action to show Franco in a rare generous mood, and one paper went so far as to announce lyrically that England had sent us a terrorist and had, thanks to our reforming prison administration, returned her a good citizen. Needless to say, Stuart, on release, showed not the slightest intention of giving up the struggle for freedom and all that the Spanish government had sent back to England was a relentless enemy.

From *Franco's prisoner* (1972) p.149–155, published by Rupert Hart-Davis, 1972.

Review of the manuscript of
The Christie file: memoirs of an anarchist by Albert Meltzer

In a moment of somewhat inaccurate lyrical ecstasy one newspaper described Stuart Christie as the best known anarchist since Peter the Painter.[1] If indeed that worthy were really an anarchist, it is a commentary on Fleet Street that it knew not Kropotkin, Malatesta, Tarrida del Mármol[2] and a score of other visitors to these shores since, not to forget several generations of British anarchists. But to Fleet Street fascinated by its own caricature of anarchism, in a perpetual alcoholic daze as to what is fact and what is its own propaganda, Stuart Christie was a gift to them since the day he presented the image to them of one who went, kilted and sporraned, to the sound of pibroch, armed with *skhean dhu*,[3] into sunny Spain in order to do battle with General Franco; or however else they ring the changes.

His book[4] is as much of a witty comment on Fleet Street as

---

1. Pseudonym of Jānis Žāklis (1883–?) Latvian (ex-Social Democrat) anarchist. Subject of *A Towering flame: The life & times of 'Peter the Painter'* by Philip Ruff (Breviary Stuff, 2019). The phrase seems to have been used in the wake Stuart's acquittal in the Stoke Newington Eight trial. See 'Press comment on the anarchists' *Black Flag* Vol.2, no. 15 (January 1973).
2. Fernando Tarrida del Mármol (1861–1915), Cuban-born Spanish anarchist who lived for many years in exile in Britain.
3. A pibroch is a variation on a theme for bagpipes, the *Skean dhu* is an ornamental dagger worn as part of Highland costume.
4. In the 1968 Coptic Press catalogue a book by Stuart titled *Spain from the inside* was projected as 'Our anticipated best seller...'. The updated version, due to be published by Michael Joseph in June 1976, would not appear until it was co-published by Cienfuegos and Partisan Press in 1980.

anything else; and he demolishes that propaganda factory with great gusto. He carries the reader along with him as he explores that desert of lies: the reader may be unaware until finishing the book that he leaves not only the propaganda factory in ruins but many of the cherished pillars of State which have their foundations in the sands of that desert.

To tell a story involving his experiences in Spanish and English Prisons, to have to go through the distressing story of Spanish repression and British frame-ups, ought to make for sad reading; but instead he tells it all with unexpected good humour and even at times knockabout rumbustiousness. Few political books manage ever to be readable, but he tells his story in a laconic style that makes it eminently so.

Seldom has the mickey taking of Fleet Street and the world press been so neatly served back at them: this is 'man biting dog' with a vengeance and a venom none the less deadly for being supremely comic.

Lewisham, London (early 1980s). A cheery Albert Meltzer (modelling his Sanday knitters jersey) on the balcony of his Lewisham high-rise with Stuart. Photo by a dear New Yorker friend and comrade, from Stuart Christie.

He presents a picture of the Special Branch at work against the Angry Brigade which makes for compulsive reading; not least because the casual way in which he shows how people angry with the Gas Board because their gas is cut off in the middle of winter do not appreciate the machinations of the British secret police.

Above all, this is a book of a committed Anarchist. No one can doubt the strength of his convictions however flippant the way in which he deals with his enemies. It is the anarchism of the international revolutionary movement and it is firmly in the tradition of the indigenous working class movement, something which seems to some a contradiction but isn't. Whether they are convinced or not, nobody reading through it can ever regard anti-anarchist propaganda in the same way again. The solemn package deal left libertarians and pacifist sectarians are going to hate it no less than the authoritarians – which will surely come out in the reviews. I fear he does not take great pains to hide his contempt for them; his fault, indeed, is embarrassing frankness – even about himself. But there emerges from the book the portrait of an authentic revolutionary, caring immensely about freedom but quite prepared to stop for a wee dram of whisky; prepared to rush into the fray but joking about the enemy meanwhile. Not, surely, an unfamiliar figure in our proletarian history.

Albert Meltzer

Stop Press: Michael Joseph, the London publishers who initially commissioned *The Christie file*, have decided – on the advice of their legal advisers – that they cannot now proceed with the publication of this title and they write to say they hope a 'more courageous publisher can be found.' Our present financial position prohibits us from proceeding with the book at the moment, but if we do manage to raise sufficient funds for this title by sub-scription we shall publish it ourselves at the earliest opportunity.

From *Cienfuegos Press Review of Anarchist Literature 1976* (*Cienfuegos Press Anarchist Review*, no 1.)

Stuart Christie 1946–2020 Anarchist activist, writer and publisher, by John Patten

Stuart Christie, founder of the Anarchist Black Cross and Cienfuegos Press and co-author of *The floodgates of anarchy* has died peacefully after a battle with lung cancer.

Born in Glasgow and brought up in Blantyre, Christie credited his grandmother for shaping his political outlook, giving him a clear moral map and ethical code. His determination to follow his conscience led him to anarchism: 'Without freedom there would be no equality and without equality no freedom, and without struggle there would be neither.'[1] It also led him from the campaign against nuclear weapons to joining the struggle against the Spanish fascist dictator Francisco Franco (1892–1975).

He moved to London and got in touch with the clandestine Spanish anarchist organisation Defensa Interior (Interior Defence). He was arrested in Madrid in 1964 carrying explosives to be used in an assassination attempt on Franco. To cover the fact that there was an informer inside the group, the police proclaimed they had agents operating in Britain – and (falsely) that Christie had drawn attention to himself by wearing a kilt.

The threat of the garrotte and his twenty year sentence drew international attention to the resistance to the Franco regime. In prison Christie formed lasting friendships with anarchist militants of his and earlier generations. He returned from Spain in

---

1.   From the introduction to *The art of anarchy* by Flavio Costantini (Cienfuegos Press, 1975).

1967, older and wiser, but equally determined to continue the struggle and use his notoriety to aid the comrades he left behind.

In London he met Brenda Earl who would become his political and emotional life partner. He also met Albert Meltzer, and the two would refound the Anarchist Black Cross to promote solidarity with anarchist prisoners in Spain, and the resistance more broadly. Their book, *The floodgates of anarchy* (1970) promoted a revolutionary anarchism at odds with the attitudes of some who had come into anarchism from the sixties peace movement. At the Carrara anarchist conference of 1968 Christie got in touch with a new generation of anarchist militants who shared his ideas and approach to action.

Christie's political commitment and international connections made him a target for the British Special Branch. He was acquitted of conspiracy to cause explosions in the 'Stoke Newington Eight' trial of 1972, claiming the jury could understand why someone would want to blow up Franco, and why that would make him a target for 'conservative-minded policemen'.[2]

Free but apparently unemployable, Christie launched Cienfuegos Press which would produce a large number of anarchist books and the encyclopedic *Cienfuegos Press Anarchist Review*. Briefly Orkney became a centre of anarchist publishing before lack of cashflow ended the project. Christie would continue publishing, and investigating new ways of doing so including ebooks and the internet. His christiebooks.co.uk site contains numerous films on anarchism and biographies of anarchists. He used Facebook to create an archive of anarchist history not available anywhere else as he recounted memories and events from his own and other people's lives.

Christie wrote *The investigative researcher's handbook* (1983), sharing skills that he put to use in an exposé of fascist Italian

---

2.   *Edward Heath made me angry*, p. 239.

terrorist *Stefano delle Chiaie* (1984). In 1996 he published the first version of his historical study *We, the anarchists: a study of the Iberian Anarchist Federation (FAI), 1927–1937*.

Short-run printing enabled him to produced three illustrated volumes of his life story (*My granny made me an anarchist*, *General Franco made me a 'terrorist'* and *Edward Heath made me angry* 2002–2004) which were condensed into a single volume as *Granny made me an anarchist: General Franco, the Angry Brigade and me* (2004). His final books were the three volumes of *¡Pistoleros! The Chronicles of Farquhar McHarg*, his tales of a Glaswegian anarchist who joins the Spanish anarchist defence groups in the years 1918–1924.

Committed to anarchism and publishing, Christie appeared at many bookfairs and film festivals, but scorned any suggestion he had come to 'lead' anyone anywhere.

From KSL: Bulletin of the Kate Sharpley Library No.102, September 2020.

Christie's partner Brenda died in June 2019. He slipped away peacefully, listening to 'Pennies From Heaven' (Brenda's favourite song) in the company of his daughter Branwen.

Stuart Christie, 10 July 1946–15 August 2020.

From *KSL: Bulletin of the Kate Sharpley Library* No. 102, September 2020.

The Kate Sharpley Library and Stuart: an appreciation

The Kate Sharpley Library Collective were deeply saddened to hear of the death of Stuart. From our very earliest days Stuart was a mentor and a supporter and we want to acknowledge his generosity and kindness. We shared his political outlook and his approach to history and we are proud to stand in that tradition. We know it just wasn't us he helped on historical and philosophical matters. A seventeen year old from Scunthorpe would get a response from Stuart equal to any learned professor who wrote to Stuart looking for help. Carrying on the work of Miguel Garcia and Albert Meltzer, Stuart was responsible for bringing to life literally hundreds of anarchists and militants who had, until his work, been forgotten in the pages of history. It was an amazing feat of historical scholarship. He brought them back because he came to understand that anarchism wasn't about great thinkers and writers but was something made by the efforts and sacrifices of ordinary people. He encouraged us think about that beautiful ideal of anarchism in a different way than you read in most of its histories.

It would have been easy for Stuart to play the role of hero and champion. He rejected that and any other idea of him being a leader, which shows the measure of the man. To us he was a friend with a delicious sense of humour overlaid with a magnificent generosity of spirit. It seemed he would always be there, chasing us up for the most obscure references or telling us to read books we had never heard of. Sadly that was not to be. We loved the man, not the legend that has crept into some coverage of his death and we send our love and support to his family. He would have been the first to say that without you and Brenda he would have been a lesser person.

Stuart and Brenda, Highgate Cemetery, Summer 1968.
By Ken Sutherland. From the Stuart Christie photo album
on the Kate Sharpley Library website.

From *KSL: Bulletin of the Kate Sharpley Library* No. 102, September 2020.

Stuart Christie has died after a lengthy illness by Joan Busquets

(Scotland) July 1946 – [Chelmsford] August 2020, at the age of 74). I made Stuart's acquaintance back in 1965 in Carabanchel prison (Madrid). Since then, we have never lost touch.

Stuart was convicted in Madrid on 2 September 1964 by a court martial and sentenced to a twenty-year prison term; his co-accused, Fernando Carballo Blanco was sentenced to thirty years. Both were charged with Banditry and Terrorism for having attempted to mount terrorist attacks on the Franco regime. Stuart was released in 1967, thanks to international pressure brought to bear with help and support from VIPs such as the English philosopher Bertrand Russell and French philosopher Jean-Paul Sartre. Upon his release, after having served three years, and once back in England, he carried on with his activism within the libertarian movement. He resurrected the Black Cross (the Anarchist Prisoners' Aid Association) and launched the paper *Black Flag* with his inseparable comrade Albert Meltzer. He published a range of books by Spanish writers such as Antonio Téllez's life of Quico Sabaté[1] and José Peirats's three-volume study *The CNT in the Spanish Revolution* (translated by Paul Sharkey with corrections, notes and editing by Chris Ealham) or the historical fiction novel *The man who killed Durruti* by writer Pedro de Paz.

His death has robbed me of a comrade, a co-worker upon whom I could always rely. Let me say that Stuart spent his entire life championing the memory of the maquis, in which he was an indefatigable pioneer.

Salud, comrade, rest in peace.

---

1.   *Sabaté: guerrilla extraordinary*, translated by Stuart.

Along with the comrades from the Berga local (the Centre d'Estudis Josep Ester Borràs, the Ateneu Columna Terra i Llibertat and the CGT of Berguedà) I want to send our deepest and most heartfelt condolences to his daughter and nearest and dearest,

Joan Busquets, Former *maqui* [guerrilla] (20 years served in prison) 16 August 2020.

Juan Busquets Verges and Stuart Christie, Ceret, 1994.
Photo from Stuart Christie.

From B. Llibertari, the web page of El Pèsol negre: The News Portal of Bages and the Berguedà: http://www.bllibertari.org/ha-fallecido-de-una-larga-enfermedad-stuart-christie.html. Translated by Paul Sharkey.

Stuart Christie, comrade and friend by Octavio Alberola

The news of Stuart Christie's death arrived by phone halfway through yesterday afternoon from comrade René after he asked if I had heard the bad news and after I quizzed him brusquely: Who's dead? I could tell from his tone of voice that it must have been somebody close who had passed away.

René's answer stopped me in my tracks, because even though Stuart had told me a week before that the cancer had left him still hoarse and that the findings of his medical tests were none too encouraging, it never at any moment occurred to me that he would be taken so quickly. I am surrounded by several male and female comrades – more or less of my own age – who are in none too rude health and at my age (due to turn 93 shortly) the thought that one's days are numbered is just 'normal'.

But in Stuart's case, how could this be when he was eighteen years my junior? Besides, we had both been working on joint projects and both had been determined to plough ahead with our battles with the world of authority and exploitation.

To me, his death represents not just the loss of a comrade and friend but an end to long years collaborating on joint actions and initiatives designed to expose the injustices of the world in which we live and the fight for a fairer, freer world. A world that is possible for all of us who have not given up on wishing and trying to work towards a consistent practice of active, internationalist revolutionary solidarity.

We have known many years of brotherly relations ever since our first meeting back in August 1964 and up until 2020, without interruption. Half a century of our lives in tandem, one way or another, working on behalf of a common cause, heedless of borders. That struggle, though centred on the Spanish people's political and social vagaries, initially under the Franco dictatorship and later under this phoney democracy spawned by the Transition/ Transaction, has at all times carried the imprint of an internationalist revolutionary outlook.

The evidence of that, in Stuart's case, was the time he spent behind bars in Spain and England, and in the case of Brenda his partner, in Germany[1] and, in the cases of Ariane[2] and myself, in Belgium and France.[3] Experiences that bear witness to struggles that knew no borders as we knew that a characteristic of freedom is that it is the right of every man and woman.

So how could I not feel impelled to remember it now that our fraternization with Stuart has ended with his death? As well as with the death just a few days ago of the German comrade Doris Ensinger, the partner of Luis Andrés Edo, with whom Stuart shared some of his prison experiences and with whom he rubbed shoulders in their struggles; obviously, speaking for myself, the loss of Doris in a way represented the final ending of my fraternization-in-struggle with Luis. A finale that started some years back with Luis's own death.

The fact is that in the case of Doris's death too I was stopped in my tracks, startled by the news of her demise communicated to me by Manel, as barely a week earlier she had sent Tomás and me an email to let us know that she had been abruptly recalled to

---

1. Brenda was arrested in May 1981, accused of involvement in an attack by the FIJL on Iberia airlines in May 1970. She was released after an international solidarity campaign.
2. Ariane Gransac, French anarchist, writer and artist, and Octavio's partner.
3. Alberola and Gransac were arrested in Belgium in 1968 and accused of plotting an attack on the Franco regime. In 1974 they were arrested in the wake of the Suárez kidnapping (and acquitted in 1981).

the hospital and undergone a transplant operation ... But was now back home and feeling well ...

Meaning that yet again I am brought face to face with the tenuousness of our existence and the need to preserve the memory of what we strove to be and do, to the very death.

Perpignan, 17 August 2020

Octavio Alberola and Stuart Christie, Venice, 1984.
From the Stuart Christie photo album on the
Kate Sharpley Library website.

From RojoyNegro_Digital el Mar, 18/08/20; 15:02 http://rojoynegro. info/articulo/memoria/octavio-alberola-se-despide-stuart-christie. Translated by Paul Sharkey.

Stuart Christie, the Eternal Young Rebel Always in the Fight for Life by Xavier Montanyà

Stuart Christie was born in Glasgow in 1946, too late to enlist in the International Brigades and go off and fight alongside the Spanish republicans in the 1936–39 war. As a child, though, he befriended some Scottish miners who had fought with the International Brigades in that faraway war that he was to take so closely to his heart. A war for ideals that were and are universal. He used to listen in wonder to the tales they used to tell. Taking a pride in them. Such conversations moulded his sensibility to life and struggle.

He did not know it yet, but Stuart would later be ready to carry on with their fight. He would try to complete his friends' task in Spain. From then on, that was to be his mission and his life. A commitment to the struggle that would be deployed across many fronts. Internationalist, revolutionary anti-fascist activism, direct action and history, publishing and investigative journalism. Stuart Christie was the real thing, a free man.

As he was to put it in the first volume of his memoirs *The Christie File: Part 1, 1946–1964: my granny made me an anarchist* (2002), his granny 'by her example and the wisdom she showed [...] gave me a clear moral map and inculcated in me an inerasable ethical code – a sort of secular Calvinism – which led me directly and inexorably through the political and ethical quagmire to anarchism – to me, the only honest non-religious ideology which aspired to social justice without seeking social, political or economic dominion over others.'[1]

---

1. *My granny made me an anarchist*, p. 52.

On reading the first edition of that book, his friend Noam Chomsky was to write: 'His fascinating personal narrative is a remarkable portrait of the late 20th century, seen through discerning eyes and interpreted by a compassionate and inquisitive mind.' And in private, if memory serves, was to comment tongue-in-cheek: 'Who would have guessed that the good-looking young lad on the cover would finish up as a dangerous terrorist and all through the fault of his granny.'

Professor Paul Preston also teased about the title whilst highlighting and praising the book's values: 'What exactly Stuart Christie's granny is being made responsible for is rather a lot. Given that the opening scene of this riveting autobiography is a bitterly funny account of his trial for attempting to murder General Franco, it seems that the poor lady is being saddled with more responsibility than is fair. As this marvellously readable and often moving book reveals, the real responsibility lies in part with the post-1945 break-up of a social system based on deference.'

Whether it was thanks to his granny, the miners and workers of Glasgow or his learning about the Spanish Civil War – 'the most important moral reference point in the whole of the 20th century' – as he put it,[2] Stuart was to commit himself wholly to everything he did. Heedless of the risks. With every action and every publication.

He must have had a lot of guts to volunteer at the age of 18 in the summer of 1964 to enter Spain on his own, hitch-hiking, carrying a load of explosives to be used in an attempt on General Franco's life in Madrid. Only a year before the regime had used the *garrote vil* and fake evidence to murder the young libertarians Francisco Granado and Joaquín Delgado for having made the very same attempt. Less than a year had elapsed since then.

---

2. *General Franco made me a 'terrorist'*, unnumbered page titled 'On anarchist resistance' before p. i.

The Francoist police were infuriated. Police cooperation between France and Spain, between De Gaulle and Franco was very intense. De Gaulle was afraid of OAS[3] personnel who had fled to Spain and Franco of the Spanish anarchists living as refugees in France.

Yes, he must have had a lot of guts. Or he might have been a bit of a nutter. Might have been Stuart, in fact. In his eyes the judicial murder perpetrated on Granado and Delgado was not about to stop him; quite the opposite, it made up his mind to act. It acted as a detonator. Rather than being scared or reckoning, as most people in Spain and abroad did, that he was not about to run the same risk, he volunteered his services in a further action designed to eliminate Franco, an action planned by the secret anarchist Defensa Interior (DI) agency; he made contact with Octavio Alberola in Paris. These young anarchists believed that the removal of the General would lead to the progressive crumbling of the regime which was at the time riven by internal differences between the various ideological factions of which it was comprised. They did not achieve their aim but were to show the whole world – especially the prisoners and the exiles – that Franco was not untouchable and had not frightened everyone off. He still had his enemies and there was a fresh generation prepared to fight him.

The plan scarcely got off the ground. Most likely the victim of some informer or 'plant', Christie was to find himself arrested upon his arrival in Madrid with the explosives, just as he was about to pick up a letter containing further instructions. This led also to the arrest of Fernando Carballo, the activist he was due to contact. There followed arrest, interrogation, torture, Council of War, a twenty-year sentence and imprisonment. Until after three years, he was released in 1967 thanks to a special pardon. In diplomatic

---

3.   Organisation Armée secrète (Secret Army Organization) right-wing armed group opposed to Algerian independence.

terms, Stuart's case was very delicate. International pressure was to play a very important part, whether coming from the British government or from a long list of intellectuals that included Bertrand Russell and Jean-Paul Sartre.

Fernando Carballo was not released until the 1977 amnesty.

Carabanchel prison, where he served three of the twenty years to which he had been sentenced, proved to be, as he himself admitted, a veritable university education. Stuart was a discreet and blunt sort. He may well have learnt the ideas of the 'anonymous militant' and the 'enlightened labourer' from his friend and comrade Luis Andrés Edo, whom he met there behind bars. Allow me to place it on record here too that Luis Andrés Edo's partner and Stuart Christie's friend Doris Ensinger passed away just a few days ago in Barcelona.

Stuart always shunned the limelight. And was not one to preen himself on his own importance. When setting out or writing down his own story and that of his comrades, he always paid special attention to human details and anecdotes. He was politically and historically rigorous, to be sure, but he was at all times prompted by an easy-going, intense curiosity about people and the world that opened up to him in the labyrinthine ways of clandestinity, repression, imprisonment and activist struggle.

Stuart Christie had a dry, twinkling sense of humour and a sardonic approach that drained the mythology out of and breathed oxygen into the harshest of stories, injecting sense and truth into them. Like some elegant cavalier, he shied away from and was oblivious to the heroics and delusions of so many who nearly always finish up slavishly welcoming the praises of the establishment in return for discreet abdications and silences.

Stuart chose to caption *My granny made me an anarchist* with a quotation from the English mathematician and philosopher William Kingdon Clifford which in my eyes sums him up to perfection:

'There is only one thing more wicked than the desire to command and that is the will to obey.'[4]

The Second Wave of International Brigaders

Christie always did what he thought needed doing. The stories he had heard from those Glasgow miners pointed the way to him. At the age of eighteen he too was to enlist as a volunteer in the underground struggle against Franco and, just as they had done way back in 1936, he was to gamble his own life for his libertarian anti-fascist ideals of justice and freedom that were his life's blood.

Stuart Christie plus other British, French, Italian and Portuguese anarchist comrades were, during the 1960s, to make up a little second internationalist wave of young activists ready to offer up their lives to the clandestine fight against Franco. Compared with the International Brigaders of 1936–1939, they were but few, a handful. Anarchists and anti-authoritarians. With no Communist Party behind them. Indeed, it was against them, the communists having years since washed their hands of the armed struggle, on Stalin's orders.

Those keen to learn the full story of this history as set out by Stuart can refer to *Franco made me a 'terrorist'*, this being volume two of Stuart's memoirs *The Christie file*, the opening volume of which was *My granny made me an anarchist*; the third volume was *Edward Heath made me angry* (2004). The latter volume covers the years 1967–1975 when Christie was charged with membership of 'The Angry Brigade' which, between 1970 and 1972 carried out a series of bomb attacks (around twenty five of them) across England, without ever causing any personal injury.[5]

---

4. This appears in a slightly different form ('one thing in the world') in an essay on Clifford (British philosopher and mathematician, 1845–1879) by Frederick Pollock *Fortnightly Review*, v. 31, n. 149 (May 1879) p. 684. It is quoted in *Liberty and the great libertarians* by Charles T. Sprading (1913).
5. A woman was cut on the leg when one of the bombs exploded.

Franco Made Me A Terrorist

When Stuart's book was about to be released in Spanish in 2005, I wrote this comment for the newspaper *Avui*: 'There is much to recommend this book. It is an account of events which, with the benefit of hindsight, one can see from the viewpoint of the protagonist, without losing a single iota of his enthusiasm or commitment. It offers a portrait of a certain Spain that was just starting to wake up economically thanks to the tourist trade and it comes from a young 18 year-old European alive to the cultural and counter-cultural developments of the day. It offers his personal reflections, complete with historical rigour, on that reality and in full detail.

'But as far as I am concerned, the most salient factor here is the personal insights which are of course subjective but highly focused in their detail, profiling the repressive liturgy of Francoism and its goons: the police, the military, the prison officials, the chaplains, etc. His account of his imprisonment, his entry into the dungeons of the DGS[6] in Madrid, the interrogations, the character of his questioners, the head of the DGS Intelligence Service, Eduardo Blanco, and the superintendent from the Brigada Político-Social, Saturnino Yagüe. These are pages of huge historical value in terms of the exactitude of the facts, the accuracy of the descriptions and the denunciation these constitute today of that machinery of repression.'

Christie closed his foreword like this: 'It cannot begin to reflect the vicious, cruel and bloodthirsty nature of the Franco regime and its prisons between 1939 and the early 1960s, but I hope that my own highly subjective experiences in Spanish prisons will connect the reader in some way with the experiences of others and prompt some thought about the struggle to be human and the hundreds of thousands of brave people who fought, suffered, died

---

6. Dirección General de Seguridad.

and lost loved ones in the selfless cause of resisting the reactionary, priest-, gun- and prison-backed ideology that was Francoism.'[7]

There are other books by Stuart that deserve a mention: books such as ¡Pistoleros! The chronicles of Farquhar McHarg (Vols 1–3), Stefano delle Chiaie: portrait of a 'black' terrorist and We, the anarchists! A study of the Iberian Anarchist Federation (FAI), etc.

In the late 1960s Stuart Christie and Albert Meltzer were to launch the Anarchist Black Cross in support of the Spanish anti-Francoist resistance and anarchist political prisoners; and the newspaper Black Flag. Stuart also did important work as the publisher of the Cienfuegos Press and Christie Books. Not to mention the trojan work invested over the years into creating the Anarchist Film Archive, the best and most comprehensive on-line digital film archive, I believe. A thousand films on the 1936–1939 war, Francoism, anarchism and revolutionary movements.

London, Stuart Christie and the Shade of Xavier Vinader

In the end, everybody finishes up finding himself. In the end, everybody finishes up in the know. Given such forever undergrounders as Stuart Christie and Xavier Vinader,[8] it is all but impossible now to carry on in ignorance of authentic history.

It is worth remembering that Vinader, while in exile in France, had come under threats from the GAL[9] and that the Batallón

---

7. *General Franco made me a 'terrorist'*, p. ii.
8. Xavier Vinader (1947–2015), Spanish reporter whose coverage of far right activists and infiltrators operating in the Basque Country resulted in his being charged with 'moral authorship' in relation to ETA's killing of two of the people he named. He was sentenced to a seven-year jail term for 'professional recklessness' but fled the country before negotiating his return and surrender in 1984. He served two months in prison before being pardoned. Went on to become president (1990–1993) of Reporters Without Borders NGO.
9. Grupos Antiterroristas de Liberación (Anti-Terrorist Liberation Groups) armed right-wing group used against ETA by the Spanish government.

Vasco-Español[10] attacked his apartment in Barcelona. Luckily, he was out of the country at the time. Xavier Vinader, a journalist who had lifted the lid on the then embryonic GAL, and an expert in the Spanish and European far right, was one of the targets of the Black International operating right across the continent. Stuart got wind of this and made every effort to protect him and offer him support.

When Xavier Vinader died, I wrote a book called *El cas Vinader, el periodisme contra la guerra bruta* (*The Vinader affair, journalism versus the dirty war*, Editorial Portic, 2015), in the course of which I contacted Stuart to follow up a few leads which had been left out of the documentation due to problems with cross-matching them.

When I asked him about his dealings with Vinader in London and the threat of far-right attacks hanging over him, his response was: 'Sure, we met up lots of times over the years, especially in 1983. I frequently dropped in on him at his hotel in Marble Arch. We would have dinner together and chat about matters of mutual interest with regards to far-right plots and activities in Europe and the connections with European special services agencies. Primarily about the GAL and "plants", informers and provocateurs. I wrote a book *Stefano delle Chiaie: portrait of a 'black' terrorist* (Anarchy Magazine, London 1984). I believe that delle Chiaie was living and operating in Spain at the time. And I had just published *The investigative researcher's handbook (towards a Citizens' Intelligence Agency)* which had triggered a scandal in the British media (TV, radio, press). In line with another book that I had published earlier *Towards a citizens' militia*, which had a similar impact ...Vinader's was a pretty boring life in London. He was living in a noisy hotel filled with Saudi families! You can just

---

10. Batallón Vasco-Español (Spanish Basque Battalion) was another 'flag of convenience' for armed right-wing anti-ETA attacks.

imagine ... I don't remember him being particularly paranoid, but it was obvious that he was careful about his security and was aware of everything going on all around him...'

One day, I was chatting with Xavier Vinader and the Scotsman's name came up. 'You know Stuart?' Vinader asked me. His face lit up. 'Sure, I have warm memories of him. When I was in exile in London because of my trial, Stuart Christie and a comrade of his refused to let me go out on my own. They used to escort me everywhere...'

Months after that, as I was still gathering documentation for my book, I stumbled across an article by Vinader for *Interviú*, published from London in his 'My Exile Diary' column. It was the title that caught my eye – 'Thank you, friend Stuart! Thank you, Jaén journalists!' The article opened with a description of his frame of mind, pretty downcast after a year in exile. The conditions upon which he might return to Spain had yet to be sorted out and the delay was really hitting home. And then, as if harking back to a time of peace and brotherhood, he mentioned Christie. Here is the excerpt in which he mentions him:

'Stuart Christie is a Scottish friend well familiar with Spanish prisons because, during the dictatorship, he had to spend a long time there after he was arrested with a suitcase laden with explosives meant for Generalissimo Franco. A few months back, in the tiny living room of his house in Cambridge, over a glass containing a good dose of Glenmorangie, one of the oldest and most renowned malt whiskies produced in the Scottish Highlands, Stuart told me that he had no difficulty understanding how I was feeling: "If you were in prison you would at least have an end-date for it all. You would have a time-table and schedule by which to get your life organized. But in your position, that is not on. Living the way you do, waiting for some solution whereby you can slip back to Spain quickly, is tough, very tough. Like being in prison. Maybe worse, in my opinion. But bear up, bear up. Sooner or later it will be over. There is nothing else for it." I took his advice to heart. And will carry on bearing up.'

That text had a hidden meaning, Vinader was secretly negotiating his homecoming and would hand himself over to the Spanish authorities, as he was to do a few weeks later. He was allowed back. I sent off a copy to Stuart without delay. He was delighted. 'I wasn't aware that he had written that!'

And now to bring this article to a close. History has no end. Let me say my goodbyes. Thank you for so many things, Stuart. As a Glasgow anarchist friend of yours once said, be it in Heaven or in Hell, they're getting their best arguments ready for you.

From https://www.vilaweb.cat/noticies/stuart-christie-letern-jove-rebel-sempre-en-combat-per-la-vida. Translated by Paul Sharkey.

Stuart Christie: In Memoriam
by Chris Ealham and
Julián Vadillo Muñoz

Not an easy year, 2020. For a variety of reasons, we are watching the disappearance of a generation that marked this country's recent history. Whether as a result of the Covid-19 pandemic or to terrible illnesses, we have lost a part of their first-hand accounts of events of import.

One such individual who left us recently was Stuart Christie. On 15 August, Stuart's heart stopped beating following an awful illness that finished him off in short order. His death triggered a flurry of condolences and memories, indicating the importance of the man we had lost. We are grateful for this short space in which to remember Stuart in his proper context, in the terms of the importance of the work he did and its implications for our recent history.

In all of the obituaries of Stuart that have appeared, whether in the general press or in more militant publications, there has been one thing highlighted above all others: Stuart Christie was the British anarchist who back in 1964 attempted to assassinate the dictator Franco at the Santiago Bernabeu stadium. And, to be sure, Stuart, whose acquaintance with anarchism had been building for some time by that point, had been in touch with Spanish exile circles in France and had volunteered to take part in an attempt that might end the life of a dictator who had been ruling over the country through heavy repression since 1939. Stuart set out all of these details in an autobiographical book about the incident called *General Franco made me a 'terrorist'* (published in Spain as *Franco me hizo terrorista. Memorias de un anarquista que intentó matar a un dictador*). No need, therefore, to labour that point, upon which so much ink has been expended. So, let us refer the reader to Stuart's work in the round.

There was much more to Stuart Christie than somebody who tried to kill Franco. Born into a working-class family in Glasgow, it was in his very earliest youth that he came into contact with local anarchist groups and, enthused by his study of anarchism, he had no hesitation in contacting various libertarians around the world. He always subscribed to the working-class anarchist tradition. As mentioned, his association with the Spaniards during the 1960s was overshadowed by the execution within Spain of Francisco Granado and Joaquín Delgado, anarchists from the Libertarian Youth, who were executed by *garrote vil* in August 1963.

The fact that he failed in his attempt to eliminate the dictator did not spare him from a passage through Spanish prisons, having dodged the death penalty. In Carabanchel, where he came upon lots of anarchists and communists, though no socialists (as he liked to point out) he worked in the prison print-shop, learnt Spanish and studied for admission to a British university. In spite of all of which he secured his release in 1967, thanks to international pressure bought to bear to get him released, a lobby that involved such first-class intellectuals as Bertrand Russell or Jean-Paul Sartre.

On returning to the United Kingdom, Stuart carried on working in the field of anarchism and was in the sights of the British police who fabricated evidence showing him to be a member of the notorious Angry Brigade. Even though none of the charges could be made to stick and he was acquitted, he spent 16 months in custody in what was one of the lengthiest trials in British history.

But there was more to Stuart than his committed activist anarchism which prompted him to resurrect the Anarchist Back Cross to defend libertarian prisoners worldwide. Realizing that the best way of spreading anarchist beliefs is through education, and in line there with anarchism's most classical values, he committed himself whole-heartedly to the study of anarchist history, launching one of the most significant imprints in the field – Cienfuegos Press – and publishing out of the Orkney Islands, in remotest Scotland, due to persistent police harassment in London. And not just books, but also newspaper projects as vehicles for his beliefs.

There is so much that we might highlight about Stuart. He was the first in his family circle ever to attend university; in the early 1980s he made his way to Queen Mary College (University of London) where he studied History and Political Science – and that decision too was influenced by his contact with Spanish anarchist exiles in London; at the Centro Ibérico he made the acquaintance of Paul Preston[1] who was then lecturing at that university. And then there was Stuart's preoccupation with familiarizing himself with the history of anarchism, often focusing on the history of Spanish anarchism. Out of this came one of the few books currently in existence dealing with the Iberian Anarchist Federation (FAI); *We, the anarchists: A study of the Iberian Anarchist Federation (1927–1937)*, published (in translation) in Spain by the University of Valencia Press, along with lots of other writings. From very early on, Stuart was concerned at the resurgence of far right groups across Europe and at the strategies these employed in the 1970s and 1980s. Given the panorama in Europe and worldwide with the rise of such groups, such vigilance remains relevant.

Likewise, his first-born venture, Cienfuegos Press, was followed by Christie Books, an imprint that he carried forward right up until his death. He was a highly educated man, a tireless, yet patient publisher, a great lover of words with a belief in their ability

---

1. Paul Preston, British historian specialising in twentieth-century Spain. See his tribute on page 238.

to work changes in human beings. And it was not just any old imprint, as Christie Books, ahead of the curve where E-publishing is concerned, made classics of anarchist history accessible on-line, translated into English by Christie, relying on those versed in the history of Spanish anarchism. Thanks to Stuart, we got to know English-language versions of books such as *The CNT in the Spanish Revolution*,[2] the complete works of Antonio Téllez (to date the leading expert in the anarchist maquis) or lesser known but no less significant works such as *¡Teniamos que perder!* by García Pradas.[3] Here we ought to highlight the great work also carried out by his good friend Paul Sharkey, a fine translator.

Stuart was a loyal fellow, loyal to an ideal, a cause and to his friends and comrades. But allow us to highlight something else from Stuart's curriculum vitae. Above all else, this dyed-in-the-wool Scottish anarchist, was a kindly person, with a great sense of humour. Affable and approachable, fond of hearing and lending an ear. Who never hesitated to put a question when there was something he did not understand and who was constantly learning.

The international anarchist movement has lost a great stalwart. And the loss of the man, the activist and the intellectual will be sorely felt.

May the earth sit lightly upon you, Stuart.

Historians Chris Ealham and Julián Vadillo Muñoz

From *Todo Por Hacer* (Madrid) September 2020 https://www.todopor hacer.org/stuart-christie. Translated by Paul Sharkey.

---

2. By José Peirats, edited by Chris Ealham, translated by Paul Sharkey and Chris Ealham.
3. José García Pradas (1910–1985), Spanish anarchist and writer. The title of his memoir translates as 'We had to lose!' Stuart published this as an ebook in 2016, with an introduction by Julián Vadillo Muñoz.

Memories of Stuart Christie
by Paul Preston

I knew Stuart for nearly fifty years. He was a great person to have as a friend, funny, open-minded and loyal. We met in the anarchist centre in Hampstead[1] along with Miguel García. In the early eighties, he came to Queen Mary where I was a lecturer and did a degree in history and politics. Needless to say, I and his fellow students learned more from him than he did from us. When he moved to Orkney, we kept in touch over the phone and I followed his various publishing efforts with avid interest. As an historian of the Spanish Civil War, what he made available in English was absolutely crucial for teaching. In the 1990s, we had a whale of a time when he started to publish *Pravda Digest* and *House Magazine*, the journal of the two Houses of Parliament. If ever there was testimony to his open-mindedness that was it.

---

1.   Centro Ibérico/ the International Libertarian Centre.

Memories of Stuart, from MH, a London comrade

I think I first met Stuart when he was attending Queen Mary College in London's East End. It was a time of intense class conflict – the miners strike was happening and the printworkers' dispute at Wapping, just down the road was about to kick off – it was experiences through these (and many other small disputes) that made me an anarchist. I was there escaping from a dull industrial suburb on the edge of SE London. He was there because it was where Paul Preston taught and there was a very good course on modern Spanish history. Preston had bucked the trend in Spanish history by not denigrating the anarchists (they could hardly be ignored in 20th century Spain). I eventually took this course myself, and the lecturer enjoyed pointing to a book on the reading list, *Sabaté –guerrilla extraordinary* by Téllez, translated by Stuart Christie: 'He's on this course, you know.'

We set up an anarchist group at the college, Stuart was supportive, but was commuting from Cambridge at the time so understandably could offer little else. I remember there was a rumour going round that the college would offer him a job in the Spanish history department; when I asked him about it he typically downplayed the chances of it happening. He was right, of course, and I suspect that he would have been ill-fitted to a life of academia.

When we formed a DAM[1] local in SE London, Stuart would regularly attend our social events, mainly because a lot of them centred around Albert Meltzer. Albert would joke that the 'laird'[2]

1. Direct Action Movement, British anarcho-syndicalist organisation, founded in 1979.
2. Scots for 'lord', a gentle joke, painting Stuart as the hero of an adventure novel by John Buchan.

might come along and support it, and he always did. I could tell they had their disagreements, but the bonds of affection between the two were strong – his was not a solidarity of words, but deeds. The last time I had much to do with him was in the immediate aftermath of Albert's death. He was generous with his time, but also with his money – helping us to keep *Black Flag* going. This was more important than it might seem as Stuart remained unemployable because of his history, so was always looking for ways to make some money, usually publishing. Despite what he's best known for – the big name actions, it always struck me that at heart he was very much an everyday anarchist who would get involved in whatever needed doing including the unglamorous stuff as well.

Death of a Mentor by Jessica Thorne

Stuart Christie, 10 July 1946–15 August 2020.

The death of Stuart Christie on 15 August 2020 has already led to an outpouring of touching tributes and obituaries. With his untimely departure, the international anarchist movement has lost one of its most committed and dedicated activists. Indeed, the 'measure of the man' has been encapsulated by how many of us, from brief, often remote encounters, felt in some way attached to him by the warmth, intensity and generosity of his character. Stuart was an anarchist of the highest calibre; iron-willed, yet self-critical, fiercely independent in mind, but always motivated by a collective and egalitarian vision of social change.

My own personal correspondence with Stuart began during the final year of my degree in 2015. It was during this time when I wrote to Stuart with (in hindsight) poorly formulated questions for my dissertation, catchily titled *The Angry Brigade: student radicals, 'The society of the spectacle' and media representations of 'red terror', 1968–1972*. I half-expected Stuart to direct me to his collection of memoirs, or snub me as an 'academic chancer', rather than respond to each question in kind. But to my surprise he took the time to share his present-day thoughts on every detail of my enquiry. After my initial haphazard encounter, Stuart and I would correspond with one another for the next five years regarding new publications, archival exchanges, elusive primary sources, Spanish anarchists, and experiences in prison.

Indeed, in a more personal sense, Stuart's death represents the loss of an irreplaceable guide and mentor. Historians constantly mull over the partiality of the 'narrator-as-witness'. Rarer perhaps are those occasions when we reflect on how a narrator informs and motivates our own retelling of the past. I encountered Stuart's memoirs when I was twenty years old. At this time I was already jaded by the petty intrigues of 'radical' student politics, riddled with class-born anxiety, and all too accepting of a precarious future. With Stuart, I was confronted with a person who, from an early age, was both assured of his own place in history, while also willing to take a leap into the unknown.

This 'unknown' was the Iberian anarchist movement in Franco's Spain. As an undergrad History student in 2015, this territory was unfamiliar to me too. Yet three years after I became personally acquainted with Stuart, I would end up undertaking a PhD on the topic. Unlike more conventional trajectories, my fascination with Spain was not stoked by Orwell's *Homage to Catalonia*, or Ken Loach's *Land and freedom*, but the unlikely and extraordinary tale 'of a west of Scotland "baby boomer"'.

Stuart had spent most of his teenage years with his mother and Grandparents in Blantyre, a small isolated pit town, located to the East of Glasgow. Familial ties crossed with class politics in Stuart's political formation. Along with the influence of his grandmother, the values of whom, Stuart later recalled, 'married almost exactly with that of libertarian socialism and anarchism',[1] Blantyre was home in the 1950s to a confident working class. Centred around the NUM[2] and the local Miners Welfare Institute, politics in the local area was synonymous with the Labour Party and the Communist Party of Great Britain. At the age of sixteen, as an apprentice working for a dental laboratory in Glasgow, Stuart had become politically active in the Young Socialists (the youth section of the Labour Party). But it wasn't long before Stuart became

---

1.   'The woolly-jumpered anarchist', Stuart Christie interviewed by Duncan Campbell, *The Guardian* 23 August 2004.
2.   National Union of Minewokers.

disillusioned with the procedural nature of Party life. Once exposed to 'the machinations and power struggles within the Glasgow Labour Party', Stuart's idealistic and reflexive attachment to Party socialism was crushed by its culture of 'office-grabbing', 'local political power plays' and 'contending sectarian power agendas'.[3]

After exiting the Party, Stuart became involved in the Glasgow Federation of Anarchists and the anti-nuclear Committee of 100.[4] A split from the 'celebrity-and-politician dominated' CND, the Committee of 100 mobilised against nuclear armament and militarism with direct action. Yet Stuart was drawn to questions bigger than those immediately posed by single issue campaigns. If war, imperialism, and violence came with the territory of the modern State, then perhaps it was the State that was the problem. As Stuart recalled in an interview in 2004, 'I began to see a lot more clearly that it wasn't the weapons themselves that were the problem, it was the states that possessed them'.[5]

Throughout Stuart's teenage years, and indeed for the rest of his life, he returned to the same question: Spain, Spain, and yet again Spain. As with the rest of the industrial belt of Glasgow, Blantyre was laced with a proud anti-fascist history. The small pit town was home to Thomas Brannan, Thomas Flecks, and William Fox, all three of whom fell on the battlefield in Spain as members of the International Brigades. This local connection to Spain evoked Albert Camus' famed representation of the 'Spanish drama' as a kind of 'personal tragedy'. Between the age of fifteen and seventeen, Stuart would bear witness to fierce debates outside the local Miners Welfare Institute on the 'politically sore' topic of war and 'social revolution' in 1930s Spain. It was here where he

---

3. 'Looking back at anger', *3A.M. magazine* https://www.3ammagazine.com/politica/2004/apr/interview_stuart_christie.html

4. The Committee of 100 was set up in 1960 to promote mass non-violent demonstrations against nuclear weapons.

5. 'Looking back at anger', *3A.M. magazine*

would learn about 'libertarian Barcelona', the anarcho-syndicalist CNT, the days of rebellion and street-fighting during the 1937 'May Days' episode,[6] and the brutal military defeat of the Republic in 1939. Yet Stuart would not look back on Spain with a wistful, melancholic gaze. Indeed, he refused to accept it was a lost battle. When he read that two young Spanish anarchists had been executed by the Franco regime for oppositional activities in 1963, he was overwhelmed by the same sense of duty that had impelled anti-fascists to arrive in Spain in 1936.

On Saturday 1 August 1964, Stuart bought a single ticket for the morning boat train from London to Calais and from there headed to Paris: the 'emigré capital' of Spain's Republican and anarchist diaspora. Arriving late in the afternoon at the Rue de Lancry, Stuart met with exiled members of the Federación Ibérica de Juventudes Libertarias (Iberian Federation of Libertarian Youth). He was to take part in a clandestine mission to Spain organised by the anarchist and CNT-backed 'Defensa Interior' committee. Far beyond the more customary exile activity of delivering banned publications, newspapers and leaflets, Stuart was entrusted with transporting a kilo of *plastique* (plastic explosives). If successful, Stuart's courier mission would have led to the political assassination of General Franco.

'As things turned out, It was fortunate I planned to be away some time and didn't buy a return ticket',[7] Stuart later recalled, as he was consequently apprehended by the Brigada Político-Social on 11 August (BPS, Franco's political police) and taken into custody. After spending four days beaten and interrogated in the dingy basement cells of Madrid's police headquarters, Christie was sent to Carabanchel prison where he would stay on remand,

6. From 3–7 May 1937, there was street fighting, chiefly in Barcelona, in a defeated attempt to preserve the revolutionary structures of July 1936 and resist the reconstruction of the Republican state.

7. *General Franco made me a 'terrorist'*, p. 1.

while the *consejos de guerra* (Franco's special military tribunals) decided on their verdict. On 5 September, Christie received a note through his cell door stating the details of his sentence: 'twenty years for military rebellion and terrorism'.

Stuart's detention reaffirmed his anarchism. In Carabanchel, he found almost instant political fraternity with the hounded, post-civil war generation of anarchists in Spain. But the world of prison challenged his idealism:

'Before I went to prison my world-view was simple and clear-cut – black and white, a moral battlefield in which everyone was either a goody or a baddy. But the ambiguities in people I came across in prison made me uneasy and I began to question my assumptions about the nature of good and evil. I came to recognise that apparently kind people sometimes had a duplicitous side to them that was amoral, treacherous, self seeking or brutal, while those with a reputation for cruelty sometimes showed themselves capable of great selflessness and generosity of spirit. This didn't make me cynical, but it did make me less judgemental about my fellow human beings. Also, it was hard to fan the flames of righteous anger in the face of the sheer ordinariness of people.'[8]

The 'sheer ordinariness of people' in Franco's prisons crossed with Stuart's steadfast rejection of scholarly and popular representations of Iberian anarchism as 'Manichean', 'primitive', or 'fanatical'. As Stuart would go on to write, 'these men and women were not fanatics. They were ordinary rational and dignified people who lived deliberately and passionately, with a vision and a tremendous capacity for self sacrifice; they had been abandoned by the Allies in the "post-fascist" world of the Cold War and deprived of diplomatic or democratic means of resisting Franco's state terror'.[9]

---

8.   *General Franco made me a 'terrorist'*, p. 89.
9.   *General Franco made me a 'terrorist',* p. 13.

Stuart returned to England in 1967, following a successful international campaign for his release and some awkward diplomatic pressure. But he never lost sight of those he met in prison. Shortly after his return, he refounded the Anarchist Black Cross (the ABC) with Albert Meltzer. With its initial premises set up in Coptic Street in London, the ABC provided a support network for Franco's anarchist prisoners while also operating a 'Spanish Liberation fund' to subsidise activist groups throughout the country. Its activity was divided into two tasks; first to provide material support, in the form of 'food parcels and medical supplies', and latterly to aid the Spanish Resistance movement with 'everything it needs, including '[print] duplicators, typewriters and guns'.[10]

In the years following his release, Stuart would continue to pay heavy penalties for his close affinities with Spanish anarchists. In February 1968, after a series of bombs exploded outside embassies in London, Stuart was raided by the British Special Branch and, thereafter, subject to round-the-clock surveillance outside his London flat. Four years later, Stuart would be indicted on conspiracy charges and was accused of being a member of the so-called 'Angry Brigade' (a group responsible for a series of bomb attacks in Britain in the early 1970s). Along with banks, boutiques, a British army reserve centre, and the 1970 Miss World Contest, the 'Angry Brigade' had claimed the machine gunning of the Spanish Embassy and the bombing of an Iberia Airlines office. The reason for Stuart's arrest in 1972 was because of the string of explosive incidents focused on Spanish targets. From the moment of Stuart's re-entry into Britain, he was viewed by the Special Branch as the main Anglophone conduit of the Spanish resistance, and thus guilty by association.

---

10.   See 'A special appeal to all who consider themselves to be revolutionaries' on page 35.

Stuart would be held on remand in Brixton prison, while the trial of the 'Stoke Newington 8' evolved into one of the longest criminal trials in English history (lasting from 30 May to 6 December 1972). As Stuart awaited trial, his mind returned to Spain. With the invaluable moral and material support of his wife Brenda, his collaborator Albert Meltzer, and his Black Cross colleague and ex-prisoner Miguel García, Stuart translated into English Antonio Téllez's *Sabaté: guerrilla urbana en España, 1945–1960*.

After Stuart was acquitted by jury in 1972, he made the decision, following a 'tip off' from a Special Branch officer, to leave London. In 1976, Stuart and Brenda headed to Orkney,[11] where their daughter, Branwen, was born. Here, with the help of Brenda, Meltzer and others, he set up the 'Cienfuegos Press' publishing house, where he translated and published a number of elusive Spanish texts. Prisoner solidarity work with the Black Cross would also continue. By the mid-1970s, the Anarchist Black Cross had taken on a much broader internationalist remit, aiding political prisoners with parcels, letters and donations not only in Spain, but in France, West Germany, Italy, and Northern Ireland.

Even when the tumult of the 1970s came to a close, Stuart maintained his revolutionary zeal. In 1980, a year after Thatcher's election, he published a controversial (and still probably illegal) A4 brochure entitled, *Towards a citizens' militia: anarchist alternatives to NATO and the Warsaw Pact* (1980). This resulted in an apoplectic response from the national press, who ran with the headlines 'TERROR BOOKS UPROAR', 'SCOTS BOOK OF DO-IT-YOURSELF GUERRILLA WAR', and 'ISLAND OF ANARCHY'.

In later life, as well as being an assiduous archivist, writer, and publisher, Stuart became a vital scholarly authority on Spanish anarchism. For professional historians of twentieth century Spain,

---

11. In 1975 they moved to Yorkshire, followed by the move to Orkney in 1976.

We, the anarchists! A study of the Iberian Anarchist Federation 1927–1937 (2008), was received as a welcome Anglophone addition on many undergraduate reading lists.

Stuart was not content with writing the political history of the CNT-FAI with a narrowly conceived concept of the 'political'. His method of writing history was always empirical, but never crudely positivist or detached. This was testament to his open mindedness. He understood that the radical character of Spanish labour movement during the first half of the century was not a result of 'ideological brainwashing' or arcane vanguards. Instead, Stuart understood the politics of the CNT-FAI as being rooted in the experience of the Spanish working class.

In 2019, I was contacted by the MayDay Rooms[12] regarding a collection of Spanish materials Stuart had recently donated to the archive. I knew I would be familiar with many of the texts in the collection. And sure, I was. But I was taken aback by the number of handwritten inscriptions on his books, messages of deep and profound gratitude, by famed members of the CNT-FAI. I knew the extent to which Spain had left an indelible mark on Stuart; now I was confronted with the mark Stuart had left on the lives of those in Spain.

To the end, Stuart cut through the inertia of our times with a perpetual desire for engagement. Whenever I presented Stuart with finds from the archives, he would inevitably give them life and, in one of his own expressions, provide me with 'another link in the chain!' But he always saw his own contribution to History as 'small'. What I would describe in my work as 'transnational networks of anarchists', he would simply call 'friendships'. He did not consider himself a specimen for study. He lived his politics. He brought people together, many of whom were separated by national and linguistic boundaries. His generosity and loyalty

---

12. Radical archive and building in London's Fleet Street.

dissolved the remoteness of our encounters. Moreover, despite being half a century older than me, our conversations were rarely unidirectional or top-down. He listened, and if I doubted myself, he built me up, urged me forward.

Above all, Stuart left me with the feeling that even when the odds are stacked against you, you only really need a handful of people to make the impossible happen. Stuart was certainly one of those people.

Jessica Thorne is a PhD student at Royal Holloway, researching transnational anarchist resistance to Franco's Spain 1950–1975.

Stuart Christie in London.

Some reflections on Stuart by John Barker

I only got to know Stuart Christie in A Wing HMP Brixton, the Victorian prison on Jebb Avenue in 1971–2. We were both on re-mand for the same conspiracy rap and there his name, what he had done to try and kill the fascist dictator Franco, gave him in-stant respect in the jail, something the others of us had to earn over time. He had been at that time working as a gas fitter and had a history of work whereas I was an ex-University person with little of the nous that Stuart had. I've written a little about this time but just to give a brief impression, while outside there was work-ing class confidence and hedonism in the jail screws were ex-army and the Governors at various levels ex-colonial police or military. Something had to give and Stuart's rep and wise thinking enabled us to be part of forcing change to the benefit of cons (prisoners) especially in the matter of Visits with a wave of sit-downs.

As a teenager I'd read a lot about the Spanish Civil War, knew a girl whose dad was an anarchist refugee from it and not just heroized Durruti[1] but believed here was a case of an individual who could have changed the course of the war had he not been killed. But I was not an anarchist and even though we shared a belief in active resistance to the fascisms evident in Spain and It-aly – a time when in both states comrades were being executed by the state officially or unofficially – we argued over theory and his-tory. I couldn't stomach Bakunin and he Marx but when it came to the politics of the prison we acted as one. And something else, the great thing about Stuart as comrade and friend is that he was always cheerful and ready to make things both happen, and to

---

1.   Buenaventura Durruti (1896–1936), Spanish anarchist.

work. Even when in later life he had a lot less luck with a hip replacement than I, he was saving and expanding the wonderful film library – big Respect to Colin Sellens also – he created at Christie Books and was full of support and suggestions about self-publishing and ebooks. He and Brenda had worked hard and mastered all the technologies needed to make radical publishing work.

It was the same in our six month long trial when things could have gone badly wrong for him, a Grade A miscarriage of justice, he was the one who could find a lightness of tone needed while Brenda saved us a lot of grief one way or another by working long nights to produce our own transcripts of the trial. This unforced cheerful can-do nature mattered and matters. It is not from a blindness to the horrors of the capitalist world and its supporting states but sat and sits with the real anger he felt and without which there is going to be no transformation for the good. With Stuart there was never any need to say, Don't Let The Bastards Grind You Down. In recent years on social media he put himself on the line in asserting the rights of Palestinians and showing the systematic nature of Israel's settler colonialist dynamics and its leading role on the technologies of repression.

What with one thing and another I didn't see much of him for some years though I did what I could for the international anarchist prisoner support group the Black Cross which Stuart had made both active and effective. Then, having been out of the game again for a while and after a decade of being fucked about with the manuscript of my own prison 'memoir',[2] Stuart tired of prison reform literature said Lets just do it. And then some years later at the time of the US-UK invasion of Iraq in 2003 he published a very different work, 'Frankenstein and the Chickenhawks' on Christie Books. I remain grateful for the space and time he gave me. In these years too we both participated in work by the artist

2. *Bending the Bars*, Christiebooks, 2002.

Duncan Pickstock. One involved doing a mock version of Desert Island Discs. What music we chose separately was very different and Stuart had a wide knowledge of Scottish music and culture, folk and comedy I was completely ignorant of but in the course of the recording, one of my choices being Georgie Fame's 'In the Meantime', we found out we'd both knocked about in the Pink Flamingo in Wardour Street, one of the few all-nighters around 1966–7 and where Georgie played Hammond organ.

That 'knowledge' of Stuart was a wide and rich culture of music, books and film that was always just popping up at the right moment when we talked which a lot of the time was on the phone in recent years. I last saw him early this year before the lockdown in London. We gave a quick-run down of our aches and pains but nothing sounded serious and then went to MayDay Rooms[3] which he had never visited but to which he had given books. The Statewatch office there was open and though he had little time Stuart was both impressed and thought of spots where if he dug around at home he might find something to add.

We talked too of the dragged out business of his moving house which had been in his mind since the death of Brenda last year and to be close to his daughter and grandchildren and should have been completed. His illness and death was sudden, leaving little time to enjoy the move. I miss him and shall miss him and his final Toodleoo at the end of a phone call. I hope too that he by his life makes clear that it is not some 'natural course of things' that one loses one's youthful revolutionary commitment, rather that as in his case he was constantly finding new ways to express it.

---

3.   Radical archive and building in London's Fleet Street.

From the funeral: Duncan Campbell's tribute to Stuart

Now, Stuart, I wonder what you would make of all of us gathering here today? It would be good to hear the sort of jokes you'd doubtless make, as you always did in the midst of catastrophe and loss. What wisdom would you have to offer us? I am sure that you would have something both perceptive and funny to say. No-one knew better than you how to find laughter in the midst of sadness and how to find the light in the darkness.

I was a student in Edinburgh when news came through that a young Scottish anarchist was facing the death penalty in Spain for an attempt to assassinate the dictator, Franco. My first ever demonstration was marching down the High Street by torchlight in protest against Stuart's arrest and the possibility of his execution.

He describes his release from Carabanchel prison in Madrid so well in his wonderful memoir, *Granny made me an anarchist*: 'we had a celebration drink in the shade of the wall with a *botijo* of wine I had stashed but it was tinged with real sadness. I was about be freed and break up our little band of friends.... Following well-established prison tradition, I divided my belongings among my friends. In some way this helped assuage the strange sense of guilt I felt at leaving friends behind while I went off to pick up my life in the outside world. When the time came we shook hands, hugged emotionally and said our farewells.'[1]

Once released, as was typical of Stuart, he started to campaign for those still behind bars and when and if they were finally

---

1.   *Granny made me an anarchist* (2004 Scribner edition), p. 234.

released made sure that they knew they would always find a welcome awaiting them in Britain.

This attitude of empathy, this lack of self-regard typified Stuart. When he was locked up again, accused of being part of the Angry Brigade and then acquitted, thanks to his eloquence in the witness box in the Old Bailey trial, his thoughts were again of those convicted who would face years more in jail. 'The feelings of euphoria I experienced,' he wrote, 'were tempered by the desolate faces of John, Anna, Jim and Hilary.'[2]

There were many, many accomplishments in Stuart's life. One was the loving relationships he had with his loyal and brave mother, Olive, and his remarkable grandmother, Agnes Ring – who surely never had an idea that she would one day be internationally famous as her long-haired grandson's moral compass.

By his actions in Spain he alerted the world to the fact that, long after the Spanish Civil War had ended, Franco was still executing, torturing and disappearing his opponents. In the countless responses to the news of Stuart's death that have flooded in from around the world – from Latin America, from Greece, from Australia – many have come from Spain – from comrades of his generation but also from young people now discovering for themselves the evil that Franco wrought.

Through his defiant eloquence in the witness box in the Angry Brigade trial he demonstrated the great importance of the jury system – for the jurors not only acquitted him but asked the judge for compassion for those convicted.

With his staunch friend and comrade, Albert Meltzer, he wrote *The floodgates of anarchy*. Together they would launch the Anarchist Black Cross which helped to provide for political

---

2. *Granny made me an anarchist* (2004 Scribner edition), p. 398. John Barker, Anna Mendleson (1948–2009), Jim Greenfield and Hilary Creek were the four of the 'Stoke Newington Eight' who were convicted.

prisoners in Spain and elsewhere in the shape of books, food and medicine.

With Miguel Garcia, one of those fellow-prisoners in Spain and a beneficiary of Black Cross, he would launch the Centro Iberico and the International Libertarian Centre in London. Another achievement that brought people together from different worlds.

With Brenda, his partner for life, he set up Cienfuegos Press on Sanday in the Orkneys and they achieved much by their dedication and hard work there to give a voice to anarchists around the world.

Another achievement in the Orkneys was the *Free-Winged Eagle*, a publication whose first edition in 1979 – price 30p – called for 'an autonomous Orkney, based on self-managed collectivism, individual freedom, solidarity and fun!' Yes, of course, fun.

When the family had moved to the south coast of England, he was the editorial voice of the *Hastings Trawler*, under the pseudonym of Francisco Ferrer i Guardia, who had been a free-thinking anarchist Barcelona educationalist active at the end of the 19th century.

And by setting up the Anarchist Film Channel there, he challenged the old stereotypes. 'Hollywood and the mainstream film industry tends to depict anarchists as flaky, obsessive, rabid, demonic, repellent stereotypes – such as Hitchcock's *The Secret Agent* or *The Man Who Knew Too Much*,' he said at the time of the launch.[3] 'If they are presented sympathetically, it is done so usually in an Ealing comedy sort of way with bumbling, ineffectual, endearing dreamers – caricatures such as Alastair Sim and John Chandos in *The Green Man*.' Indeed, Stuart was neither bumbling nor ineffectual – but endearing, well, certainly.

---

3.   From 'A revolution in cinema?' by Duncan Campbell *The Guardian* 24 November 2006.

His book, *Granny made me an anarchist* was another great achievement. As a memoir, it stands alongside those of Laurie Lee and Brendan Behan. Just reading it again now you can hear Stuart's voice on every page. And there was his fictional voice, too, in *¡Pistoleros!, the chronicles of Farquar McHarg*, published by another of his achievements, Christie Books.

FREE-WINGED EAGLE

30p

NUMBER ONE | LONGHOPE ORKNEY | WINTER/SPRING 1979.

STOP PRESS STOP PRESS STOP PRESS

Shock Horror Drama as Eton educated Orkney politician declares 'nearly classless society.' Lord Lieutenant commits suicide in car boot after revelations that autonomous workers' councils had cast the entire Orkney Islands Council adrift in Scapa Flow on board the "Lyrawa Bay." Militant shopkeepers, angered by the way the State system had cheated them for so long, were seen erecting a hoarding above the entrance to what was only a few days ago St. Magnus Cathedral, bearing the legend 'Workers' Distribution Warehouse.' In the country, collectivisation of the fields is taking place, and black flags are flying everywhere. All political power has been abolished, save that of the workers' horizontal organisations, and the above-mentioned Eton-educated politician was last seen being consoled by a group of sycophantic Fleet Street hacks, anxious for a juicy story, in a well known London . . . . cont. page 94.

WHAT WILL **YOU** DO WHEN YOUR LOCAL ATOMIC FAST BREEDER REACTOR **BLOWS UP** — RELEASING FISSION MATERIAL OVER **THOUSANDS OF SQUARE MILES?**

THE ONLY CULL WORTH HAVING — FOR AN AUTONOMOUS ORKNEY, BASED ON SELF-MANAGED COLL-ECTIVISM, INDIVIDUAL FREEDOM, SOLIDARITY AND FUN !

First issue of *The Free-Winged Eagle* from the Kate Sharpley Library.

But I know that Stuart would see his greatest achievement as Branwen and through Branwen and Andy his adored grandchildren, Merri and Mo. His emails were often accompanied by photos of them and the perceptive remarks he attributed to them. We used to tease him that one day they would write *Grandad made me an anarchist*.

To me as a teenage student, Stuart was a heroic figure and to me now as, like Stuart, a septuagenarian, he remains a heroic figure. He never became cynical or defeatist. He never forgot his comrades nor his cause. He never lost his sense of humour.

A few years ago I saw Stuart give a talk at a university in London. There were many young people in the audience some of whom had little knowledge of his life. But as he spoke and told his story you could see the admiration and amazement on their faces. Here was man who was prepared to risk his everything for his principles. To them he was a shining example of Granny's instruction not to be a bystander to life. And never has it been more important in this world that we now inhabit to follow that credo and make sure we are not bystanders to what is happening around us.

There have been many tributes to Stuart – whom Billy Connolly once described as 'windswept and interesting' – from around the world.

Many of Stuart's family are here today, proud of their father, grandfather and brother. In his memoir Stuart recounts his farewell to his own father, who had left many years earlier but returned and with whom Stuart had made his peace. 'As I left him for the last time I kissed him on the brow. His last words to me were "Never fear, the sun will shine again tomorrow."' The sun will shine again tomorrow and we are all of us here blessed by the sunlight that Stuart brought to all our lives and the lives of so many, many people around the world – and that will shine on forever in our memories.

From the funeral: Tribute by Ron McKay

Whenever I think of Stuart I smile. Not today of course. But I will again. And always.

People may pass but love remains, as do the fond memories. Some of which it would be inappropriate to recount today.

I first knew of Stuart when I was a junior reporter on a Lanarkshire local newspaper and someone, not me, wrote a piece about this young lad from Blantyre with unfeasibly long hair. It must have been a quiet news week. I mean we were all trying, but Stuart romped the tonsorial stakes, it was down to his oxters. That's armpits in the patois. Stuart's mum was a hairdresser. I don't know what she made of it all.

We had some similarities in our lives. We were both largely brought up by Grannies, in Glasgow. His Dad went out for a packet of fags and came back 20 years later, I never had one. We were working class, although he was from the West End which was a smidgeon above where I was from in the north of the city.

We were bright, we were into music and fashion, although of course we'd never admit the latter. Although Stuart was always well turned out.

At that time, in the Sixties in the city, you were either into politics or gangs, although I guess politics is a kind of gang warfare in your best clothes. If you were young then Glasgow was a pretty violent place. It wasn't a choice of either getting physically stabbed or metaphorically in the back, but there was a lot to be angry about and to rebel against.

It was the height of the Cold War, before and after the Cuban missile crisis, and politics could get pretty rowdy. The then Labour leader Hugh Gaitskell[1] turned up at an anti-nuclear demonstration at Queen's Park and wasn't just shouted down, hundreds of people – including our Stuart of course – tried to pull him off the stage and he was only saved by a line of polis[2] and stewards. Stuart's picture appeared in the *Daily Record* next day.

The next I heard of Stuart was when he was back in the news for trying to blow up the bestial, fascist dictator Francisco Franco. A lot of men from the previous generation, from Glasgow, had fought in the International Brigade, which was one of the motivations which inspired Stuart in his attempt.

Of course, later he was associated with a different brigade, the Angry one, but that had a happier outcome. His adult life was splattered with headlines but it was the small print of it which was important, his decency, loyalty, acerbic and self-deprecating humour, his utter dependability, his love of family, his wide-ranging knowledge, from Glasgow comedians to philosophy, although he was a bit remiss on fitba'.[3] He was the kind of person most of us aspire to be and fail. He was at my side in several projects, he was there for me in the bleakest time. I relied on him. Quite simply I loved the man.

In 1974 we holidayed together in a remote cottage up a small track outside of Oban and while we were there a Spanish anarchist group had captured and ransomed a Francoist banker. When Stuart returned to London he was told by an unusually friendly Special Branch officer he wasn't safe in the city. So he and Brenda decamped, first to Yorkshire, then to the small Orkney Island of Sanday and a house called Over The Water where Branwen was born.

Sanday at the time might have been some prototype of an anarchist society. There were no police on the island, only occasional

---

1. Hugh Gaitskell (1906–1963).
2. Police.
3. Football.

visits which were well telegraphed, and I'm not sure anyone had car insurance or license.

Pub licensing hours were decreed by the last person standing. Once, when the police turned up from the mainland at the Kettletoft Hotel and insisted on turfing us out, Stuart kept the two sitting in the car busy while someone else, ok it was me, let down their back tires and we sped off. Anarchism in my experience requires a lot of heavy arm lifting. And exuberance.

Anyone who hasn't read it should get a copy of his partial autobiography, *Granny made me an anarchist*, a rollicking account peppered with cultural and political reference points, from the Jeely Piece Song and 'hingies' to Leslie Howard, Buñuel and *Just William*. It's also extremely funny.

The last time I saw Stuart was in Glasgow in February, we had a couple in the Doublet and then a curry in the Shish Mahal next door, and we planned a sort of loose commemorative trip to Spain, retracing more than 50 years later the route he had taken, with a few cultural and bibulous diversions obviously. But it wasn't to be.

There's so much to remember him for, and smiles will return. For all of us. There's a phrase of his that will stick with me for ever and remind me of him every time I hear it. He used it whenever I asked him how things were going or how he was. Ticketty Boo he'd reply. Ticketty Boo.

From the funeral: Pauline Melville's tribute

Well, Stuart always said that August was an unlucky month for him. It was in August, 1964 that he was taken out of circulation by the Spanish authorities. It was in August, 1971 that he was taken out of circulation by the British authorities and it was in August, 2020 that he was taken out of circulation in the most drastic and irreversible way. I don't know what authority organised that but, whoever it was, as his granny might have said: 'May hell slap it into them.'

Just after he died I got an email from someone I didn't know who had got hold of my email address. It said:

'Dear Pauline, So sad. My condolences on the loss of a true comrade. I had not seen Stuart for 45 years but shared a room with him, courtesy of Her Majesty, for a while. He looked and often acted like a Scottish d'Artagnan.[1] He was a true comrade, positive, friendly and cared deeply for those who needed help or, more likely, he would help them to help themselves.'

As for me, I first caught a glimpse of the Scottish d'Artagnan in his 'windswept and interesting' days in the late sixties. We brushed up against each other briefly in the damp, cramped basement of a north London, commune-come-squat where there was a printing press that we both needed to use. He told me later how much he disliked that ideologically driven household. Stuart was never one to let rigid political ideology get in the way of basic humanity. Always warm, always generous, always humorous and always courageous.

---

1. D'Artagnan appears in *The three musketeers* by Alexandre Dumas (1802–1870).

When Stuart was eighteen he was charged, in Spain, with banditry and terrorism. When I was eighteen I was charged, in France, with undermining the morale of the French Foreign Legion. So it wasn't surprising that we should become firm friends later on in his life.

We didn't meet again for about thirty years. I'd become a novelist and he was looking for help in finding a mainstream publisher for *My granny made me an anarchist*. The three books that document his personal life are a treasure trove of personal, social and political history, packed with photographs and quotations from Burns to Bakunin, Shakespeare to *Just William*, Glaswegian childhood songs to Samuel Beckett.

He was never self-serving, never tried to climb the greasy pole of a career, entirely lacking in ambition for himself but with huge ambition for social and political justice for everybody else. He had an international reputation. Anarchists I met in Venezuela, on his behalf, held him in awe. Anarchists in Bolivia felt the same. They saw him as a shining beacon, an example of how to live a life of courage and principle. He remained a committed anarchist to the end, believing that people could flourish without government. He contributed what he could to that end as a writer and publisher. Testament to that are some words from the man himself via his emails showing how he never stopped working at it:

'Well, nothing exciting planned today other than working on a dozen or so pages on this book I'm doing about the last days of the Spanish Republic.'

Or:

'Just finished another book on the anarchists in the Russian Revolution and about to start another on the Anarchist Red Cross, precursor to the Anarchist Black Cross.'

Stuart was a man of astute political awareness and he could be a lot of fun. Once when we were passing two posters of a

Conservative and a Labour candidate during an election campaign, he took one look and said: 'Dearie me, if it's no' bugs it's fleas.'

He loved his family, to use one of his own phrases, more than tongue can tell. He nursed his wife, Brenda, during her final illness. He was greatly appreciative of Andy, Branwen's partner, who helped him so much with that last move to Chelmsford and equally grateful to his sister Olivia for providing him with shelter around that time. As for Branwen, who has inherited his big heart, even a man as eloquent as Stuart would struggle to find words that could express the depth of his love for her and he was near to bursting with pride over his two feisty grand-daughters, Merri and Mo. In fact he used to produce these hilarious satirical sketches for Facebook with photographs of Merri and Mo adjacent to a text beginning 'Hey Gramps' in which they'd spout high-flown political and philosophical theory from Marx or Kropotkin interspersed with requests for a go on the Bouncy Castle and a chocolate biscuit.

To finish I'm going to read a very short poem by Lorca, another man who fell foul of Spanish fascists and was murdered by them in 1936, oddly enough also in August. It just reminds me of Stuart's fellow-feeling for humanity and his optimism that somehow, even in death, the window is always open to possibilities.

The poem is called:

Leavetaking
If I die,
Leave the balcony open.
A child is eating oranges,
I see him from my window.
The reaper is reaping wheat,
From my balcony I see him,
If I die,
Leave the balcony open.

But Stuart would probably want to end with a smile. Once, for some reason, he sent me some photos of humorous sayings found on Mexican gravestones. One of them might even be relevant to him. It said: 'Rest in Peace. Now you are in the Lord's arms. Lord, watch your back.'

From the funeral: Branwen's Words For her Father

Dear Dad, Do you remember, in every birthday or father's day card I sent you, I'd always write 'thank you for being my rock'. And you were. My constant, my everything, always there for me, no matter what, my right hand man, my biggest supporter, my confidant, my best friend, loving me unconditionally. Always. Your love, understanding and support, unwavering, unflinching, always with me, undeniably. Ever present. Thank you, what a gift.

Every text, card or email you'd send me you'd always sign off 'luvyaa bns, dad, kiss kiss'. Bins was your text shorthand for billions. Some time ago, I casually text back saying 'dad, you don't always have to sign off like that, I do know it's you sending the message you know, exclamation mark, smiley face' and thought nothing more of it. The next text I received from you, minus the luvvya bns, dad, kiss kiss, jarred, I missed it, as if it were written by someone else. 'Put it back dad, it doesn't seem right, I miss your sign offs' and with that, normal texting service was resumed. Thank you for loving me bins.

I swell with pride when I read and hear so many wonderful tributes to you dad, the outpouring of love is of huge comfort to me. I hope you know how loved you were and are, how special you are to people, how your actions and not only the 'big actions', of which there are many, have influenced and affected so many people some of whom you've never met. Your kindness, warmth and big heartedness, how you'd endeavour to help people in any way you could, how you'd love to introduce people to each other, bringing people together, joining the dots, creating new links in the chain, always pushing forward. Thank you. I'm so proud of you dad, so proud, your strength and courage, your unwavering commitment to social justice, for always following your heart, your grace and compassion, your moral compass, your humility, your ability to love easily and forgive easily but most of all I am proud to call you my dad. Thank you. The love you and mum poured in to my childhood and growing up was the greatest gift of all. The happiest of times in the happiest of homes, surrounded by the two greatest people I have ever known. Thank you.

Branwen, Brenda, and Stuart Christie. Photo from Branwen Christie.

It breaks my heart our girls didn't get more time with you. How they adored you dad, how they'd cry when you'd have to go home, how they'd argue over who got to sit next to you at dinner, 'just one more story Grumpa, pleasssseee'. The sports days, nativities, school fairs, holidays, what I wouldn't give for us to share more time, make more memories and to take more trips to the swings. The last gift you bought Merri was a diary, written in the front sleeve underneath a Scottish toast you signed off 'Your ever-loving Gramps, who's always with you'. I hope so dad, I hope you are, please always be with us. Please. I remember you saying, 'You'll always have me, love, as I'll always be in your heart'. Thank you, dad, we will carry you in hearts, always and forever. Pushing forward, just as you did. Thank you for being my rock dad, luvyaa bins, your Bran xx.

The Stuart Christie Memorial Archive

After the funeral, friends, family and comrades of Stuart Christie came up with a plan to commemorate his life by creating a physical and online archive. Fundraising for the archive, which started online in February 2021, met its target the next month.

To reveal the richness of Stuart's life and the many histories he was a part of, we intend to establish a memorial archive in his name. The Stuart Christie Memorial Archive will be housed at the May-Day Rooms in Fleet Street in London. [...]

The memorial will include photographs, letters, personal momentoes, art works, his writings, as well as the output of his publishing arms, Cienfuegos Press, Christie Books and his Anarchist Film Archive.

The archive will also be available online. With the money raised from you, we will be employing a part-time archivist and researcher. Jessica Thorne, a doctoral researcher, whose work focuses on anarchist prisoners in Franco's Spain, has already started work on the archive. Stuart's daughter Branwen is contributing personal photographs and letters.

Much of the material will be new, including letters from Carabanchel prison in Spain where he was incarcerated after his failed attempt to assassinate the dictator Francisco Franco, as well as early childhood photographs. It will cover his involvement in the Angry Brigade trial, his period on Orkney – and his newspaper, the *Free-Winged Eagle* – with previously unseen photographs.

[Updates on the project can be found online (look for @ArchiveStuart). When the fundraiser hit its target, Branwen thanked all the donors. We'd like to share a few words from her message.]

'If you knew dad, you'd know he was always keen to help or at least point people in the right direction, probably with an anecdote or two and a couple of film and book recommendations to boot! That's why we feel this memorial archive seems so fitting. We are so cheered that so many of you were behind us from the start and have faith in the project.'

A handful of the books Stuart wrote and published. Photo by the Kate Sharpley Library.

A time for anarchy...

We wanted to give Stuart the final word. This is one of the many amazing pieces (published and unpublished) collected for the Stuart Christie Memorial Archive. As well briefly describing his political 'trajectory' it gives Stuart's political credo: 'The main attraction anarchism has for me is that it is the political philosophy which best encapsulates my ideas of freedom and social justice.'

Despite the legion of sects and all the jargon used by socialists to define where they stand politically, there are essentially only two schools of revolutionary thought and praxis – one authoritarian and the other libertarian.

The essential difference between the two is that Marxism requires absolute control of the state apparatus in the hands of the party for an indefinite period of time until the 'proletarian' revolution has been successfully consolidated. After that they promise, on their honour, that the state will wither away.

Anarchists, on the other hand, know that the only thing likely to wither away in such a 'revolutionary' state will be their freedom. The Marxist state would be much more omnipresent and oppressive than its predecessor, and the transformation of the economy to a centralised statist one with its accompanying ideologically buttressed bureaucracy would ensure it remained the permanent arbiter of political and social life.

Anarchism is more an attitude towards life than an ideology. An anarchist is someone who believes that *no one* has the right to be another's master; is prepared to resist all attempts to suborn him- or herself to the arbitrary authority of statist power politics and whose positive aspirations are for a free and self-managed society as the only possible basis on which to build a more just and equitable world.

Most people oppose 'undemocratic' government and dictatorships. Anarchists take that one step further. They oppose 'representative democracy' on the grounds that real power does *not* lie with the elected representative but with the machinery of the state, the civil service.

In their turn, the elected representatives are not effectively answerable to their constituents other than once every five years. Genuine democracy is only possible when *everyone* is involved in the decision making processes and, where elected representatives are necessary, they must be answerable to those on whose behalf they speak, listen and negotiate.

To many people, the word anarchist conjures up the vision of Joseph Conrad's sinister madman Karl Yundt[1] dressed in a dark havelock coat and black felt sombrero shading the hollows and ridges of his wasted face, waving a bomb or a jar of anthrax about to wipe out an entire city.

'...I have always dreamed of a band of men absolute on their resolve to discard all scruples... strong enough to give themselves the name of destroyers. No pity for anything on earth, including themselves, and death enlisted for good and all in the service of humanity...' If Conrad's words were written today they would be more likely to refer to the SAS.[2]

The malevolent image of the anarchist results from a century of emotive conditioning. Not only is it unpalatable, but it is dangerous in its consequences [for the state] for anarchism or anarchists to be presented in *any* light other than that of wrecker,

1. Yundt appears in Joseph Conrad's *The secret agent* (1907).
2. Special Air Service. Stuart's 'The golden road to Samarkand' in *Cienfuegos Press Anarchist Review* number 6 is 'A speculative look at [...] the Special Air Service Regiment as a warrior elite and potential "parallel enforcement body"'.

terrorist or harmless eccentric. That anarchist attitudes are gaining wider currency is recognised by western policy makers who are distinctly uneasy about the way things are going at the moment. In proportion to the extent to which authority as a social tool is rejected, the credibility of the state is diminished – it is seen to be superfluous to society's requirements.

Writing in the *Police Journal* (January 1982), the dean of academic studies at Bramshill Police Staff College warned: 'Another feature of society likely to continue is the persistent scepticism towards all authority, and mounting demands for "accountability" and "open government" ... this proliferation of pressure groups, which has been very much a feature of recent years in this country, seems likely to continue to the point of endangering the basic unity of the country.'[3]

Coming from a Lanarkshire mining background, as I did, with its strong local anarchist tradition and the still vivid memories of the Spanish Civil War among the miners who fought in the International Brigades, anarchists were always present and active in local political and industrial activities. However, my first response to anarchism was indicative of the insidious influence the Communist Party and Marxist groups in general have on attitudes to anti-authoritarians. I rejected it as a middle-class anachronism which had outlived its time.

Later, though, after some years among the Young Socialists and members of the Glasgow Communist Party and as an US-DAW[4] delegate to Glasgow Trades Council I came to the conclusion that perhaps the anarchist miners who first introduced me to politics were right after all.

The main attraction anarchism has for me is that it is the

3.   'Bramshill Meets the Challenge' by I. A. Watt, *Police Journal* vol. 55 issue 1, p.67–70 (January 1982).

4.   Union of Shop, Distributive and Allied Workers (formed by merger in 1947).

political philosophy which best encapsulates my ideas of freedom and social justice. There is an excellent quote by William Kingdon Clifford which captures the spirit of anarchism for me: 'There is one thing more wicked than the desire to command and that is the will to obey.'[5]

I was very conscious of the strong bond of solidarity between the Scottish working class and the anti-Francoist movement in Spain. I was quite outraged and bewildered by the fact that he was the last of the Axis dictators still entrenched in power.

Further, he was toadied to by the Western democracies, and was embarking on a brutal and savage campaign of repression against the Asturian miners unparalleled since the Civil War itself. And there was apparently no international body capable, or interested in, exerting any influence on the Franco regime.

Under those circumstances and against that sort of background with my good Protestant upbringing which imbued me with solid Presbyterian values of good and evil – I came to the conclusion that if he wouldn't leave the stage of history gracefully then he'd have to be helped off. The final and decisive straw for me came when two young Spanish anarchists[6] were garrotted (execution involving both strangulation and the breaking of the spinal column by mechanical means) following the bombing of Spanish Security HQ in Madrid.

As for the Angry Brigade, I suppose it came into being as a direct consequence of the heady – euphoric almost – atmosphere of the late 1960s and early 1970s. Then it seemed all the conditions were right for the final confrontation with the forces of reaction. I

---

5. This quote appears in a slightly different form ('one thing in the world') in an essay on Clifford (British philosopher and mathematician, 1845–1879) by Frederick Pollock *Fortnightly Review*, v.31, n.149 (May 1879) p. 684. It is quoted in *Liberty and the great libertarians* by Charles T. Sprading (1913).

6. Delgado and Granado (see glossary and Stuart's tribute to Antonio Martín Bellido on page 182).

imagine the Angry Brigade, and the numerous other people who were, at the time, involved in direct action of one sort or another, saw themselves as potential catalysts and as expressing the anger and exasperation of a generation denied power or influence over the events which affected and most concerned them.

No doubt the sort of groundswell of popular consciousness which gave rise to the AB may be invoked again at some time in the future. Whether or not the 1980s sees the rebirth of such organised groups depends on how the state responds to, and accommodates popular disaffection. Certainly groups calling themselves revolutionary will continue to let off bombs or kidnap or assassinate those they consider to be 'enemies' of the people, but any justification terrorism – as practised today – had as a tool for social change has long since been debased.

Stuart at 'Over the Water' on Sanday, August 1980.
Photo from Stuart Christie.

From *City Limits*, 22–28 April 1983.

Index